Life and Death in a Small Southern Town

Life and Death in a Small Southern Town

Memories of Shubuta, Mississippi

Gayle Graham Yates

Louisiana State University Press
Baton Rouge

Published by Louisiana State University Press
Copyright © 2004 by Louisiana State University Press
All rights reserved
Manufactured in the United States of America

An LSU Press Paperback Original

Designer: Laura Roubique Gleason
Typeface: Minion
Typesetter: Intergrated Book Technology, Inc.

Library of Congress Cataloging-in-Publication Data:

Yates, Gayle Graham, 1940–
  Life and death in a small southern town : memories of Shubuta, Mississippi / Gayle Graham Yates.
    p. cm.
  ISBN 978-0-8071-2937-1 (pbk. : alk. paper)
  1. Shubuta (Miss.)—History. 2. City and town life—Mississippi—Shubuta. 3. Shubuta (Miss.)—Social conditions. 4. Shubuta (Miss.)—Biography. I. Title.
F349.S5Y38 2004
976.2'673—dc22

                                                           2003021053

The paper in this book meets the guidelines for permanence and durability of the Commitee on Production Guidelines for Book Longevity of the Council on Library Resources. ∞

To the people of Shubuta,
especially

Cleo Powe Cooper

James B. Johnston

Mary McCarty

and Syble Meeks

Contents

Acknowledgments • ix

Introduction: Beautiful Town ... Ugly Town • 1

TROPE 1: TOWN • 22
TROPE 2: AUNTIE'S TRUNK • 23
Chapter 1: Shubuta's People • 26

TROPE 3: THE HOLY LAND ... HOLY LAND • 58
TROPE 4: "MAMA'S MAMA WAS ALL DUTCH" • 62
Chapter 2: Shubuta's History • 67

TROPE 5: FLOWER GARDENS, QUILTS, AND CROCHET PIECES • 112
TROPE 6: THE LANG HOUSE • 115
Chapter 3: Church and School, Depot and Town Hall • 116

TROPE 7: THE HANGING BRIDGE • 134
TROPE 8: THE PHILLIPS ARCHIVE • 136
Chapter 4: Documents: Shubuta Memory in Maps, Pictures, Letters, and Buildings • 139

TROPE 9: OL' MAN WEEMS'S NICKELS • 157
Chapter 5: Interviews: Shubuta Memory in People's Own Words • 160

TROPE 10: OVER THE PRAIRIE TO MATHERVILLE WITH MY CHILDREN • 181
Chapter 6: The New Shubuta • 186

Notes • 201

Notes on Sources • 211

Acknowledgments

While I worked on my "Shubuta project" for periods of time over twelve years, the people of Shubuta, my family, friends, and colleagues have thoroughly supported me in bringing my work from the vagueness of a wish to write it to the finished form of a book. I am grateful to all of them.

There would be no book if all the individual people named here—and others, too, who live in Shubuta today, have Shubuta relatives or ancestors, or care about Shubuta—had not opened their doors, their scrapbooks, and their reservoirs of memory to me. I thank the Shubutans, every one.

Librarians at the Mississippi Department of Archives and History in Jackson, the East Mississippi Regional Library in Quitman, the Waynesboro Public Library, and the library of my university, the University of Minnesota, were quite generous in giving me their help. The University of Minnesota Graduate School, the College of Liberal Arts, and the American Studies Program all enabled me with funding, leave time, and staff assistance for this book. I especially appreciate the help of a sequence of graduate student assistants: Elizabeth Anderson, Josephine Fowler, Lynn Bronson, and Kelly Kuhn-Wallace.

Opportunities to read three papers from this work at professional conferences were useful to me, and I thank Danièlle Pitavy-Souque of the University of Burgundy in Dijon for one such opportunity, Tony Badger of Cambridge University and the Southern Studies group of the European Association for American Studies for another, and the American Studies Association at its Boston meeting for a third.

Friends and colleagues who read some or all of the manuscript and gave me advice about it include William G. Brockman, Graham Howes, B. J. Stiles, Kelly Kuhn-Wallace, and Jean W. Ward.

My family members, as always, are my very best source of support. My husband, Wilson, and our four children, birth and in-law, Natasha Leigh Yates and Ian V. Scheerer, M. Stiles Yates and Tina Schultz Yates, make life good even at its low moments. Natasha read the manuscript through and Wilson read parts of it, and both helped me make it better. I thank all of you with love.

Errors here, and I am sure there are many, though I have tried hard to clean up all the mistakes I found, are all mine.

Life and Death in a Small Southern Town

Introduction
Beautiful Town ... Ugly Town

> *I placed a jar in Tennessee,*
> *And round it was, upon a hill.*
> ....
> *The wilderness rose up to it,*
> *And sprawled around, no longer wild.*
> —Wallace Stephens, "Anecdote of the Jar"

On the banks of the Chickasawhay River in the piney-woods section of southern Mississippi is a town called Shubuta, and it is a beautiful town. Shubuta is beautiful in its natural setting with live oaks beside the river bearing their Spanish moss, with the woods around it in springtime filled with dogwood and redbud and new leaves of baby green, bronze, and rose red. The gardens at homes both modest and fine hold cold-weather camellias and pansies, early spring pear trees and azaleas, and later summer roses and lilies, marigolds and zinnias. Autumn brings goldenrod to the ditches and chrysanthemums to the gardens. Even in winter, the pine trees retain their vivid green, the stubble of broomsage is a golden brown, and lawns remain slightly green even with the occasional crusting of hoarfrost or thick patches of iced puddles or ice-skimmed ponds.

Shubuta is beautiful in memory. Boys, dead from old age now, remembered for their lifetimes their climbing its water tower and surveying the beauty of their town. They remembered from around the turn of the twentieth century the pranks they played, banging their shoes on the upstairs floor to convince their mothers they were going to bed, before they shimmied out the windows and down the sides of their houses to meet each other in the darkness. Together they would go, harmlessly, to the campfire of the camping country people who had come to town to trade and at night sat around their campfires telling stories to one another. Women remember the births of their babies and the loving care of the intellectual doctor who had made an unprecedented perfect entry-test score at Millsaps College and who taught them birth control. Decades later they laugh gently at the joke on him when his wife had four children, the last two twins.

Shubutans remember Eucutta Street, their Main Street, with its two rows of frame shop buildings, later brick, facing one another, and its well of continually running water in the middle of the street, drinking pipes for people, a watering trough for their animals below. Fires were so frequent on the one-block length of commercial wooden buildings on Eucutta Street that an executive in New York of the fire insurance company that insured them told Robert C. Weems, the Shubuta agent, facetiously, "That Eucutta Street must have been miles long for all the fires that have been on it!" Even so, to young people in Shubuta in the 1910s and 1920s, Chester Mathers and Elsie Jones Cross among them, it was exciting to get up in the night and go downtown to watch fires burning. One heart-pine timber building would go up in flames, igniting another and another, sometimes burning down every structure on the block of a whole side of the street before the fire could be put out. Fires burned on the street of commercial buildings and the residential streets alike, with town center buildings or homes, one or two or even a whole row catching fire and the flames sweeping, cracking, and leaping high into the night sky. In memory from a safe old age, it was even beautiful.

There was beautiful architecture in Shubuta: houses, shops, the depot at the railroad tracks, hotels at one time, and churches. Today standing in century-old glorious beauty are the Shubuta Baptist Church and Shubuta Methodist Church buildings, both built in white frame "Carpenter Gothic" style, with gables and towers and carved bargeboards under the eaves, both built around 1891. Each is kept in careful repair and is tended reverently. Both have thick new carpets, restored good wood furnishings inside, and outside polished stained-glass windows, fresh white paint, and lush lawns with well-tended trees and shrubs. A half-block apart, they sit next to U.S. Highway 45, today's Main Street through Shubuta.

Shubuta is beautiful as a town and as a natural landscape. Shubuta is beautiful in memory. It is beautiful in the recollections of the people for whom it has been home. It is beautiful in the ways it has come to life as a town, the ways it has grown and decayed, changed and constrained, remained the same and moved on. It is beautiful in its history, its vitality, its locality.

Shubuta is beautiful in the stories of its people. We see this beauty in their tall tales, their legends, and their lies, but most of all, the truth of the matter is in the stories of their lives.

The geography, demography, and economy of Shubuta bear similarity to many small U.S. towns of the nineteenth and twentieth centuries. Their beauty is in their function as rational, orderly, and serviceable. Like many towns Shubuta was first established on a source of transportation, the river. Its location on the Chickasawhay River where the river forks with Shubuta Creek is about one hundred miles from the coast of the Gulf of Mexico and thirteen miles from the Alabama state line. The Chickasawhay River flows south into the Pascagoula River, which in turn empties into the Gulf, making Shubuta a place that once had a navigable river from its site to the open waters of the Gulf.

The earth around Shubuta, except for the more fertile bottomlands beside the creeks and river, is red clay soil and, hence, not as good for agriculture as that on the opposite side of the state in the Mississippi River delta. Even so, subsistence farming and plantation culture flourished in an agricultural economy for a few decades before the Civil War, and productive farming continued for a few more decades after it. Also, the land is not as good for hardwood growth as for the pine trees that were within its virgin forest and that grow quickly now when planted on its cut-over land. Today R. L. Toney has beautiful stands of pine trees he planted on his property around Shubuta.

Shubuta's population in the 1990 Census was counted as 577, down from 626 in 1980. With the 2000 census it was up to 675. Shubutans say that its population was as high as 2,000 soon after the turn of the twentieth century when it was an expanding sawmilling town. A 1926 promotional flyer for agriculture and industry in Clarke County, Shubuta's county, claimed the population of Shubuta was "more than 1500 persons." A town booster story published in a newspaper in 1974 claims that in the 1880s Shubuta was the largest town between Meridian, Mississippi, now Mississippi's second largest city, and Mobile, Alabama, the port city eighty-eight miles away.[1]

People "traded" in Shubuta, too. For more than a century, farm families came to Shubuta to do their shopping from several adjoining counties in both Alabama and southern Mississippi, Jasper and Jones Counties among them. Celebrating his 108th birthday in 1996, Ed Graves from Ellisville, forty miles southwest of Shubuta in Jones County, remembered that before the railroad came to Ellisville some people went to Shubuta from there by oxen-pulled wagons to trade. In fact, it was truly trade, exchange of goods for goods and services, for the farmers brought farm produce to sell to the merchants in town, as well as bought what they needed from them. On 22 November 1918 just before Thanksgiving and just as World War I was ending, W. H. Patton & Son closed an advertisement with an accounts-due notice, saying, "We insist on your bringing in the cotton or the money." The ad points out that "We are unloading to-day one of the finest if not the finest car [meaning railroad freight car] of flour we have ever had—plain and self-rising—in 12, 24, 48 and 96 lb. sacks and barrels and halves in wood. Also car of salt in 25, 50, 100 and 200 lb. sacks. A car load of Pittsburg [sic] steel net and barbed wire rolling. Have a car of extra heavy oats. Stock of dry goods, clothing, hats, under wear [sic], shoes, hardware and groceries complete."[2]

The ad continues by telling the customers what they should bring in, together with prices the Pattons will pay: $25.00 a ton for velvet beans, $1.85 per bushel for "white sacked corn," and $1.55 per bushel for "heavy slip-shucked sound corn in ear." They will buy cotton at market price. They also want "ribbon cane molasses, if well strained and good body, $1.00 a can," as well as peas, peanuts, turkeys, eggs (50 cents a dozen), and cottonseed. They offer the service of grinding corn for their customers.[3]

As this ad suggests, Shubuta has served its people, sometimes beautifully, with commerce, community, and security of place.

Shubuta is ugly, too, with its share of ugliness both natural and moral. Its people have experienced the ugliness of fear, grief, and hatefulness. Shubuta mothers used the word *ugly* as cautionary to their children: "Don't you all act ugly now, you hear?"

Ugly results, too, came from natural disasters, economic distress, or both. Down near the river are some houses that flood almost every spring when the river rises and leaves its banks. Their African American occupants must cope with near-yearly water damage to their floors and furnishings, but they know poverty too deep to move to other homes. Other black Shubutans live in trailers, as mobile homes are called there, or shacks or old crumbling houses on the west side of town or out of town and down the road from town, knowing poverty and job loss and inadequate education. Whites and blacks alike suffer from the urban economy having passed them by, taking jobs and services to the cities and regional centers. Shubuta has been "urbanized" and standardized like all of the rest of the country. Once an agricultural trade center, then a boom sawmilling town, and for some decades a financial and trade center again, by the beginning of the twenty-first century the town's major employers were one branch factory employing fewer than three hundred semiskilled workers, two small locally owned factories with thirty-nine and seventeen employees respectively, and two sawmilling and timber operations. The old and prestigious Bank of Shubuta has another name as a part of a merger. The first main food store that was a part of a supermarket chain opened and closed in the 1990s, leaving only one small local market in the town where several fine grocery stores had once flourished. Shoe repair, eyeglass fitting, and dry cleaning are not available in the town at all, though out on the highway there was briefly a self-service laundry business marked "Washatera."

Shubuta no longer has a school of any kind after a long town history of education, both private and public. Along with education, most government services and health care must be obtained now, as well as most shopping done and even leisure activities pursued, in Quitman, the county seat of Clarke County, fifteen miles to the north; in Waynesboro, the next large town fifteen miles south on Highway 45; or in more distant cities of Meridian, Laurel, or Jackson, rather than in the town of Shubuta itself.

Ugly fear of a kind holding many Americans grips Shubuta, too, fear of violence, fear of drug trafficking, fear for personal safety. Some Shubutans keep guns in their homes for self-protection and at night lock front doors that before were never locked. They say, "Shubuta is not like it used to be."

Shubuta knows the collective honest griefs of all Americans. Some of its sons died in wars. The cemeteries of the Tribulation Baptist Church, black, and the Shubuta Cemetery, white, hold graves of Shubuta men killed in World War II. Shubutans participated in the Civil War, both World Wars, Korea, and the Persian Gulf War; and a Green Beret from Shubuta, Allen Trotter, was called to service in 2001 for the war against terrorism. Families represented in Shubuta have been to even more wars. William Thomas Sellers, a retired Shubuta man, spent four years in the Navy, three in the Army, and twenty-five in the Army Reserves. He says men in his family have been in every U.S. war since the War of 1812. They fought in the Battle of New Orleans in the War of 1812, were at the Alamo, in Creek Indian Wars and the Civil War, as well as both World Wars. This participation in wars is an irony because his first Sellers ancestors, eight brothers, Quakers, who did not believe in bearing arms, came to Pennsylvania on the same ship with colony founder William Penn.[4]

Daughters of Shubuta have traveled abroad—though seeing Havana, much of Cuba, Panama City, and the Panama Canal as a cruiseship tourist in 1928, seasick on the Caribbean, Mary Weems said woefully, "I would give a thousand dollars if I were in Shubuta now."[5] Some Shubuta women have stayed home, some willingly, some without any choice. Shubuta's daughters, too, both wed and unwed, have given birth. They have worked, women and men, in the homes, the fields, the shops and the offices, the businesses, schools, and the factories, by their labor making their town, their lives, and their living.

Shubuta has participated in American and world history.

Shubuta knows its share of prejudice, both inside itself and against it. The greatest of this, but not all of it, is racism. Shubuta like most of the United States practiced racial segregation until the 1960s, and some Shubutans, like some other Americans, harbored racial hatred after that; but some white Shubutans, like many white U.S. southerners, have experienced unfairly being scorned or blamed for all of U.S. racism. It is the usual paradox: some of them are guilty, but not all of them. In the years of the civil rights movement, summer voter registration workers were recruited for Shubuta at the University of Wisconsin at Madison. By the mid-1990s, the town librarian, the chief of police, a bank officer, the postmaster, and two of the supervisors at the supermarket were black; and by the last local election of the 1990s, a Shubuta-born black man, Clyde Brown, was elected mayor of Shubuta along with two black people elected among the five aldermen.

The landscape is ugly, too, in some places near Shubuta where the trees have been overcut, leaving dead treetops and a new growth of thorny brambles to choke the hacked and stumpy earth, and where red gullies have been washed in the sparse topsoil in now-abandoned fields. The red dirt in much of the region was never rich for large-scale farming, though it sustained the family living of hardworking oxen-, horse-, and mule-driving farmers of an earlier era. Now even the bottomlands by the creeks and rivers have been given up to some cattle raising and to timber. Oil has come in small portion to some landowners, bringing momentary wealth to a few, but the oil wells and trucks and power lines and tanks are ugly on the landscape and the roads. Hunters around Shubuta find deer in the woods, wild turkeys, quail, raccoon, squirrels, and rabbits to their liking, and armadillos and opossums to their disgust. One can only imagine the virgin glint of green glory of the piney woods before the cutting, before the logging, sawmilling, and timber removal and the flourishing of farms and towns that brought down the original trees. However, today even the fields and streams of the vicinity of a long-ago agricultural time have largely given up much of their beauty, just as the virgin pine of the beautiful piney woods is long ago gone from Shubuta.

Shubuta was considered to be an "aristocratic" town through most decades of the twentieth century. Shubuta's leading families, including the Ledyards, Floyds, Heidelbergs, Pattons, MacCormacks, Weemses, and Hands, had wealth and manners, music and art and professional education, good architecture for their houses and for their Methodist and Baptist churches, political connections and travel experience far beyond Shubuta, a secure bank, stores, and land. They were "cultured people."

When I was a child, there were few country people who moved into Shubuta. Rather, rural people went into town on Saturdays for shopping, "to trade." One or two generations before that, the farm people had gone to town twice a year, in the spring to get planting materials and in the fall to sell their cotton and corn and other crops and to buy farm and household provisions.

Shubuta was stratified town and country.

In town, there were merchants and their families and managers attached to the railroad and the sawmill businesses that made up a middle class; but most of white Shubuta was upper class, the "cultured people," with a large black underclass, descendants of slaves from the Lang Plantation, the

Horne Plantation, and other smaller farms in the region. In my childhood Saturdays were "trading day," the day the farmers and farm workers would go into town to buy tools and fertilizer and livestock feed that they needed for their farms and those foods their families did not grow for themselves. Shubuta streets would be lined with white men with hats shading their leathery necks, some of them sitting on sidewalk benches, whittling or spitting tobacco and talking, and black men, women, and children standing around on the streets, laughing, and talking with their neighbors, all going in and out of stores for their weekly shopping.

Shubuta was also stratified black and white.

The white men sat if they pleased. The black people stood or kept walking.

My Town

In this story of a town, I am a player, not an onlooker, for Shubuta is my town and the voice of Shubuta articulated here is spoken through my voice. Yet, Shubuta itself, the town itself, is the key player, and supporting it are the Chickasawhay River and Highway 45 and the U.S. government and the State of Mississippi and all of the people over all of the time that Shubuta has been their hometown. This is a narrative of a place called home and the river and the road, the town, the sky, and the stars of home. It is my story, Shubuta's story, and the story of all Shubutans, a tale of a place made up by its people, created, governed, escaped, and returned to by its own. It has its particulars as well as its generic connections with towns everywhere. In the Chickasawhay River at Shubuta, the catfish swim deep in the river bottom's muck, and, as in Eden, the snakes crawl out of the trees by the river, live oaks hanging with Spanish moss, venomous water moccasins, able to poison paradise. The law and the land and the story all rise from the river. This is my town, Shubuta.

Born at home five miles out in the country in a rural community called Hiwannee, thus born a "country" person, my birth was attended by Shubuta's Dr. Albert Hand, who lived on "Silk Stocking Row," as people called North Street, where the families of professional men and business owners lived, with his Tennessee-born musician wife, "Miss Rhoda."

In the U.S. South in my childhood and even to some extent today, both married and single women were addressed as "Miss" with their first names, in contrast to the title "Mrs.," which was used only with the family name of the married woman or for the married woman with the name of her husband. This was a kind of affectionate or familiar means of addressing a mature woman. Thus, she would be "Miss Rhoda," "Mrs. Hand," or "Mrs. Albert Hand." Men, likewise, were addressed by a title and a first name. Because he was a doctor, Albert Hand was called "Dr. Albert." The Weems brothers who were his contemporaries living in Shubuta, sons of the turn-of-the-century bank founder George S. Weems (1859–1935), were known, especially to children and across social classes, as "Mr. Bob" (Robert C. Weems, 1885–1977), "Mr. Jim" (James A. Weems, 1892–1983), and "Mr. George" (George S. Weems Jr., 1890–1969).

I knew Shubuta peopled with Hands and Weemses as my town from birth and childhood. When I returned to do research for my Shubuta book, I read in the town government minutes dated the night before I was born, 5 May 1940, that Dr. Albert Hand, alderman, had been present at the town council meeting. I imagine, pieced together from the stories I have been told, Dr. Hand going home from the town council meeting to his comfortable house and then being fetched first thing in the morning by my father. Out in the country, since we had no telephones until I was a teenager in the 1950s, when a birth was pending, the men went to town in their cars or pickups to get the doctor. After I was born early in the morning, the doctor expressed delight with my mother that I was the girl she wanted, and then, on May 6, my first day of life, he no doubt went back to Shubuta and spent the day seeing patients in his office in town.

Shubuta is the place, also, where I knew I was loved. I went to Dr. Hand's office once when I came home from college with a broken heart. He attended to me medically and then paced across the room of his clinic with his hands clasped behind his back, turned back around to me dramatically and declared, "Girlie," as he affectionately called all his women and girl patients, "I can't imagine anybody not loving you!"

In addition to being a player in Shubuta's story by birth and love, I came to this creative narrative of the town after higher education and much travel.

I wanted to understand the place of my childhood the way I had come to know many other places of the world through formal education. I wanted to grasp professionally how "my place" has changed with the specifics of our history and our time—the civil rights movement and racial desegregation, urbanization and mass transportation, electronic communications, air travel, globalization. I came to realize that I wanted to know emotionally and personally, too, what has happened to Shubuta.

I lived away, came back for visits, went away, and returned again. But to write about the town, I returned to Shubuta with a project, a new eye and ear. Through the 1990s, I spent much time there with a scholar's plan and a writer's questions, and suddenly, Shubuta looked entirely different. In Shubuta, I interviewed people, had lunch with my mother's friends and with black people whom I had not met before. Then, during the more-than-a-decade in which "Shubuta" was my project, I went off to southern Africa, Munich and Amsterdam, Berlin, England, and Israel, as well as to Minnesota, where I am a professor, and thought about Shubuta with fresh vision and comparative insight. I was learning in the most fundamental of ways, with my heart as well as with my mind.

I came to this project, too, through readings of a lifetime. Since I was a little child, reading has been my primary way of knowing. The works that suggested "Shubuta" to me were village studies, stories about towns, and sociology books on the town.

Bessie Head's book, *Serowe: Village of the Rain Wind,* is the single most important work that influenced my writing this one. My daughter, Natasha, was given Bessie Head's books for her Peace Corps Volunteer orientation to Botswana, and she gave them to me. A fiction writer of exceptional talent and power, South African–born "coloured" novelist Bessie Head, child of an illicit union of a white neurotic South African woman and her family's black stable servant "boy," wrote the history of her country of exile, Botswana, in *Serowe* by means of interview biographies of the villagers in that place she had chosen for her exile home.

Bessie Head, in turn, had been influenced in her method and style for her village book by the English sociologist Ronald Blythe, in his village study, *Akenfield.* I, too, loved reading *Akenfield,* in which Blythe, like Head, reports interviews with villagers by occupational groups to provide a composite portrait of a Suffolk village. The village studies of both Blythe and Head are as pleasing to read as any fiction.

Another important source of inspiration for my work is Eudora Welty's *The Golden Apples,* a story cycle about the imaginary small town Morgana, Mississippi. In fiction, in *The Golden Apples,* Eudora Welty paints the portrait of a Mississippi town with the strokes of genius for social order and history, people and place as brilliant as any sociologist. The Morgana townspeople and their streets and woods and churches, their politics and foibles and fancies, their cruelty and survival, can be compared with African Serowe and English Akenfield and overlaid on Shubuta to show Small Town, USA.

No doubt Bessie Head and Ronald Blythe in writing about Serowe and Akenfield and Eudora Welty in creating Morgana loved their subjects, as I do mine. No doubt they have felt ambivalence, too, such as mine, over the colonialist past, the feudal past, the racist past, and the sexist past of these places that we love.

Geographer Yi-Fu Tuan, who was my colleague at the University of Minnesota, guided my thought about the capacity of place to be mythic in his book *Space and Place.* Myths are stories that break open meaning. Tuan suggests that *space* designates a location, while *place* reveals meaning. *Space* is a spot on a map or the inhabited physical environment, while *place* carries all the attachments, associations, loyalties, and feelings people engage with a location. Folklorist Henry Glassie in his Irish village study, *Passing the Time in Ballymenone,* taught me to be respectful of people being studied on their own terms. Likewise, historian David Hollinger influenced me in his thinking in *Postethnic America* to consider the political narrative in the United States as singular and unifying, the story of *a people,* while the American ethnic narratives are many and multiple, the stories of *peoples.* For me, in my story of Shubuta, place and stories meet, as do the political people and the ethnic peoples of the United States.

For more than a decade I went back to Shubuta and stayed for periods of time in the house out in the country that I inherited from my parents, working as a researcher on my town. My research plan was haphazard. I meant to interview people, do a "survey" about events and attitudes, look at census records in the state library in Jackson and at newspapers and court records in the county seat town of Quitman. While I did those things and learned from them, I discovered that far more important were the unexpected moments of revelation opened up by a Shubuta person, or the offhand passing on to me by someone of old clippings and pictures and, in almost incidental ways, their giving me leads to new sources, human and archival. "Hanging out" with Shubutans at the post office, the library, the Nutrition Center, or Meeks Shoe Store proved more valuable than planned meetings for my project of learning. Riding around in their cars to places Shubuta people volunteered to take me proved very instructive as well. It became a journey, rather than a project, a journey with its destination unknown, a journey into meaning, the meaning of our town, and, in turn, the meaning of our human selves.

Shubutan Janette Hudson was my first interviewee, and she generously shared with me Shubuta history that she had gathered for a church history booklet on the Shubuta Methodist Church.[6] Janette Hudson, in her sixties then, was the widow of Tommy Hudson, who had died at the age of 39. She lived alone in a 1905 house across the street from the home where her parents-in-law had lived and next door to "Miss Mary" Weems's house on Eucutta Street. A dignified, attractive, and reserved woman with graying hair, handsome clothes, and a pleasant smile, Janette took quite seriously my request to learn from her about Shubuta history. When I arrived for our interview on a cold winter afternoon, in addition to hot drinks and homemade food for us, she had the gas space heaters on in her high-ceilinged rooms, and she had numerous documents out for me to see. She also gave me a dozen names of people I should talk to. She showed me maps of Shubuta made of the town by the Sanborn Fire Insurance Company in the late nineteenth and early twentieth centuries. In doing so, she at once increased my knowledge enormously, and much that she told me that day formed the nucleus of what I was to expand upon in later times for the development of my book.

My beloved and locally revered aunt Erma Mathers, who lived in Matherville most of her adult life, had grown up in Hiwannee, and had gone through high school in Shubuta, accompanied me on several of my interview visits. She knew and was known by almost everyone in the town and its surrounding rural communities. Thus, she opened doors for me and helped me ask the right questions for people to unlock their store of memories and banks of knowledge to me. In many a home we went into, the people would have on the wall a framed crocheted panel piece with their name in crochet letters, gifts made for them by Aunt Erma for an anniversary, a birthday, graduation, or celebration of a baby's birth. Each member of my family has similar crocheted works in frames on our walls, along with tiny fine-thread baby booties laced with pink and blue ribbons for babies yet to be born. My aunt was very enthusiastic about my writing and expressed her excitement about what I was doing to any and all her friends. She had been president of her 1925 high school graduating class in her Shubuta public school; to be able to attend that school, she had come in from her Hiwannee home in the country and lived with her aunt. She gave me her 70-year-old high school memory book, a seventy-four-page album of notes, pictures, programs, autographs, newspaper clippings, and cards around her senior year in high school, along with many other bits and pieces of paper memorabilia, as documentation for my research.[7]

Sometimes I despaired that I would not be able to get enough information to arrive at mature insights about the town. For example, I worried about how I would handle the lynchings that had happened in Shubuta, not wanting those horrendous events to dominate my narrative, but also not wanting to minimize their gravity in the town's past. I was concerned about the potential for my becoming sentimental or nostalgic about some of my material and thus diluting the effectiveness of what I might write. Once my husband said to me, "You love those people too much to tell the truth about them." While I do love Shubuta and its people, I did not want him to be right that I could not tell the truth about what I was learning.

Over and over again, I was frustrated when people gave me already published material about Shubuta when I asked for documents or family archives. There was the forty-eight-page town booklet *Shubuta,* by Frank L. Walton, published in 1947, of which I was offered several copies and of which I already had a copy that had been in my family home among my father's belongings. There was a feature from the Wayne county newspaper on Shubuta's celebrating the nation's bicentennial that I saw several times. But I struck gold when Syble Meeks, a lifelong friend of my family, brought out a stack of newspapers and handed me copies of the *Mississippi Messenger.* Did I know that Shubuta had a daily newspaper for many years? she asked me. I had not until that minute. Cassandra Cameron, the young African American librarian for the new Shubuta Library, was introduced to me by Patsy Toney, a white community leader of the town whom I had known for most of my life; and Cassandra became an important link for me with people and resources new to me from Shubuta's black community. She helped me find more vantage points for understanding Patsy's, Syble's, her and my town, Shubuta, than any of us had quite had before.[8]

Cassandra Cameron's Town

When I was introduced to Cassandra Cameron in February of 1990, she was in her late twenties and had been recently appointed to her job as librarian in the new Shubuta Public Library. It was a ten-hour-a-week job, and the library was a modest one-room space in the corner building across the street from the Town Hall. The library itself was more a gesture to reading than it was a useful library. From the standpoint of history-making, Cassandra herself was significant, for she was the first black officer employed in Shubuta.

On my first day at the library, its holdings seemed to me to be very modest indeed. There were a number of children's books, many of them appearing to be secondhand. Shelves contained a quite limited collection of a miscellany of books for adult readers, and they too seemed to be used ones. One whole bookshelf was made up of *Reader's Digest* condensed books, volumes many public libraries reject as donations. What Cassandra pointed out to me that first day that interested me most was a glass case, a kind of curio cabinet, containing a display of old pictures, diplomas, scrapbooks, and family keepsakes. She said that this material, which was a collection of family archives, had been given to the library recently by Miss Helen Phillips, an 82-year-old woman living in Meridian who had lived in Shubuta as a child and whose family had been prominent in town, her grandfather Joshua M. Phillips having been the minister of the Shubuta Baptist Church, her grandmother Georgia Dees Phillips, a teacher and writer for the newspaper. The Phillips family archives were to be a generating source of information for me at that beginning time for my project.[9]

That 1990 day with Cassandra Cameron proved to be the first of many days over several years that I joined her at the library and later at the Shubuta

Senior Nutrition Center in the same building, when she was appointed to head it. Through her I met and interviewed people, many of them older black people I would not otherwise have been able to meet, and I learned of her life as it changed and developed with a changing Shubuta.

When Patsy Toney introduced me to Cassandra, I wanted to meet her as a member of the younger generation of adults who had come of age in Shubuta after the civil rights movement. In the library, I talked with her about her job there and asked if I might interview her with her parents the following day. She agreed to the interview and gave me driving directions by which to find her.

I set out the next day in my car, and my directions to Cassandra's home said that I was to go about seven miles out into the country on the road that was Eucutta Street through town. Later I was to learn that this community was called Beaver Dam. I drove out of town on the two-lane blacktop road with no median line and with foliage of close trees hugging the road's shoulders. The ubiquitous red dirt of the region shone through some near gullies, at times washing dryly down to the road. My directions said to go by the oil field, that I would see a sign past a hill for Tribulation Baptist Church, Cassandra's church, that I was to go three or four more miles after that to find her home, a green trailer, or stationary mobile home.

At that time Cassandra and her two young children shared that trailer home with her parents, O'Dell Cameron and Bertha Carter Cameron. Cassandra's mother was an invalid, having suffered a stroke recently. At the time of the interview, she was wrapped in a faded warm blanket, sitting up in a recliner chair. When I arrived O'Dell Cameron was finishing his lunch, sitting in the same central room of the trailer with his wife and daughter, eating from an aluminum foil pie pan.

We four talked of education, of Cassandra's degree from Jackson State University, and of her parents' teacher certification from Jackson State, which they had received after a few months' training, not by a degree like Cassandra had earned, and their subsequent schoolteaching. We talked of fishing and hunting around Shubuta, of childhood in the woods and along the river.

Later, after Cassandra's mother had died, Otis Bumpars, another of my interviewees, told me that as a child Bertha Carter had walked seven miles into town to school each day to the segregated black school on the west side of Shubuta. Besides being teachers, in the 1960s she and her husband had gone to meetings and organized within their community for black voter registration, civil rights, and desegregation.

Their church, the Tribulation Baptist Church, was a very important force in their lives for the Carters and the Camerons. Cassandra Cameron took me to visit the building and the churchyard right after my visit with her family. I saw the handsome chancel furniture, the old pieces hand made by parishioners, newer pews, as beautiful, made with saws. I saw the baptistery, the baptismal pool for immersion in Baptist practice, the pride of the congregation. Cassandra told me that before it was built her congregation held baptisms in the nearby creek or river where the riverbed muck had sometimes included leavings from previous visits by cows. Her mother had made her a white dress for her baptism as a child. Both of us laughed shyly as we simultaneously had the mental image of the immersion of the young girl in her new white dress in the mucky river. In the cemetery among the gravestones were markers for Carter men killed in World War II. Cassandra pointed out the burial places of these war-dead relatives of hers.

Church and school citizen effort blended in Cassandra Cameron's life, and she benefited both from her parents' teachings and their civil rights leadership. A young child at the time of the one civil rights march in Shubuta, a 1967 march protesting segregation around their Head Start program, Cassandra remembers watching the march through the streets of town, remembers the controversy over desegregating schools, and understands the benefit she gained when she became the first black government employee in Shubuta, the town librarian.

The Camerons and Carters were among the very few black Shubutans with some college education and, as such, were among their community's leaders. Their economic circumstances and material goods—a small trailer home for five people, foil-piepan dishes—were indicators of the limits still there at the top of Shubuta's black middle class. Cassandra's new quarter-time job as town librarian in the small, ill-stocked single room on Eucutta Street in town was more a source of pride than of income.

Later in the decade, after both her parents had died, Cassandra added another government job in the back room of the same building, becoming the supervisor of the five-day-a-week noontime meal service in the Shubuta Senior Nutrition Center. She served the meals daily at the center and sent them out to shut-ins, white and black both, but as late as 1997 the word *Niger* [*sic*] was scratched deeply into the metal of the center's air-conditioning unit. Prejudice was not dead yet.

Some Townspeople

In my goings and comings to and from Shubuta in the 1990s, I met and talked casually with a number of people like William Thomas Sellers, who told me about his family's U.S. military record and other stories of his family and Shubuta. I attended public events with other people like Methodist minister Dr. Shaw Gaddy and went to still other people's homes like that of Mrs. Cleo Cooper when I was invited. I spent productive time informally visiting in Shubuta places, walking alone on the town sidewalks, and putting my head into shops and offices. Sometimes I would drive my car around town and out into the country very slowly, paying attention to whatever and whoever was there, sometimes tape-recording my observations. I behaved like the part-time Shubuta area resident I was, shopped in town, mailed my letters and packages at the Shubuta post office window, and cashed checks at the bank. I bought milk and eggs and orange juice at the convenience store in Shubuta on my drives through town from the Meridian airport to my house on Highway 45 each time I arrived in the evening for a stay. I drove often to Waynesboro or Quitman for purchase and service needs not met in Shubuta, and I attended services at my Methodist Church in Shubuta when I was in town.

My work when I was in Shubuta was that of a full-time research scholar. Interviews were at first the most important part of the work; and besides interviewing Janette Hudson, in my researcher role, I formally interviewed more than a dozen people with tape-recorded and transcribed records of those interviews. I also learned from papers, letters, clippings, and pictures that the people giving them to me often would not have thought of as documents, though I did. Likewise, people's remembered or family transmitted stories were instructive for me of both their lives and those of many Shubutans no longer living.

In my text, I mention numerous people and acknowledge interview and site visit sources; but in the course of my book becoming my own storytelling, I came to find certain people's Shubuta voices and Shubuta frames of reference other than my own helpful to add, so large sections of interview reports or frequent mentioning of a short list of Shubutans came to be important to the text. Cassandra Cameron was one of these people. The others are, in alphabetical order: Otis Bumpars; Elsie Jones Cross; James and Phyllis Johnston, husband and wife; Aubrey and Ollie Jones, husband and wife; Mary McCarty; Charlie D. Meeks and Syble Meeks, father and daughter; and Mary V. Weems and her father, George Stephenson Weems.

Otis Bumpars is a black man who was in his seventies during the 1990s. A lifelong Shubutan, he experienced the full range and impact of racial segregation and its lifting in the town by the 1970s. Over his working life, he had been a laborer at farming, sawmilling, road work, railroad work, and timber hauling. In 1942, as a late-teenage county prison work gang member, he was forced to participate in a crew required to bury the bodies of the two young-teenage victims of the 1942 lynchings and to keep the cover-up quiet in the community.

Elsie Jones Cross died in 1999 at 103.[10] She came to Shubuta in 1915 with her mother and father, her father being in the sawmilling business that flourished at the time. As an unmarried young adult in the 1920s, she worked on Eucutta Street at the Hudson Drug Store and enjoyed the social life of Shubuta's upper-class young people. When she married Robert Cross, she went to live a few miles out of town in the Lang House, the antebellum mansion on the Lang Plantation, which her father-in-law and her husband after him owned by that time. The Lang House was in the Langsdale community, and Elsie Jones Cross kept the post office in one room of the mansion for many years. Farther "across the prairie," as the road to Matherville was referred to, her friend Erma Mathers kept the post office in a store that had once been the commissary of the Horne Plantation. On the red-dusty gravel road the mail carrier brought the mail each day from Shubuta to these small community post offices. In Matherville, there was no grand house or other sign of there having been a plantation site there, though the structure next door to Erma Mathers's was the rambling old nineteenth-century house of the Mathers doctor who had named the town and served its medical and civic needs in the first half of the twentieth century. That house, now in very poor repair, is owned and occasionally occupied by Chester Mathers, a retired career military officer and son of the doctor. The Crosses, along with all the Matherses and Horne descendants, went to church in Matherville at the Geneva Presbyterian Church.

James Johnston was postmaster in Shubuta for thirty-three years, from 1955 until 1988. He and his Maine-born wife, Phyllis, met when both were in military service during World War II, and they have lived in Shubuta continually from when they made it their home after their wartime service. They brought up five daughters in Shubuta. James Johnston's grandfather, Arista Johnston, was born in Clarke County in 1849, into a family that had bought land in Mississippi and Alabama from the federal government in the Chesterfield District of South Carolina. Living in Alabama for the years of his youth and through the Civil War, Arista Johnston moved back to the family's Mississippi land in 1869, married, and became a leading citizen in the Shubuta community. James Johnston's father was a dentist and his mother a grocery store owner; and James and Phyllis now live in the house where his parents lived on Eucutta Street in the second block west of downtown. The Johnstons and Patsy and R. L. Toney are the only two representative couples of the economic leadership class of the twentieth century still living in Shubuta, R. L. Toney's father having established the very successful Shubuta Tie and Timber Company in 1919. The Toneys live on the east side of the center block of town on Eucutta Street about as far on that side as the Johnstons live to the west.

Aubrey and Ollie Cooper Jones also came from families that settled around Shubuta after buying land from the government in South Carolina in the 1830s. Aubrey Jones was mayor of Shubuta from 1937 until 1943. He liked the fact that he had put in the town water works system when he was mayor. Before that, the town paid a man to clean the household toilets and other facilities at each house in the town city limits—the *Mississippi Messenger* reports in the town financial statement of 18 October 1918 paying Archie Brown for "cleaning closets" from $25.00 to $27.50 each month; there had not been waterworks as a public utility before. The Cooper and Jones families had come with the earliest migration of white people, Aubrey Jones's grandfather settling in 1836 on the land Aubrey subsequently owned in what was later known as the Red Hill community. Ollie Cooper's father was the well driller in Shubuta. Aubrey Jones was an entrepreneur as well as a farmer and a town politician. Following other work, he had the feed store in Shubuta in midlife, and when he retired he bought an orange grove in Florida and was successful there. The pride and joy of both Ollie and Aubrey Jones were their two daughters, Edith and Claire, whom they thoroughly enjoyed bringing up in Shubuta, even claiming to build their new big house out on the highway for them when they were teenagers.[11]

Mary McCarty is a black professional woman, a civic and church leader in Shubuta today. She was in her fifties through the 1990s when I interviewed her, had lived "up north" and taught high school in an all-white suburban school before moving back to Shubuta to live with her mother in her family home. She is a social studies teacher at Waynesboro High School. She went to Rust College, the then-all-black Methodist Church–related college, right out of high school in Shubuta and sang in the college's world-famous a capella choir. She is a genial and generous woman, highly intelligent and welcoming, who both volunteers and is recruited to serve on local and regional government boards and church agencies.

Charlie D. Meeks was the shoe repair man in Shubuta and ran the shoe shop on Eucutta Street from 1941 until the early 1990s. His primary identity, however, for most of those same years was that of the youth leader for the Shubuta Methodist Church. Several generations of Methodist teenagers found "Mr. Charlie" their adult friend and social leader, as well as their spiritual mentor, in that youth group. He lived in his old family home on the farm several miles north of Shubuta on Highway 45. His wife, Gladys, to whom he was devoted, was a semi-invalid for many years; she did not go to church with him very often, which townspeople found remarkable for such a devoted churchgoer husband. The Meekses had one daughter, Syble, who with her father was a pillar of the Shubuta Methodist Church. Gregarious and delightful, everybody's friend, a person with a high level of organizational skills, Syble Meeks lived at home with her parents until her father's death in 1993. She worked in the shoestore with her father, and after he was unable to repair shoes any longer, she kept the store open for a few years. The interview I had with "Mr. Charlie" in 1990 was several years after his wife's death and was as much an interview with Syble Meeks as with him.

Mary V. Weems died in 1992. She was not one of my interviewees. She would not have thought it seemly to talk about oneself on a tape recording. She was, nevertheless, one of the leading figures in the town of Shubuta for much of the twentieth century. Her father, George Stephenson Weems, founded the influential Bank of Shubuta in 1902, and she worked in the bank for several decades. Her mother, Mary Virginia, called Molly, for whom she was named, was a member of the Shubuta Hand family, another family, along with three branches of Weemses descended from cousins, among the core group of twentieth-century leading business and professional people in Shubuta. "Miss Mary" Weems lived in Shubuta all her life, though was able to travel frequently, once "around the world," and as a single woman in late years of her life occupied her big family home alone. Her oldest brother, Robert C. Weems, and his wife, Suzie, lived next door and there brought up their four children, none of whom remained in Shubuta. "Mr. Bob" was the bank president; and the younger Robert C. Weems, born in 1910, now living in Reno, Nevada, and retired from being a university dean, enjoys the memory of helping his father nail onto trees and posts "in much of the territory" advertising signs for the bank that said, "Your Money is Safe in this Bank."[12] Mary V. Weems was college educated, having earned a degree at the Methodist women's college in Brookhaven, an institution that was merged into Millsaps College long ago. She was a kind and loving woman, a philanthropist whose gift-giving came from her heart, a loyal and supportive friend, a reliable and trustworthy family member. She was also a good and firm businesswoman, a strong civic leader, and a wise and principled person in all her dealings, both public and private. She had a merry laugh, twinkling eyes, and the grace needed to make good social conversation of whatever kind the occasion demanded. She also had a regal bearing, a patrician countenance, and impeccably good manners.

These are the people it turns out I mention most often, I feature, as it were, in my story of Shubuta.

TROPE 1: TOWN

Town is a special word in the vocabulary of U.S. democracy. *Town* is generic for constellations of people, for congregations of citizens, for civic organizing. Town is the place people come into from the country, from the farm, the river valley, or the hills. Town is the building-block unit and the historical antecedent of city: urban places first were towns.

Town is a unit of government, too, an authority for making laws and keeping peace, for providing clean water, service, schooling, and heed to or neglect of citizen opinion or need. On some U.S. maps, town is a municipality of fewer than 10,000 people.

Town is also a unit of cultural geography. It is a specific place with a name on the map of memory of human persons and a way of being that is both general and particular. For many Americans, though far fewer than in 1900, town is still the place where they live: home, hometown.

Our hometown on the Chickasawhay River in piney-woods southern Mississippi is Shubuta. For Shubutans, past and present, those from the surrounding countryside communities of Langsdale, Matherville, Chapparel, Hiwannee, DeSoto, and Eucutta, too, town is the one-block-long commercial street of Shubuta. Also, for Shubutans, town is the visible boundaries of the legal corporation limits, the police station and the jail, Town Hall, the post office, the library, the train station, grocery store, banks, and gasoline stations. For Shubutans, as for other Americans, town is the invisible compass of fidelity to a place. Town is the limits of place. Town is the structure of place, the aesthetic lines and colors of place. Town is a boundary and a launching pad. Town is where we believe we belong.

TROPE 2: AUNTIE'S TRUNK

When history buff Chip Mitchell was 15 years old and his great-great-aunt Mary Weems was moving from her big old family home in Shubuta to a Jackson nursing home under the medical care of Chip's father, Chip helped his mother and others of his Weems relatives clean out and pack and move generations of Weems family belongings out of the house. The grand old house, described as "massive" in the county newspaper article when it burned soon after the new owners bought it, sat prominently in the midst of large lawns in the first block going west after the commercial district of town on Eucutta Street.[1]

In the house there was the cherry corner cabinet in the dining room that had unstained wood under its claw feet, signifying that it had stood there in that corner holding china and crystal behind its glass doors since the house was built. There was a spot on the wallpaper in a bedroom where at a young child's height the great-great-aunt the children called "Ty," born in 1901, had written her name, "Sarah." There were the porch swings and fans under which Chip's grandmother Alice had come from next door and played and swung as a happy child in the summertimes of childhood. There were the couches and curtains, as well as the dishes and chairs and glasses and linens with which Mary V. Weems, noted on the 1900 census records as a child as Mary V. Weems Jr., and the senior Mary before her, had entertained not only the family but groups from their Shubuta Methodist Church, their women's clubs, and George S. Weems's business and banking associates and those of his sons and daughters. There were books and magazines and newspapers and boxes that had come from New Orleans or Memphis in the mail and piled up over the years in the house. There was the long-case clock in the front hallway, the grandfather clock that chimed the English sounds of York, Canterbury, Westminster, and Winchester Cathedrals.[2]

Chip's mother, Mary Sue, with her sister, Sally Barksdale, and their cousins, was growing tired of so much effort and emotion around the packing and moving when Chip came out of a bedroom and asked if he could have Auntie's trunk and take it home to Jackson. "Why would you want that old thing?" Mary Sue wanted to know.

Chip did not have a good answer, but she indulged him and Auntie's trunk went to Jackson to a new home in teenaged Chip's room.

After the hubbub of settling the belongings with various nieces and nephews, great-nephews, and cousins of Weemses, the fifteen-year-old history buff gradually brought out the bits and pieces of paper and stuff of Weems legacy that he had rescued from the dustbin and annihilated memory.

Miss Mary Weems, as she was known universally throughout her lifetime to all but the family who called her "Auntie," had kept trinkets and memorabilia, travel notes and speech manuscripts and newspaper clippings of interest to her in her trunk. One item was a newspaper clipping about a Weems castle in Scotland, presumably the ancestral site. Another was a small moneybag for deposit of coins, marked Bank of Shubuta, the bank founded by her father and in which she worked. There was a Bank of Shubuta ashtray in the trunk. Souvenirs from Cuba fascinated Chip, and he found two manuscripts of talks made about a trip around the world, one on Hawaii and one on religions of India.

Mary Weems had saved a handwritten paper on Keats's poetry, evidently a college essay written when she was a student at Whitworth College, the Methodist women's college at Brookhaven, Mississippi. She had saved a speech on the planting of a tree, a cedar of Lebanon, possibly a public ceremonial speech for a planting in the town park, for the Shubuta town government minutes book records in a 1943 entry that Miss Mary V. Weems was paid $2.00 per month for "park upkeep."

In the trunk were several speeches, neatly typed out on printed letterhead stationery, some of them with typos, suggesting that she composed at the typewriter, on religious subjects for her Sunday School class or her church women's group. One speech recounts the history of the Shubuta Women's Club from its founding in 1919 until its present time of 1951.

Chip's mother's excitement rose with Chip's at their discovery of a lively historical literary gem among the contents of Auntie's trunk, a typescript of a thirty-seven-page travel diary dated 10–27 August 1928, "Diary of Annie Ruth Johnston on a Trip to the Tropics During the Summer of 1928." It was here that it was recorded that young Mary Weems, traveling with her sister, Sarah, and two families of cousins, Hands and Johnstons, lamented, seasick on the Caribbean, that she would give a thousand dollars to be in

Shubuta out of such misery. It was here that a record was made available from the eve of the Great Depression, of luxurious travel of young Shubuta women shown departing from the New Orleans French Quarter, going on a sixteen-day Caribbean cruise on the *S.S. Parisimina*. They traveled through the Panama Canal, went on shore in Honduras, Panama, and Cuba, visited the cities of Havana and Panama City, and saw the Latin American shores with banana boats loading and royal palms, coconut palms, banana plants, and locust trees growing in abundance alongside bushes of croton plants and hedges made from hibiscus. Auntie's trunk, as Chip understood, contained a remarkable material and literary testimonial to his family's past experience and the history of Shubuta.

Chapter 1

Shubuta's People

> *One of the peculiar difficulties of being a Southerner is that sometimes those we may believe to be wrong are coincidentally those we love, and we sometimes seek a solution to that problem by ignoring or even hiding the evidence.*
>
> —Josephine Humphreys, from "Southern Discomfort"

In the new, twenty-first century, people in Shubuta are black and white, Baptist, Methodist, Presbyterian, Church of God in Christ, Covenant Church of God, and Assembly of God. There are now none who are Native Americans, even though Choctaws first lived at the site where Shubuta now is and its name is Choctaw. There are none who are Catholics or Jews, though some Jews were early white settlers and founders of the earliest businesses. Greenhood Pond in Shubuta today is named for the first merchant who got off an early Mobile and Ohio Railroad (M&O) train going through Shubuta sometime in the mid-1850s and established a business, Moses (later "Morris") Greenhood, a Jew.[1]

Shubutans today are high school graduates and school dropouts and a very few are business and professional people who have gone to college and professional schools. They are factory workers and farm laborers, clergy, office workers, retired people, storekeepers, a doctor and a dentist, bank and store and business managers, and owners of stores, small businesses, and a lumberyard. They are mothers and fathers and children, single people, grandparents, uncles, aunts, and cousins in single family homes, nuclear families, single-person households, and empty nests.

For the last decades of the nineteenth century and almost to the end of the twentieth, Shubuta was a well-to-do town with its white leading "cultured people," wealthy business proprietors and landowners, professional men and their finishing-school-educated wives, a small middle class, and a large class of poor people, some poor whites, and many working poor blacks. Shubuta today has much less wealth held and invested locally, and a very large percentage of its population lives on low wages or close to the poverty line.

Shubutans like other Americans derive their identities from their work and families, from their educational experiences, and from race and religion, as well as from their place and time. In Shubuta, as in most of the South, both race and religion play a much larger part in setting personal and community identity than they do in eastern seaboard, midwestern, and western American locations.

This has been true from the start, though our consciousness of it has changed over time. Likewise, respect accorded to people has shifted with time from where it once lay, within class and racial and religious groups, to criteria sometimes outside the in-groups. Thus, status both attributed and achieved has fluctuated. Always, though, people honor their own particular ancestry and, usually, they honor the older people within their group.

Lisa Spencer, in her 1987 sociological study of rural elderly people around Shubuta and other parts of Clarke County, asked her twenty-four informants what gave some people higher status. Twenty-two of Spencer's elderly interviewees were white and two of them black. She disguised their names but keyed them in her records of her tapings, and I thereby learned that one of them was my Shubuta interviewee Charlie D. Meeks. She reports of the twenty-two responding:

> 32% (7 of 22) said "money"; 27% (6 of 22) said occupations such as "doctors, lawyers, merchants"; 18% (4 of 22) said "community leaders"; 27% (6 of 22) said "church-going hard workers"; and 9% (2 of 22) said "breeding and culture." Interestingly enough, the status which the informants reported to stem from the various factors (i.e., money, occupations, and church attendance) was not reported to result in different treatment. The status which was reported seemed to have been more of an attitude toward the various individuals.[2]

Spencer says that the way younger adults and children exhibit their regard for old people includes "not 'talking back,' giving them a title, giving up a chair for them, opening a door for them, lending a hand, and not letting them see wrongdoing like drinking or gambling."[3]

Tellingly by silence, race was not mentioned at all, and religion seemed incidental in these responses, signifying perhaps not that they were not important, but that they were such basic givens of the culture that they were not even brought to consciousness.

Town Ancestry from the Census

People's quest for their genealogy, a popular pursuit in Shubuta, is another way of showing respect for, or at least interest in, their elders and forebears. A simple search for the townspeople of the past yields much. I found their traces on U.S. Census records on microfilm at the state library, on the brittle papers of old school programs and letters saved and shown to me by Shubutans, in scrapbooks or bits of paper held onto by families, and in conversations with living people as they drew on and elaborated the memory of what they have been told.

More than once I drove to Jackson for my project and, in the state Department of Archives and History library, studied the archived and microfilmed data of maps and the U.S. Census for Shubuta over the decades it has been recorded and in the parts that are now open to the public.

Census data are organized in such a way that information and inferences about both ancestry and status of people's progenitors can be understood. In the 1870 Census for Shubuta, the first U.S. Census after the Civil War, and also the first after Shubuta was officially incorporated as a town, Shubutans were listed as having come from the other southern states of South Carolina, Alabama, Georgia, North Carolina, Louisiana, Texas, and Virginia. Antinette Gibbson, the 35-year-old wife of James S. Gibbson and mother of seven children—James, 14; Frank, 13; Wolis, 11; Castila, the only daughter, 9; Fredrick, 5; Emerial, 3; and an as-yet-unnamed 2-month-old baby boy—was listed as born in New York. Her husband, a farmer, whose real estate was valued at $4,000.00 and personal estate at $1,000.00, was born in Scotland. All five of the older Gibbson children were born in Alabama, but Emerial and the baby were born in Mississippi, placing the family's arrival in Mississippi, and perhaps Shubuta, between three and five years prior to 1870, just after the end of the Civil War.[4]

The 1870 Census shows that in Shubuta a white man, Josh T. Heard, listed as a "minister" by occupation, was born in Georgia. A black man, William

Brown, called a "preacher" in the listing, less respectful sounding than "minister" for the white man, was born in Pennsylvania. A black man named Moses Martin whose occupation was "blacksmith" was born in Virginia. Dayle Thomas, white, a painter, was from "Irland." Two white families next door to one another with the name of Cooper, the husbands of which were blacksmiths, Columbus Cooper, age 21, and William Cooper, age 52, presumably father and son, were born in Alabama. Dentist S. Saltenstahl, age 60, was born in South Carolina. The 42-year-old physician in the town, whose real estate was valued at $11,000.00 and personal estate at $1,000.00, was born in Mississippi.

The white man with the largest net worth in the year 1870, $13,000.00 in real estate and $5,000.00 in personal estate, was Morris Greenhood, age 45, born in Austria. His household was shared by his 26-year-old wife, Sarah J. Greenhood, and their five young children, Fannie, 8, Willie, 7, Emma, 5, Maria, 3, and Esteer, 1, and with three black servants with the same last name as theirs, Mary Greenhood, 15, Amus Greenhood, 33, and Lagie Greenhood, 40. Morris Greenhood was a merchant, the man who had arrived on the M&O Railroad as "Moses Greenhood" and established the first store in the newly platted town.

Another 1870 Shubuta merchant was born in France, Meyer Alexander, who had a wife, Elizabeth, and eight children.[5] A woman, Eliza Parker, age 40, was listed as a lumber merchant, with real estate valued at $13,000.00 and personal estate valued at $1,000.00. She was born in Alabama. Her household was shared by a 46-year-old woman, Mary, and 10-year-old child, George B., with the same last name. Other merchant households were those of Isaac Champenois, 56, and John Champenois, 29, living in adjacent houses and presumably father and son. (The Census form has a box to check for "Head of Household," and where a man is present in each listed household, the man's name is always checked.) The Champenois men were born in Alabama, as was the 13-year-old daughter of Luisa and Isaac Champenois, Duzila, who lived in their home. However, Fannie and John Champenois's three young children, Louisa, 7, Valberg, 4, and Isaac, 1, were all born in Mississippi, as were the three black servants living in Fannie and John Champenois's home, Sallic Holmes, 35, Mary Collins, 11, and a third one not further identified by name.[6]

By 1880 "Jno. F. Champenois," presumably the same 29-year-old John from the 1870 Census, was the secretary of the Board of Trustees for the Shubuta Male and Female Academy, listed as such on the program for its "Closing Exercises" for "Wednesday Evening, June 30, 1880." The program featured band music, speeches and "compositions," enactment of a scene from "Lady of the Lake" called "Chamber of Horrors," and a three-scene drama called "Mrs. Harley's Wax-Works." Both "Master Isaac Champenois" and "Miss Lulu Champenois" had parts in "Mrs. Harley's Wax-Works." It is reasonable to suppose that these were the 1870 Census's 1-year-old Isaac and 7-year-old Louisa now grown up to be schoolchildren of 11 and 17.[7]

By the 1900 Census far fewer Shubutans had been born beyond Mississippi and Alabama. Some older people had been born in Georgia, North Carolina, and South Carolina, but none in northern states, and only one family had been born in a European country. The five-member family of Elizabeth B. and Adolph T. Bell had all been born in England. Adolph Bell was the only Shubutan listed as a minister in 1900.[8]

By the 1900 Census, the names of all the white families that were to be government, business, and professional leaders of Shubuta of the first half of the twentieth century were in place, names like Floyd, Stovall, Howze, Patton, Weathersby, Ledyard, MacCormack, Hudson, Heidelberg, Nettles, Hand, and Weems. Professional people show up along with the merchants in the census records. Sixty-two-year-old Charles Stovall is listed as a journalist. Sharing his home with his wife, Mary E., and his 36-year-old son, "Jno. E.," a printer, as well as their black cook, Della Williams, he is the town publisher. He owned the daily newspaper, the *Mississippi Messenger,* established in 1879, and presumably employed his son as printer.[9]

Robert M. Hand, 47, is the only physician in Shubuta on the 1900 Census. Thirteen-year-old Albert P. Hand, later to be a physician himself, "my Dr. Hand," and a partner with his father and husband of musician "Miss Rhoda," is occupied with "school" as a budding adolescent in 1900, as was his older sister, Caroline. The fact that she was to live to be 100 and to teach hundreds of young Shubuta children in the third and fourth grades in the Shubuta School is confirmed by a single-page 100th birthday tribute from "Auntie's trunk," "A Living Tribute to Miss Caroline Hand," by the Reverend Ralph Savarese. Caroline Hand's being listed at "school" in the 1900

Census is a reminder that Shubuta's upper-class white girls as well as boys were educated in the town. The "Prospectus for 1900–01" of the Shubuta Institute and Military Academy, of which George S. Weems was a trustee, says, "Girls admitted to class relations upon the same terms as boys, provided, however, that they be placed, by parents and guardians, under the exclusive control and direction of the Faculty in their boarding arrangements, their social privileges, and their correspondence."[10]

The academic year on the prospectus is from 10 September 1900, to 24 May 1901, making it a nine-month school year, an unusually long calendar for small towns in that time and place, many others and nearly all public schools being eight months or less. The other trustees were D. W. Heidelberg, president; S. H. Floyd, secretary; Thos. A. Ledyard; J. M. Nettles; A. Johnston; and J. M. Beard.[11]

Girls being educated in that excellent private school came about at least in part through the agency of young Albert and Caroline's mother, Annie, who as a girl near the end of the Civil War in Shubuta determined to become educated after-hours in the boys' school. She succeeded in being well schooled and soon taught in the school for girls.[12] Apparently, coeducation eventually followed in the school, for the Shubuta private school is subsequently called the Shubuta Male and Female Academy, and later still, the Shubuta Institute and Military Academy.

George S. Weems was 40 years old in 1900, the census records. It was he as much as any other who was responsible for the twentieth-century prosperity of Shubuta. Only two years later he was to establish the Bank of Shubuta and the cottonseed milling company, the bank in particular being a key institution in Shubuta's future economic stability. Two of his children who were to succeed him in working in the bank and living in Shubuta for their lifetimes, Robert C., and "Mary V. Jr.," were 15 and 6 years old at the time of the 1900 Census.[13]

"Capitalists" Form the Bank of Shubuta

At eight o'clock one Tuesday evening early in the year 1902 "in the elegant and spacious parlors of Mr Geo S Weems [sic]," the Bank of Shubuta was created along with a cottonseed oil mill by Shubuta's financial leaders. In announcing the establishment of the bank and mill, the *Mississippi Messenger* boasts in its headline, "Both the Creatures of One Hour's Conference Among Local Capitalists."[14]

Born and brought up in DeSoto, Mississippi, George Stephenson Weems married a member of the Hand family, Mary Virginia, and moved to Shubuta eight miles away not long after the birth of their first child, Robert Cicero Weems, in 1885. The Weems and Hand families were already financially secure from their DeSoto, Stonewall, and Enterprise years of landowning, business, textile milling, and finance; and when he came to Shubuta, George Weems opened a store. His "mercantile business" was housed on Eucutta Street in a three-story building, which had an elevator. It was the centerpiece business on Shubuta's main street.[15]

On the night of the bank founding, thirteen men or pairs of brothers subscribed $21,700.00 to the establishment of the "Shubuta Oil and Manufacturing Co.," and ten individual men or pairs pledged $11,000.00 for the bank's beginning. While they claimed that they had the funds among them to begin these enterprises, they said that they wanted the mill and the bank to be available to the community and the surrounding trade area, so they were making the stock available to people in other towns and communities. The newspaper reported proudly that this was for "building up financial and manufacturing enterprises for the advancement and accommodation of the commercial and farming interests of the towns, vicinities and districts tributary to Shubuta, and for the convenience and accommodation of the public at large in transacting the general business that centres [sic] at Shubuta."[16]

The men, Shubuta's "leading capitalists," determined to capitalize the mill at $35,000.00 with the possibility of increasing to $50,000.00. They put the stock for the mill at $50.00 per share and opened their books for subscriptions in their first meeting up to $20,000.00, with "$15,000.00 in shares to be offered to other vicinities and districts." Of the $21,700.00 subscribed that night, the three shareholders who put in more than $1,000.00 each were W. L. Weems, S. H. Floyd, and George S. Weems, each contributing $5,000.00. The other pledges were W. H. Patton, $1,000.00; Patton Bros., $250.00; John Martiniere, $1,000.00; Ferrill Bros., $1,000.00; T. R. Gates, $250.00; D. W. Heidelberg, $200.00; W. M. Smith, $1,000.00; Dr. W. O. McNeill, $1,000.00; S. D. Owens, $500.00; and Dr. Hand, $500.00.[17]

When these Shubuta capitalists turned to setting up the bank, which the newspaper said would be called "The Shubuta Bank," they decided to set its capital at $25,000.00 "with privilege of increase to $50,000.00 and business to be opened on $15,000.00 paid in." The same three men who contributed most to starting the mill, George S. Weems, W. L. Weems, and S. H. Floyd, were the major funders of the bank as well, this time with $2,500.00 each. The *Mississippi Messenger* reported that this stock, too, would "be offered to parties in the districts tributary to Shubuta, but if not taken outside will be gladly taken by capitalists in Shubuta—one party will be only too glad to take it all; but the policy is one of a general community of interest and accommodation to commerce centreing [sic] at Shubuta where business is gradually increasing. The receipts of cotton here this season is near one third in excess of last season. Shubuta capitalists have contributed largely to the upbuilding [sic] of enterprises in other towns and cities, and now they believe it is their duty to be generous to their own people."[18]

Another meeting was set for "Monday evening March 24th at 7:30," again in George S. Weems's parlors.[19] Apparently the group made their capital pledges quickly, for an account in the archives of the bank tells of the first deposit slip having been dated 30 September 1902. The deposit was from W. L. Weems and it was for $2,449.97. The archives, watched over by a family member of a later bank owner, Nerva McCaskey, contain both a desk and a clock bought by Mr. Weems for the bank in 1902. The desk is a tall accounting table, the kind at which the banker stands to work. It was reportedly bought secondhand in 1902, evidence perhaps for the truth of the many stories of Weems's renowned frugality. The clock is a pendulum clock.[20]

The archival record shows the bank building was located, beginning in 1912, at the corner of Eucutta Street and Station Street, that is, across the street from the railroad tracks a short distance from the depot building. That lot was bought for $400.00 in 1912. When a fire destroyed the building in 1916, it was rebuilt by the same architectural plan at a cost of $6,364.86.[21]

The fact that the Bank of Shubuta did not close during the Great Depression of the 1930s is legendary among old-timers from and around Shubuta. The genealogy book of the Hand family, of whom the Shubuta doctors and George S. Weems's wife were members, spends half its entry on the senior George Weems on that point:

George founded and was for many years president of The Bank of Shubuta. During the bank "holiday" of the great depression, George refused to close, saying he could handle any "run" on the bank. After the government forced the closing of all banks for inspection, the Bank of Shubuta was found to be one of the strongest in the country.[22]

Asked by me for Shubuta stories on a May day in 1996, the eight white men at the men's table at the Shubuta Senior Nutrition Center lunch, each of them over 70, told how the Bank of Shubuta did not close during the Depression. This was still a source of great community pride. "But those Weemses wouldn't give us loans," one said. "They kept the money in the bank."

Shubuta Townsperson Otis Bumpars

When I interviewed him in 1996, black Shubutan Otis Bumpars, 77 years old, talked banking. He was illustrating the change in the way black Shubutans were treated at the time of his young manhood in contrast with the present.[23]

He said that "since I've been grown I've told several fellas" that when he was young if he had gone to the bank and asked to borrow a hundred dollars, "they would have laughed at me, or might have even put me in jail. How was I going to pay a hundred dollars back?"

"It is different now," he says. "If I go down there [to the bank] and tell them I want ten thousand dollars, they'll tell me to come on in and let's talk. No doubt I'll get that ten thousand dollars. Then, I'll have to worry about paying it back."

Otis Bumpars had spent most of his life in Shubuta, only living away a few miles up the road in DeSoto as a "little boy," he says. I was first introduced to him by former Shubuta mayor Florence Busby, standing by the gazebo over the town's historic watering place for people and animals, now located across Station Street from Town Hall on the Eucutta Street intersection near the railroad. This well was dug a few decades into the twentieth century after the flowing well in the middle of the downtown Eucutta Street was shut down and its pipes capped.[24] Today's well is near the edge of the Toney family's crosstie and pulpwood yard by the railroad, the Shubuta Tie and Timber Company, which was organized in 1919 by J. E.

Toney Sr. Florence Busby and I were with Patsy Toney on a day the two of them were driving me around and showing me Shubuta businesses in the town when we stopped to speak to Otis Bumpars and his brother, Andrew. Andrew Bumpars was making a holiday visit to his family, and it turned out that he now lives and works in Colorado Springs, Colorado. "Small world," Patsy Toney said. Her "Number 2 son," Barry, who now lives in Plano, Texas, also had lived in Colorado Springs, "Number 3 son," Brad, being the only one still in Shubuta, since his oldest brother, Buddy, R. L. Jr., lives in Jackson. Brad runs the Shubuta Timber Company. One son of Shubuta poor and black, one affluent and white, both today cosmopolitan and prosperous in Colorado and Texas.

On the day of our interview, I met Otis Bumpars at the town public building housing the library and the Senior Nutrition Center. We were with Cassandra Cameron, who had set up the meeting for me. Otis spoke with me comfortably with a great deal of candor and dignity. A dark-black man with expressive, deep-set eyes, he is a wonderful storyteller as well as a well-informed source of information. He spoke with the resonances, vocabulary, and pronunciation of the rural South, at times a speech pattern shared by whites and blacks, at times with some particularities of the black community. He said "mens" for the plural of *man*, like black people do and whites don't. He said he knew my father. At times he sounded like my father. He said "ou-ver" for "our" the way my father and all his siblings did and the way my white interviewee James Brewer did. He called the kindling firewood made from the local pine "lidurd"—"lightwood"—the way my father and most other local people there did, white and black. As my father did, he talked about "them boys" with a chuckle in his voice, meaning grown men. My mother, and probably his wife, would have corrected him to say, "those men."

I asked Otis Bumpars to tell me about his childhood and growing-up time, his work as a young man and as a mature adult, about his church and schooling, what the town of Shubuta had been like all of his life, how it had changed, how he liked it, and what he had seen and done over his lifetime.

He told me a lot, especially about how white people and black people had behaved toward one another. He told me of ambivalence and caution, as well as celebration of the changes in the town. His summary: "When you look back at it, it was all for the better."

Otis Bumpars was one of seven children. When he married, he and his wife had seven children of their own, two of them still living in Shubuta. He said he had "fourteen or fifteen grandchildren."

As a child out in the country from Shubuta, he said his family "didn't have a decent house to live in," no electricity, only wood in a fireplace for cooking and heating. He said, "We made it, though . . . had to get out and hustle up wood, cut it and carry it in" for firewood.

To do their school work, he and his siblings would "throw a piece of 'lidurd' on the fire where there would be light from the fireplace to see how to get our lessons. We would be on the floor.

"Then, we had a lamp, a kerosene lamp to get lessons by."

His father "worked pretty regular" earning 50¢ a day "off in the woods cutting timber and sawmilling. He drove oxen."

For their food his family "growed practically everything we eat, just about it—chickens and cows. We had our own milk. We had 'ouver' hogs, had our own meat and lard, and we growed in the garden greens and peas and so forth. We would go out in the spring of the year and pick blackberries and put 'em up, peaches and put 'em up. We would can everything. The boys and all of us would pick berries, and Mama and my sisters and them would put them up. Wild berries. Go out in the woods and hunt berries. Everybody got a bucket and go out in the woods."

The boys would also hunt wild animals for food, squirrels, rabbits, and possums, "carry them home, clean them, cook and eat them."

Otis and his brothers and sisters went to the segregated black Shubuta public school. This school went through the eighth grade, and if they were able to complete eight years, that was the extent of the schooling most of the children got. The children had to walk to school four or five miles. His contemporary, Bertha Carter, Cassandra Cameron's mother, had to walk seven miles. He said to Cassandra, "Yo' mama walked from out there every day. She and her brothers C. L. and J. L.—them was the two oldest boys—they walked to school every morning and they didn't have no road to walk in. They's have to get out of the edge of the woods to get out of the mud, but they'd make it every day, raining and cold, they'd make it to school."

They studied reading, writing, and arithmetic. The teachers "learnt you your ABCs. Then, they'd put you in a primer book. After that, you would go to the first reader. That was Baby Ray and Sleepyhead, Lucy Lockett and Kitty Fisher. And 'Humpty Dumpty' was in there somewhere."

Otis Bumpars finished the eighth grade and that was the end of his schooling. After that he went to work on various farms, plowing a mule twelve hours a day for 50¢ plus dinner.

When he was older and married, he went to sawmill work and made $2 a day. "When I first went there, they put me in the place called the slab pit. Over that fire. That was the hottest place in the world. I stayed there and worked until I learned everything in that mill to do, blocksetter, edgerunner.

"When I left there, I went to the woods and drove a log truck, and I've cut logs. I've sawed logs with that crosscut saw, didn't have no power saw. Two mens on each side of the saw. . . . I pull thisaway and you pull thataway. . . . Pine, oak. We cut some of everything. All kinds of logs."

Otis Bumpars said that no matter how good a black man was in the sawmill or the log woods, he could not get the jobs or money white men did.

He said after a while he left logging and worked for the railroad for twenty years. Then he came home, bought a truck, and hauled paperwood for a while before going to work for the county in roadwork for twenty years until he retired.

When he was 19, Otis Bumpars was an unwilling and unknowingly coerced player in the cover-up of the lynching of two young boys off Shubuta's Hanging Bridge. He was a trusty convict on a road crew, and the convict boss required his crew to bury the bodies of the two black 12- or 14-year-old Shubuta boys taken out of the jail in the county seat of Quitman by a mob on a Saturday night and killed. The boys had been arrested for frightening a white girl, jailed, and then taken from jail and dragged through the town of Shubuta tied to the back of a truck. They were hanged from the bridge just outside of town known to have been the site of at least one previous lynching. Otis and his work gang were required to bury the bodies to the north of the "white people's cemetery" outside the fence and outside any recognition or acknowledgment of the community.

This indelible experience had lifelong consequences in the psyche of Otis Bumpars, as it did for all of his black community, but as an old man, he could talk of the changes desegregation brought, changes that meant jobs and open talk about wrongdoing.

"You know, used to, you had to kind of walk a chalk line. If you didn't, they liable to catch you and take you and beat you up or something. Wasn't nobody going to help you. Black people couldn't help one another, white people wouldn't.

"Now there are better ways of getting jobs. Way it is now if you're qualified for a job you get it. When I was coming up, like when I was working on the railroad, no matter how qualified you were, you didn't get it. That wasn't a black man's job. Black man didn't go no farther than a pick and shovel. Couldn't get the job being a foreman, assistant foreman. After I left, they come to be foreman. Hansen plant out there [factory in present-day Shubuta] mostly black, nearly all black. Black people over certain areas. Black person gives you your orders.... We have a black mayor now, black alderman.... Kind of runs on an equal basis down here now. If I run for office now and I win, it's just my job. I remember when we didn't even go to the polls and vote. We didn't vote. But after desegregation and everything come on, we went to voting. We all signed up to vote."

On Election Day 1998, even though there was not a local election or a major state or federal office on the ballot other than Congress, state legislators, and county officers, Otis Bumpars, just out of the hospital from getting a heart pacemaker, showed up at the Shubuta polling place and voted.

The Hand House and the Hand Family

An architectural gem of Shubuta, the Hand House, one of three homes listed on the National Register of Historic Places, was brought back in the 1970s to a restored condition and its historical beauty by Federal Judge Brevard Hand of Mobile and his wife, Allison, for their use as a second home. Judge Hand had himself never lived in Shubuta before, though his father, prominent Mobile lawyer Charles Connor Hand, had been born in that house and grew up there, and his grandparents and aunt Caroline had lived there most of their lives. His mother, also, born Irma Weems, and his mother's parents and grandparents had been Shubutans. Brevard Hand was deeded the house as a gift by Caroline Hand in 1978 after it had stood empty for fifteen years and was rapidly decaying.

Brevard Hand was born in Mobile in 1924, one of four sons, earned his undergraduate and law degrees from the University of Alabama, and was admitted to the bar in Alabama in 1949. He is a senior U.S. district judge, hearing cases in Mobile and Selma, Alabama. It was his parents and oldest brother, Charlie, as a little boy, who were a part of the travel party with Mary and Sarah Weems and Annie Ruth Johnston on the *S.S. Parisimina* for their sixteen-day Caribbean "trip to the tropics during the summer of 1928." His brother Charlie was to die in an automobile accident in Mobile when he was a junior at the University of Alabama. Brevard Hand succeeded his father in becoming a lawyer and then came to hold the distinguished post of federal judge.

Ancestors of the Hands had come to southeastern Mississippi among the pioneers who bought the 25¢-an-acre land along the Chickasawhay River from the federal government after the 1805 Treaty of Mount Dexter and settled first at Winchester on the Buckatunna Creek in what is now Wayne County and at Enterprise and Stonewall north of Shubuta on the Chickasawhay River. The son of one of these settlers, James Meyers Hand (1820–1902) was a wealthy landowner, planter, and major in the Mississippi militia before the Civil War. During the early years of the war James Hand served in the Confederate army, but was exempted from later duty under the Confederacy's "twenty-slave law": those who had more than twenty slaves were excused from duty to produce food and supplies for the troops. He had been born in 1820 near St. Stephens, Alabama, and brought as a 6-week-old baby along the Three-Chopped Way with his family, who drove their livestock all the way and came to a farm seven miles southeast of Shubuta around Matherville. Later his father bought land along the Chickasawhay between Stonewall and Enterprise, which he inherited. In 1846, James Hand married a member of one of the first families of settlers at Winchester in Wayne County, Caroline Eliza Powe, who had been born at Winchester in 1827.

Brevard Hand's great-uncle, Albert Powe Hand, was the first Hand to come to Shubuta, and he built a store, a cotton gin, and a sawmill in Shubuta, lost money on them, closed them, then built a turpentine business, lost money on it, and finally built a successful wagon-wheel-spoke factory. Brevard Hand's grandfather, Dr. Robert McLain Hand, born in Enterprise, came to Shubuta in 1876 after he had finished his medical education in Kentucky. That Dr. Hand's wife, Annie Brevard Case, had moved to Shubuta in 1864 as a 10-year-old with her bachelor uncle, Alexander Hamilton Connor, her unmarried aunts, and her brothers, getting out of Bladon Springs, Alabama, because of a slave uprising.

This was the Annie Brevard Case who was determined to be educated herself and who went to the boys' school in Shubuta after hours for her studies during the 1860s. As I discussed earlier, she was a part of the girls' school, maybe a founder, and was a teacher in the Shubuta private school where her own daughter, Caroline, as well as her sons, Albert Powe, James Miles, and Charles Connor, were schooled.

The house now known as the Hand House was bought by Annie's uncle, Alexander Connor, when they moved to Shubuta in 1864. It had been built with great care by a carpenter named Thompson for himself. The first section of two rooms in the back wing was built in 1834, the front section in 1854. In this house of her uncle, by then a judge, Annie Brevard Case and Dr. Robert McLain Hand were married on 27 December 1877. After Judge Connor's death in 1880, the young couple moved into the home and there all seven of their children were born, including "my Dr. Hand," Albert Powe Hand, and Brevard Hand's father, Charles Connor Hand.[25]

As a child I was taken to visit "Miss Caroline" a few times at the Hand House, but my 1990s visit was only an exterior "tour" given by Patsy Toney. Patsy is a lively, enthusiastic person with a ready smile, sparkling wit, access to gossip, and a sense of adventure greater than mine. (When I was in the seventh grade, my two best girlfriends and I slipped away from school without our parents' knowing it, went to her house, and the young Shubuta bride, Patsy Toney, pierced our ears for us.) She assured me that it was fine for the two of us to traipse around the Hands' houses and grounds and peek into all the windows, and she talked nonstop as we looked in and walked about, speaking knowledgeably about the architectural and social details of the building and its history.

The one-story Hand House is a Greek Revival style house with a pyramidal roof. It has a five-bay L-plan with an original gable-roofed kitchen attached to the house, making it now rectangular. With the appearance of a miniature antebellum mansion, the white-painted house has a front porch with sturdy posts and railings running across the entire front facade, and its graceful front entrance has double doors, sidelight windows, a transom, and pilasters. A wide central hall runs from the front door to the back door and has heart-pine floors now restored to their original brightness. The first section of the house was fitted with wooden pegs and the later addition with cut nails. The two bathrooms, as well as the three bedrooms, all have working fireplaces, and the bedroom fireplaces have oak mantels.

Built before the railroad, which came through Shubuta in 1855, the original house faced what became the railroad and the street ran behind it. Today the house still sits beside the railroad tracks, and in Brevard and Allison Hand's restoration two other buildings have been bought and moved to stand with it on the double lot. The second house was brought to the property to be a guesthouse in the restored Hand complex. It is the house of Brevard Hand's maternal great-grandparents, the Stovall house, originally home of the newspaper family owning the *Mississippi Messenger*. Adding air-conditioning and a swimming pool, Brevard and Allison Hand have made the complex of houses both a usable vacation place in the present and a restoration of Shubuta architectural memory of more than 160 years.

Cleo Powe Cooper

Cleo Powe Cooper's ancestors were slaves around Shubuta. Her mother's mother's name was Roseanna Chapman, Chapman being a family name shared by both some white families and some black families in next-door Wayne County where her grandmother came from. The name Cooper, Cleo's married name, is also a name of both black and white families from Shubuta; and in Clarke and Wayne Counties there are both blacks and whites named from that earliest settler family near Winchester and Buckatunna, Powe, Cleo's father's family name, as well as that of the Hand family ancestor Caroline Eliza Powe (born 1827).

Cleo Cooper said of the slave names, "The master would do the naming of them in those days because they didn't have any names. My daddy would say that his daddy was a slave, and he got his name from his master."[26]

The next generation, Cleo's parents, Morris and Daisy Powe, was free from slavery but dependent upon the white people for their livelihood. Cleo's mother did washing and ironing and housecleaning for white people. She was a maid for the Weemses for a time. Her father was a farmer on rented land.

Cleo and her siblings went to the public school for black children on the west side of town through all eight of the grades of schooling that it offered. Then, Cleo went to Hattiesburg and lived with her aunt to finish the twelfth grade. After high school, she went to Jackson State for summer school and got "a year-and-a-half of college," enough to pass the county test for licensing to teach, and she started teaching school.

Born in 1912, Cleo Powe did not marry until 1951, and in her single adult years she taught school "in the county [at the country schools], not in the city [Shubuta]. I would always board [live and have meals in a family home] and come home to Shubuta to my parents Fridays and go back Sunday afternoons. We didn't have a car, but other people did.

"I didn't have any children. I love children. I enjoyed teaching the children very much, and they liked me."

Cleo's husband was John Cooper. "He passed in 1979," she said. "I'm a widow. I live alone."

Introduced to her by Cassandra Cameron, as I was to so many people, I first interviewed Cleo Cooper rather formally in the town library while Cassandra was serving the lunches in the attached Senior Nutrition Center. Later, Mrs. Cooper invited me to her home on East Street, "a 'foth' of a mile from 'town,'" pronouncing *fourth* in the local manner and thinking only of the commercial district as "town," as most Shubutans do. She said she was born at Red Hill, "a 'foth' of a mile west of town." She said her own house is a white house, "the third house on the left going out toward the river."

There it was again. The river. Shubuta people orient themselves in a very basic way in relation to the river.

After some visits to her home on some of my return research trips to Shubuta, Cleo Cooper took me to visit her church, the St. Matthew Baptist Church, in which she is a very active member. She has participated in that church for most of her life and it is very dear to her. She elaborates on her activities: "I am the financial secretary of my church. I teach Sunday School. Well, I do extra at the church, fill in. I am very active."

Like Otis Bumpars, Cleo Cooper told me Shubuta stories from over the years inside the black community. One impressive feature that she cares about is the change in manners that desegregation and social integration between black people and white people has meant. "In the past we had to say, 'Yes, ma'am,' and 'No, ma'am' to the white people." Now she counts herself friends with white Shubuta women, calling Kathleen Stallings and Linda McInnis, "good friends." She says, "Now they say, 'Call me Linda, not Mrs. McInnis!'" and then they move on to friendly conversation: "When have you been fishing?'"

Most black people as well as many rural white people of Cleo's parents' generation literally fished and hunted and farmed for their living. That is, they did subsistence farming to feed themselves and also did hunting and fishing to provide food for themselves and their families. This hunting and fishing were not for sport, as they are today for most Shubutans, but for food.

I asked her if the boys went hunting for squirrels and girls didn't when she was a child, and she said neither. "I don't think so: maybe they didn't have any guns.

"Now I am a fisherman. I fish. I love to fish. I haven't fished now in about three years. I fell and knocked this arm out of place."

"Where did you fish?" I asked.

"I fished on the river, the Chickasawhay River."

"From a boat or from the bank?"

"From the bank, Honey! No boat! And then I fished in Mr. Toney's pond quite a bit, too. Now I would go hunting from my house, out in the back, out in the woody area. I would go out there and kill a squirrel or two or a rabbit and come back. I enjoyed that.

"I started hunting in '55 or '56. I would fish every day."

"Did your husband fish and hunt with you?" I asked.

"That's right. Just we two."

I asked her about food from her childhood. She said her father farmed on rented land, and after harvest time he would cut crossties. "We made our own food. My mother had a garden, some chickens, a corn patch, potatoes. Back then everybody made their own food. We would have a hog. My mother had turnips, collards, mustards, white potatoes. My mother loved peanuts and she would put in a peanut row. She would put in sweet corn, just anything she thought would fill up her children.

"We took corn to be ground. There was a miller down here, and he would grind the corn for us. It wasn't far from the railroad. There was a cotton gin over there."

"Did your mother make biscuits?" I asked.

"Sometimes, but she made cornbread just about every day. Daddy didn't want the biscuits. He wanted cornbread.

"For breakfast we would have molasses, pancakes, eggs, sausage, something like that for breakfast time. Then, we would have vegetables and whatnot for dinner [at noon]. She would have some type of dessert. We had cornbread. It had to be like that because times were hard."

I asked her if there was a big difference between the way white people lived and the way black people lived when she was a child.

She said, "We couldn't live as well as they were living. Because we had to get 'ouver' living from them, you know." There was that lovely local pronunciation "ouver" for *our*, reminding me of my father and my aunts and Otis Bumpars, shared speech of blacks and whites of her generation.

In 1998 I went to visit Cleo Cooper the day after Election Day, and she had been an election worker at the polls the day before, staying out late counting the votes because the voting machine had not functioned. She was tired, but elated. She knew she had done a good job, and her white friend Kathleen Stallings had been her companion poll worker. She reminisced that she had first registered to vote and voted about 1969.

The next day, as I did for several times on my return visits to Shubuta, I rode with Cleo Cooper on her noontime route to deliver meals from the Shubuta Senior Nutrition Center to shut-ins. Often she took the meals into the house for her clients, but a few times the client, usually an elderly woman, would come out to the car to collect her Styrofoam box of dinner and her carton of milk. "This is my white friend" is how Cleo Cooper would introduce me to the woman, no name, no title, just the details important to her: "white" and "friend," just an affirmation of the sea change in race relations in her lifetime.

Family Names: Shubuta McCartys, Black and White

In Shubuta as in many U.S. southern settings where the population remained stable over several decades, there are two sets of families, one black and one white, with the same surname, like the Powes. In and around Shubuta, such families and their names have included Powe and Lang, Falconer and Green,

Carter, Howze, Horne, and McCarty, among others. Underscoring recent scholarly understanding that "race" is a cultural construct far more than a biological one, these shared family names reveal shared histories. In some cases, the people designated "black" are the biological offspring and descendants of African American slave women and their white slave owners, but in general in that part of southern Mississippi, as Cleo Powe Cooper's father told her, slaves and former slaves were given and kept the European family names of the plantation masters or other slave owners for whom they worked, their African languages and names as well as their freedom having been taken from them by enslavement.

It is revelatory, for example, of this historical covering of black names with white ones, and, indeed, of obscuring of black people's personal identity, that the 1840 and 1850 slave censuses for Clarke County, Mississippi, including present-day Shubuta, list no names at all for slave persons. Rather, the names of slave owners are given and the slave persons are identified only by age, sex, and the letters B or M, for "black" or "mulatto."

In the 1990s two Shubuta families, one black, one white, with the same last name, McCarty, appeared in the celebrity pages of the *New York Times*. There is a local story there, too, and it is a story of money and education.

Oseola McCarty's picture was on the front page of the *Times* on Sunday, 13 August 1995, with another picture and a continuation of the story running across the entirety of page 11, where it is written, "She comes from a wide place in the road called Shubuta, Miss., a farming town outside Meridian, not far from the Alabama line."[27]

"Huh!" I thought indignantly as I read my *Times* that morning, "wide place in the road, indeed! What they don't know!"

A laundress in her own small home in Hattiesburg, Mississippi, Oseola McCarty, who dropped out of school after the sixth grade to care for her ill aunt, lived modestly and saved most of her earnings of her lifetime in a bank, depositing small amounts of cash regularly week after week, year after year. As she anticipated the end of her life, having no spouse or children, she decided to give her money to the University of Southern Mississippi, which is a few blocks from her home.

There were numerous surprising factors to this gift, not least of which was that Oseola McCarty initiated giving the gift herself, having had no previous contact with the university, no fund-raising phone calls. Indeed, it was not known that she had any money to give. And also, not having had any college education herself, not even high school, it was unusual that she gave the gift to a college. Even more unusual was the fact that she gave it to a formerly all-white Mississippi state university, one that she as a black person would have been barred from attending, or even one to which the next generation of her family members would have been denied admission. The newspaper reported, "It has been only three decades since the university became integrated. 'My race used to not get to go to that college,' she said. 'But now they can.'"[28]

She said she did not want to be honored by the college for her gift with a plaque or a monument or by naming a building after her. Rather, she wanted to be able to attend the graduation of a black student who made it through the university.

Oseola McCarty's gift is a major indicator of how much black southerners prize education. Her cousin, Mary McCarty, a woman in her fifties in the 1990s who lives in Shubuta now and helped Oseola McCarty plan her gift, is a high school teacher. For both Oseola McCarty and Mary McCarty's generations, public schools in Shubuta and throughout the South were racially segregated and poorly funded for black children. In Shubuta, the school year for the white school was nine months and went for twelve years, while the school for blacks had only eight grades and had a short yearly calendar dominated by the agricultural seasons, ending early in the spring for the children to help with planting and starting late in the fall after corn and cotton picking had been done.

When Oseola McCarty's gift became known, she was an instant national celebrity. Reporters went to Hattiesburg in droves. She was given numerous awards, including one from UNESCO and one at the White House. Harvard University gave her an honorary doctorate. Searching for "one good person" to counter the image of New York's Times Square as a seedy district, the 1997 New Year's Eve celebration committee chose Oseola McCarty to drop the ball at the stroke of midnight in their annual nationally televised event. Through all of this, she remained unassuming and down-to-earth, unchanged from the modest person she had been all her life. An Atlanta reporter persuaded her to publish a little book of her wise sayings and she did so in *Oseola McCarty's Simple Wisdom for Rich Living*.[29]

Mary McCarty tells of going to Washington, D.C., and the White House with Oseola McCarty:

"I was going to church, and the phone rang about 5:30, and it was Paul Laughlin from the bank. 'Miss McCarty is going to D.C.,' he said. 'Somebody from New York is going to call you in fifteen minutes.'"[30]

Someone did, and it was arranged for the two of them to go to Washington by train, since Oseola McCarty would not fly. On their return trip they were even to have a private car on the train. Then, someone from President Clinton's office called to set up the awards ceremony. "He told me it was black tie, to find a dress for her for after five. I never did go to sleep that night," Mary McCarty said. "At 2:30 I just got up and drove to Hattiesburg.

"The train trip—lunch with several black McDonald's owners—just unbelievable.

"The next day Alexis Herman, top aide to President Clinton at the time, now Secretary of Labor, and I took her shopping. We bought her this gorgeous outfit. Spent more money than she had ever spent on clothes.

"The ceremony was just a ceremony in the Oval Office, but then there was a dinner sponsored by the Congressional Black Caucus. People there included Colin Powell, Jesse Jackson, Mohammed Ali, Jack Kemp.

"We rode in a limousine from the White House with the president, just him. He's a very personable person. He's a real human being.

"The Secret Service were everywhere. He's a people-person. He went around speaking to everyone."

The unexpected outpouring of national attention on Oseola McCarty was thoroughly enjoyed by Shubutan Mary McCarty, her traveling companion.

Mary McCarty is herself a representative of high standards of conduct and profound values in her generation just as her cousin is for the older generation. She was one of my new acquaintances in the late 1990s in Shubuta, my having met by that time or become reacquainted with numerous Shubutans who welcomed me, showed enthusiasm for my project, and shared their knowledge and memories with me. Mary McCarty was a woman with whom I had instant rapport. I regretted I had not met her much earlier, for I liked her very much and knew that I could learn a lot from her. My peer in age and achievement and aspirations, she is a person of delight and warmth and sincerity. She is "genuine," my mother would have said. Patsy Toney had taken me to the Shubuta home Mary shares with her mother to meet her, Patsy working with her as a member of the area public health medical board Patsy chaired at the time. Soon after we met, both Mary and I recognized the irony that we had both spent many childhood years as schoolchildren and Methodist churchgoers in different schools and churches just a few blocks apart on opposite sides of this very small town, and yet because of racial segregation, we had never met.

Mary McCarty returned to Shubuta to live in the chestnut-tree-surrounded home with her parents after sixteen years of living in other places. The last stint of eight years away she taught in an all-white high school in suburban Chicago. She decided "it was time to come home," so she returned to the house her family built about a mile out of town on Eucutta Creek near where Oseola McCarty was born. Mary's father, Levi McCarty, who died in 1991, had been a highly respected carpenter in Shubuta. When Mary came one day in the late 1990s to my house out in the country that my father had "built" for my mother in late life, we learned that her father had built this house for my father. Her father's mother was a Falconer, relative of the Lang and Falconer families from Langsdale, her Falconer forefathers also known as expert carpenters. Her mother was a Brown, her mother's mother an Esther from the St. Luke community out from Matherville.

A social studies teacher in Wayne County High School in Waynesboro, the public school consolidated for black and white students after desegregation and consolidated town and country again in 1989, Mary McCarty is a woman who is a community leader and organizer as well as educator. She is much like the black women subjects of Carol Stack's book, *call to home: African Americans Reclaim the Rural South*,[31] savvy black rural southerners who went to northern cities for work and education, earning some money and gaining some skills, but always keeping in touch with the people down home. On their return home to the South and their families to live, they became economic, social, and political leaders of their rural and small-town communities. This is what Mary McCarty has done in Shubuta.

Mary McCarty attended Rust College, a Methodist Church–related then-all-black college, from 1959 through 1961 and sang in its famous a capella choir. She left school, married, divorced, and returned to her education to get her degree in 1967. Besides a social studies teaching certification, she has a special education certificate. In Shubuta, she is an active participant in the New Mount Zion United Methodist Church, where she is an officer, a musician, and chairperson of the worship committee. She goes to many professional workshops, as well as serves with Patsy Toney on the medical board that oversees public health services for the town and its region.

On 10 December 1997 Mary McCarty allowed me to interview her at work, showed me around her school, and introduced me to some of her colleagues and students. This was particularly meaningful to me, for I went to high school in Waynesboro and this high school was the successor school to the one from which I graduated.

Mary McCarty's memories of Shubuta as her childhood town in the 1940s and 1950s contrast in black and white with my own and with the memories from the 1920s of my 90-plus-year-old white interviewee Elsie Cross. Like Elsie Cross, Mary remembers the picture show, but her memories are of going up the stairs and sitting in the segregated balcony, entering through a different door from the white people. She claims, "We had the best seats, though. We could see better from above than they could down there." She remembers *Gone with the Wind* as the first movie her father let her go to, along with her siblings and her cousins who were her grandmother's wards. They loved it, but it went very late, so it was after dark when they got home. Even so, Levi McCarty still made them go out and get the cows in. He milked the cows himself, but it was the children's job to go out to the pasture and get the cows and drive them home. She thinks that having responsibilities in her loving family was one of the things that made her family members turn out well.

Other features of segregation in Shubuta affected her—the back-street shops for blacks' eating and haircutting, the separate schools and churches, the inaccessibility of many kinds of jobs, travel, and opportunities. Still, her family was privileged among African Americans, she remembers. Because of her father's earning a good living as a carpenter, her mother did not work outside the home and their family was seen as well-off by some other African American people. "We were not poor," she says. "We had a good house, not a great house, but a good one. He [her father] kept a good roof on it. We had food and we got to go to school. We were not really middle class like the white people, but we were not as poor as the poor."

At her school during the interview, Mary McCarty demonstrated that she is a fine teacher both in the descriptions she gave me of her work and the smiles and greetings she received from her students and colleagues. She described a Mississippi Studies course in which she teaches history, geography, music, and literature. She also teaches a world geography course, black history, and sociology. She says, "Kids are my life. I will go to bat for them—if they are right." She sponsors travel for seniors, a trip to Florida each year. She shows her leniency, though: "Kids are kids. You have to allow them to be kids." Rules were posted about her classroom the day I visited: "No gum chewing. No food in class." She said, "I enjoy the country atmosphere here, but the city is coming, change is coming. We are thinking we might have to build a fence around the campus." She says, "The hard part is lots of kids are not fired up enough about learning. They don't seem to have goals. That bothers me."

She says, "Kids learn better with videos," so she is trying to build a complete video library for her subject in her classroom. She wants students to "be somebody, be the very best they can be. Just be what they can be. Learn how to be well-rounded human beings. If I can teach them that the color of one's skin doesn't matter, that's enough. But it's hard. 'Just love each other,' I tell them, 'treat each other kindly.'"[32]

Hyman McCarty's obituary appeared in the *New York Times* in July of 1998.[33] This white former Shubutan named McCarty achieved national recognition for his achievement as a businessman, a chicken farmer, but the direction of his philanthropy took the same path as that of Oseola McCarty, a college scholarship fund.

Very early in his adulthood, Hyman McCarty developed efficient methods of raising chickens for a large market, and his enterprise at Magee, Mississippi, grew quickly to be at one time the largest in the country. This gave him great respect in the nationwide agricultural business community. The same work ethic that gave Oseola McCarty incentive to provide the best-ironed shirts and dresses possible gave Hyman McCarty ambition to grow the best chickens.

Hyman McCarty's story is not only a poor-boy-makes-good story but also an overcoming-the-odds story of childhood tragedy. As a young child, Hyman was orphaned by what was believed to be the murder of his mother by his father and the suicide of his father. He was brought up by two aunts near Shubuta and went to the public school and the Methodist Church for white people in Shubuta, where he was a part of "Mr. Charlie" Meeks's youth group. Encouraged by teachers and church leaders, Hyman McCarty went away to college and earned a degree. One of the people who gave him money to support his education was Mary V. Weems. After he had become prosperous and well-established in his business, he said he wanted to give to other students what he had been given as a young person, and he established a scholarship fund at Millsaps College in honor of Mary V. Weems with a starting gift of half a million dollars. He went to Shubuta to announce the gift at an eightieth birthday party for Mary Weems.

Mary McCarty knew "Miss Mary" Weems, too. She commented, "Now she helped a lot of people—Miss Mary did."

"Miss Mary" Weems and Her Family

"Miss Mary" was the classic upper-class small-town person, a generous, gracious, and benevolent single woman who lived out her days in the home and the town of her birth. Because of the privilege that money gave her, she was able to travel a great deal, and she bought gifts and clothing and household goods on order from New Orleans, Memphis, and Mobile, rather than being dependent on local merchants. She subscribed to city newspapers, and she played a leadership role in the Shubuta Methodist Church and its women's group, as well as in Shubuta's community as a civic leader. She was employed by her family's Bank of Shubuta.

A typical philanthropist of her time and place, she contributed generously to institutions she appreciated, largely Methodist ones: her church in Shubuta, its colleges and other institutions in the state of Mississippi. However, there was also the very personal touch with her gifts of money that dozens, if not hundreds, of Shubutans remember. I did not ask if she helped Mary McCarty with her college expenses, but I do know that she provided financial aid for several black Shubutans to attend Rust College, the all-black

Mississippi Methodist college. She gave small checks that made a large difference to Shubuta teenagers, no doubt black and white, going to Methodist state and regional conferences and camps, my age peer Gary Boutwell and me in our church among them.

Her beneficence with money was matched with parallel hospitality. A formative memory of mine was her having me alone to lunch in her big house at her big dining room table when I was about 10 years old. I remember nothing about what we ate or drank, only the ambience of her house with its twinkling chandeliers and glass-doored, polished-wood china cabinets and her total attention paid to me alone. Focusing on me as if I were a very important person, and as if I were an adult, as well, she served the two of us on china, crystal, and sterling silver and made my eyes brighten with delight. When it was time for our dessert, she rang a little crystal bell beside her plate and a black girl about my age came from the kitchen and cleared the plates just so, taking away the plates one at the time, one in each hand, and then coming back with our dessert plates, ever-so carefully and correctly putting our dessert in front of each of us. In that racially segregated society in which we lived, both the young black child and I were in training by Miss Mary for future social roles.

Mary Weems worked in the Bank of Shubuta, which her father had founded and of which her oldest brother, Robert, had succeeded their father as president. More than sixty years later, her niece, Gin French, baptized Mary Virginia Weems III, sitting in her daughter Jean's waterside living room in Fox Island, Washington, told happily of working in the bank for a year when "Auntie and Ty took their trip around the world."

"I loved the bank," Gin said. These words are nearly the same ones spoken of the Hudson Drug Store by Janette Hudson, daughter-in-law of the pharmacist of Mary Weems's generation.

Gin's daughter, Jean, was born in Shubuta because Gin's husband was away in military service during World War II, and Gin went home to Shubuta and stayed with her parents, "Mr. Bob" and "Miss Suzie." That day more than half a century later in Jean's Fox Island living room, we ate lunch with silver Jean's grandfather had given her after her grandmother's death. He let each of the grandchildren choose items from her belongings, Jean said, and wanted to give her something else when she chose the silver, because her grandmother had not really liked this silver of her mother-in-law's. I remembered my mother's account of "Miss Suzie's" death. She had fallen over with a heart attack in the dining room of their home into the arms of her husband, no doubt in the very presence of that sterling silver set. Theirs was a great love story, my mother thought.

The daughter of Gin's older sister Alice and the oldest grandchild of Robert C. and Suzie Weems, Mary Sue Mitchell, gave me copies of letters her grandfather had written to her during the 1960s. The letters tell Shubuta news—Tommy Hudson's death, his brother George's illness—and immediate family news—visits from her cousins and aunts—and make requests for favors—would she buy her mother a brooch for him for a birthday present? Always signed, "Love, Granddaddy," they thank her and her husband for gifts and holiday cards and visits, or urge them to make more visits. They are filled with affection, delight, and pride expressed about all his children and grandchildren, especially this young adult one who is emerging from college, becoming engaged and married, teaching the seventh grade at Spann School in her first job in Jackson while her husband is attending medical school. He writes near her 1963 college graduation, "Just a few more days and you will be a bachelor, pretty good for a young lady. . . . If I could enter school again, I would like to take my work under you at Spann School. . . . It is wonderful to have such a granddaughter."[34]

Only a few months later, during the year between her finishing college and her wedding, he writes of his wife's death, "It was a great comfort to me to have all the family here when Grandmother left us. . . . She is now forever with her Lord whom she served devotedly. Her life on earth has blessed every one of us. We shall cherish her love and memory forever."[35] The month before her marriage to Don Mitchell, he writes Mary Sue, "Mother and Sally should do all the work, you just report as the bride when the bells begin to ring. We wish for you and Don everything that is good, a wonderful home, and Mitchells under every rug."[36] In the fall of 1967 his letters speak of the expectation of and then the arrival of baby Sally Kay Mitchell.

He also writes of his frustration over the Kennedy administration and the pressures against racial segregation, which he and all the other members of his class had upheld in Shubuta all their lives. He breaks his characteristic gentlemanly manner when he speaks of the likelihood of black children in Mary Sue's classroom and other results of desegregation, "Maybe there will be some black spots in the days ahead, we hope not" and suggests they will smell and behave badly. He says, "Those Washington folks surely are licking us Southerners right now, and all without constitutional authority," and "It is interesting to note how much more brains the Mississippi mules have than have the Delta negroes."[37]

While deeply loving her grandfather and "Auntie" and caring for them all the rest of their lives, Mary Sue Mitchell had already ceased to share their views on relationships between black and white people while a college student; and having black and white children together in her classroom was not a problem for her.

And a generation later, when the first Weems great-grandchild, Sally Kay Mitchell, graduated from college, she entered graduate school at the Kennedy School of Government in Cambridge, Massachusetts.

James and Phyllis Johnston

James and Phyllis Johnston live in the house where James was born, on Eucutta Street in Shubuta. It is diagonally across the street from the house in which Robert C. Weems and "Miss Suzie" lived next door to the Weems family home, where Mary Weems lived alone until her final illness. James's father, Percy, was a dentist in the town, a man educated at what is now Mississippi State University and at Atlanta Dental College, now a part of Emory University. James's mother, Lydia, ran a family-owned grocery store, a "mercantile business" as old-timers called the general store, in the one-block-long commercial district of the town. James's Johnston great-grandparents were among the earliest white settlers of the farming region around Shubuta, and their son, Arista Johnston, was born there 4 November 1849. In turn, his son, later to be the dentist, Percy Walker Johnston, was born there also on 13 July 1881. Percy Johnston and his siblings went into town to school in Shubuta in a horse-drawn buggy and were prepared for college by that school. Their father, Arista Johnston, is listed among the trustees in the 1900–1901 catalogue of the Shubuta Institute and Military Academy. The next generation, Percy and Lydia Brashier Johnston's sons Percy Jr. and James, the family by that time living in town, went to the Shubuta public school and prepared for college education, both of them going to the University of Mississippi, "Ole Miss," in the early 1940s.[38]

Having lived in Shubuta for all of the more than fifty years of their marriage, James and Phyllis Johnston brought up five daughters there. All five daughters, all of them university educated, are now married and have children. James Johnston was Shubuta's postmaster from 1955 until his retirement in 1988.

Phyllis Johnston said of Shubuta, "We had built a house right next door [to James's parents, the house where they now live]. We just had a wonderful time. This was a wonderful place to raise those five girls. I wouldn't have taken anything for that."

Phyllis Johnston was not a Shubutan originally, not even a southerner. She was born and grew up in Maine. Her town was South Brewer, Maine, a suburb of Bangor. She was the middle child of nine children of John and Claire LeGasse, and her father was the foreman of the blueprint department of a large paper mill on the Penobscot River. As World War II advanced, with all four of her brothers and a brother-in-law in military service, she decided that she wanted to sign up, so she registered for the Women's Army Corps (WAC) without telling her parents. On enlistment in 1944, and with her family's knowledge by then, she was sent to Fort Oglethorpe in Georgia for training and then stationed in Macon, Georgia. That's where she met James Johnston.

James Johnston had volunteered for the army in 1942 from the University of Mississippi, where he had gone, following his older brother, Percy, in September of 1940 as a 17-year-old, "way too young," he says. "I didn't miss a dance or a party or a picture show—and my grades showed it!"

He did basic training at Fort McClellan, Alabama, was sent to Fort Benning and then to Camp Wheeler in Macon, Georgia, where he met WAC Phyllis. They dated a while and then were married, and James brought Phyllis home on the bus to Shubuta to meet his family and the Shubuta townspeople for the first time.

Phyllis remembers that it was a Saturday night when they arrived in Shubuta on the bus. "James took me right to the store to meet his mother," she says, "and that place was packed!"

"Mary Bounds and Katy Owens [women a generation older] were the first ones I met. James just told them to 'take her down to Mama's'—you didn't keep your house locked back then, and about ten o'clock he came home.

"The next day was a Sunday and I thought, 'My, Heavenly days'—there wasn't a soul around. On Saturday the streets were crowded. On Sunday there was nobody around! I just thought, 'He just brought me here to die!'

"Sunday morning we went right to church. Brother Dye was the preacher [at the Shubuta Methodist Church]. That afternoon there was a little tea reception for me, and I began to get a little more at ease. I was really nervous. It was like I was from a foreign country!"

James remembers that he had his turn at being the outsider, a "foreigner" with his southern accent, when they went to visit her family in his wife's native New England. When their first child, Ann, was about 6 months old, "we flew to Maine. There was a write-up in the newspaper about it. They said they couldn't understand me! I had to spell it out when I went to get something there in the drugstore!"

Phyllis tells her much-told story that with her Maine accent and his southern accent, she could not understand him. She says when he asked her to marry him, she could not understand what he was saying so she said Yes!

Theirs was a very close family as they brought up their five girls in Shubuta. They all participated in their Methodist Church, and the Johnston girls—Ann, Jeannie, Hope, Jimmie, and Jacque (Ann born 11 April 1946, Jeannie born 19 December 1949, Hope born 16 July 1952, Jimmie born 1 January 1954, and Jacquelyn born 26 March 1957)—walked the short distance up Eucutta Street to the public school on the east side of town. When the girls were older, James got season tickets to the Ole Miss football games for the family, and like many families of University of Mississippi graduates all over the state, they enjoyed going up to Oxford, Mississippi, for the games. Ole Miss sometimes got to play in the Sugar Bowl, and James enjoyed going to New Orleans very much for that. Laughing, he says, "Jimmie being born on January first [in 1954] kept me from going to the Sugar Bowl game—and the doctor who delivered her, too!"

When the children were younger, James says, "a big trip was to go to Meridian. After I was in the post office, Mama, Phyllis and the five children and I would, Saturdays, go to Meridian. And that would be a big treat. In

Sears or Kress's we would buy chocolate-covered peanuts or chocolate-covered raisins and eat them on the way back. That was a thrill in those days."

With their army background, and, also, like many white families in the South with Confederate Army ancestors, James and Phyllis have family archival records from the Civil War, or "the War Between the States" or "the War of Northern Aggression," James reminded me some southerners call it. James noted that there was no Civil War fighting in Shubuta, but the first unit of soldiers to enter the war from Clarke County was from Shubuta. He has a newspaper clipping about the Shubuta Rifles being mustered on 28 March 1861, and listing his great-uncle, Everette M. Johnston, second lieutenant, as among the officers.

James and Phyllis Johnston pointed out that people from Shubuta have served in every U.S. war. Phyllis remembers that even the Persian Gulf War had a Shubutan in it: "That little Nelson girl, black, a little short girl named for her grandmother, Faithy Nelson, went to the Persian Gulf."

James's brother, Percy, left Shubuta, like many of its ambitious, talented, and well-educated sons and daughters. Percy Johnston finished law school at the University of Virginia and then settled in Mobile, Alabama. He worked with an attorney uncle there for a while, then for the Gulf, Mobile, and Ohio Railroad, and then retired after a number of years as a vice president and head of the legal department of the Illinois Central Railroad.

Mention of his brother's successful adult life away from Shubuta reminded Phyllis and James of their sense of decline of the town. "This used to be a very aristocratic town, a very active town, but people went off to Memphis or Jackson or Mobile. People went off to college and then went away.

"We don't have our own school now. We don't have any local businesses any more. The Hanson plant is owned somewhere else. Mississippi Laminators is locally owned, but a lot of the businesses are not locally owned. People have moved in from the country, and most of them are factory workers or farm workers. Shubuta is different now. Too many people have left."

"Except James," Phyllis said. "He wanted to be here. He wanted to come back home." And so he did.

TROPE 3: THE HOLY LAND ... HOLY LAND

My seat companion on my Swissair flight to Zurich, the man on the plane who called the female cabin attendants "girls" and who asked me about my religion, turned out to be a big-time fundamentalist preacher and was also on our flight to Tel Aviv. None of us on my Minnesota Interfaith Women's Study Tour shared his sexist backwardness nor his evangelical enthusiasm. We were a group of well-educated Jewish, Muslim, Catholic, and Protestant women, most of us professors, clergywomen, and other professionals; and we avoided him and his brand of piety as soon as we got into the airport. However, when our plane landed in Israel, some of my group companions were ecstatic along with him and the many other conservative Christian pilgrims on our plane over the fact that they were arriving in the Holy Land.

I felt nothing.

I was somewhat alarmed that I felt nothing. I am a person of deep and wide-ranging emotions, a person of considerable expressiveness, and I felt nothing. I remembered my father's funeral and his burial in the Hebron Church Cemetery near Shubuta when I also had felt nothing and had thought I was supposed to feel a certain way. At least, I thought I was supposed to feel something.

Here in Israel I was even a little scornful of the label "the Holy Land." Much more interested in contemporary Israel and its society and culture and the Middle East peace process with the Palestinian elections under way that winter of 1996, I was, nevertheless, still interested in seeing the historical sites revered as holy places by Judaism, Islam, and Christianity. In fact, I would not have come on such a trip had it been sponsored by a Christian organization alone. The appeal of this particular trip was its organization by my perceptive Jewish activist friend, Marcia Yugend, as well as its being a group of women who were from the three different Abrahamic faiths—and, as my grown-up children said of my category, "and then, our mom."

Then, it came to me: this *was* like my father's funeral. Arriving in Israel was not something about which I had ever had great expectations. For most of my life, I had not even especially wanted to come to Israel. I was more appalled than attracted to the idea of the Holy Land from the constricting religion of my rural family and early childhood, appalled in the same way that I found my evangelizing seatmate offensive rather than saw him as a fellow traveler with a shared journey's goal. No-o-o-o, I was not like that, not like him, not like him and not like my rigid rural Methodist fundamentalist father, either.

Yet, here I was in Israel, getting ready to go to Galilee and Bethlehem and Nazareth, to "walk the places that Jesus walked," to visit the same shrines of Christendom that U.S. southern fundamentalists visit—albeit ones that are Jewish and Muslim, too, and to hear feminist speakers and to learn about contemporary Israeli politics and culture, with my urban, cosmopolitan, northern U.S. women's group.

And I was here in Israel as an urbane traveler using money to pay for my trip that had come from the sale of some of my father's land, my inheritance from my parents.

The irony was enormous. One of my feelings was shame.

My father's land outside of Shubuta, the land on which he was born and his father had been born and my brother and I were born, the land he farmed all of his life, taking charge of his family's livelihood while still a teenager when his father died suddenly, many of the years walking behind a plow-mule, the land on which he had built houses, planted and harvested crops, tended animals, and fought floods, the land from which we moved him away only after the debilitating strokes that became his terminal illness, the land his grandfather, the old Irishman who rode a white mule, had homesteaded.

I have not ever wanted to go to Dublin, either.

I wanted to go to places where people were educated and open-minded, where they wrote poetry and made art, where they made government decisions with international consequences. I wanted to visit sacred sites where people made pilgrimages. I wanted to see places whose inhabitants were worldly and wise, exercised power, and were seen on the nightly news. I wanted to be in places I had read about and seen pictures of in encyclopedias, in literature, art, and history books, in travel brochures, in the newspaper, and on public television broadcasts.

In Israel, though, one of those places, in the company of Jews and Muslims and Christians, it came to me, as it never had in the United States: my father's land in Mississippi is as sacred as any spot in Jerusalem.

It was our place, the place vested with original memory as the place from whence we came. Like the single hill in Jerusalem on which stands the Western Wall of the Temple Mount, to Jews their most sacred site of prayer in the world; the golden dome of the Dome of the Rock, the Muslim shrine where Muslims believe Mohammed ascended to Heaven; and the gray dome of the Church of the Holy Sepulchre, where Christians memorialize the site of Christ's crucifixion, my father's land is our family's site of collective memory.

Like that hill in Jerusalem and like the one at the thriving small contemporary Jewish city of Nazareth where Jesus was a boy and like the town of Bethlehem where the Palestinian flag flew over Manger Square and a large banner in Arabic and English proclaimed Yassir Arafat's political campaign promises during my 1996 visit to that place of Jesus's birth, my father's land is the place where meaning was imbued into all our lives.

Like the archaeological dig at Dan in the north of Israel where an earthen gate has been uncovered from beneath the ground dating back to the time of Abraham, the founding patriarch of the peoples of Judaism, Islam, and Christianity, my father's land is the location of our ancestry.

Like all these holy places, my father's land is the place from which we came, our place of origin, a holy place for its location of meaning in human history, our family's human history, a sacred site, for it is the place to which we return for knowledge, for the truth about who we are.

When my father died and I felt nothing, my husband said to me, "But he gave you what he loved. He gave you his land."

And, at last, I wept and, perhaps for the first time, understood my father.

In Israel, too, standing among the bougainvillea blossoms beside the Sea of Galilee in January, I understood and knew my place.

Holy ground, indeed. Land where love is possible even after death.

We visited the gravesite in Jerusalem of the recently slain Israeli prime minister, Itzak Rabin, where hushed schoolchildren were placing small stones on the tomb in respectful silence, as is the custom there.

We saw in a frame at the memorial site the blood-soaked paper from Rabin's breast pocket at the time of his death, and I remembered ritual words from my own tradition, "blood . . . which was shed for you . . ." and was moved to join the children in shared communion.

I took a tiny pebble and laid it softly on Rabin's tomb. The reverence I felt in my hand might as well have been from gravel on a road near Shubuta.

My father's friend had a different love for my father's land, the "place," as Southerners call it, and for my father. Coming to visit me there, he commented, "It is hard to come to this place. If anybody is getting in to Heaven, it is your daddy. He was so good to us. And to my parents before us."

This man had taken his oldest grandson out of school to bring him to my father's funeral. He told my brother and me that day, both of us a little awkwardly out of place in our home setting after our many years in different ones, "This boy really loved your daddy. He would bring him watermelons every summer as soon as he had some ripe, and this boy really loved that. This boy really loved your daddy."

My father's watermelons that he grew on his land *were* the best in the county and his watermelons were always ripe for that highest of American civic holidays, the Fourth of July. My brother and I enjoyed them every summer, and now their memory is a perpetual remembrance of our father and the land that he loved.

TROPE 4: "MAMA'S MAMA WAS ALL DUTCH"

As we were growing up on our farm outside Shubuta, my brother and I really only heard about our Irish ancestry. It was understandable, because while all their other grandparents were native-born, my father and his brothers and sisters had grown up in their house with their Dublin-born grandfather. It was also consistent with the dominance of the patriarchal line in typical U.S. cultural thinking. The Irishman's lore dominated the family: how he asked one sister to marry him and go to America, and when she refused, her sister volunteered, married him in her place, and sailed with him the next day to their new land; how after landing in New Orleans, he worked his way north on the railroad as far as Shubuta and then settled near there in the Hiwannee community and homesteaded the land on Carson Creek and Mill Creek on which three generations of us were born; how he rode a white mule and was known throughout the county as the old Irishman with the heavy brogue.

As children we did not have the knowledge that yields ancestry from names. Our grandmother Jones was born Reilly, and our father's mother was the granddaughter of an itinerant minister named Samuel Jones, but I only learned as an adult living in England of the pure Welshness of Jones and the Irish derivation of Reilly.

Around Shubuta when we were children, ironclad ancestry was racial and racial identity definitive. People were either black or white. Even if some tanned white people might be darker than some blacks and if some blacks were whiter than whites, we all knew instantly who was which—a gesture of lowered eyes, a specific fragrance, a footstep of a certain kind, an inflection of speech or word choice, a choice of hairstyle, dress, or vehicle, the place one lived, shopped, or traveled to, the company kept. Physiognomy told only a little of the story, but a person was clearly one or the other, no doubt about it.

Yet, in other American contexts, it mattered a great deal that a person is a fraction of one ancestry or a bit of another. For example, membership in Native American tribes or on Indian reservations and entitlement or inclusion such membership provides is often based on a fraction of ancestry in

"Mama's Mama Was All Dutch" • 63

the tribe—one-eighth or one-quarter or one-half or even as little as one-sixteenth—to be enrolled as a member. Guidelines for some scholarships and admission to some colleges are often based on a proven portion of ancestral blood.

What common sense once told, 1990s scholars have demonstrated: race is foremost a cultural category. The most delightful illustration of this was a 1998 *New Yorker* article by Toni Morrison calling President Bill Clinton the first black president. His male sexual behavior, she writes, is that which is culturally attributed to black males. The academic version of the theory suggests that culture—social norms, economic opportunity and decision making, law formulation, behavioral fashion—creates people in the shape of human-formed categories, names them by race, and limits or supports people within the boundaries of these invented proscriptions.

In Shubuta when we were children, ancestry was black and white with little room for the ambiguity or uncertainty or mixings that were actually the historical reality.

After my mother had died and before I went to teach at the University of Amsterdam for the spring term of 1995, I found a remarkable letter, returned unopened and saved for many years, that my mother had written to me and my family on our first trip to Amsterdam in 1973. The startling sentence that jumped out, a fact I did not remember ever having been told, was "Mama's mama was all Dutch."

That was new news about who I was! Schooled in my feminist consciousness of the legitimacy of tracing one's ancestry through one's female line as readily as the male, I quickly seized upon the knowledge that, seen afresh in my newfound female line, if that were emphasized exclusively, I would not be Irish or Welsh at all! If we should only trace directly back through female ancestry as the lineage that counts, my daughter Natasha, granddaughter Jessica, and I are Dutch, for our female forebears directly back through my mother's maternal line, along with "mama's mama," were all Dutch!

When I lived in Amsterdam that spring, I enjoyed imagining my great-great-great-grandmother or some earlier relative exploring the Netherlands as I was doing, walking along the city's canals, gathering armloads of tulips, sampling Dutch gin and Dutch food—well, maybe the women were not *jenever* drinkers. When I went out to the Kuekenhof Gardens and enjoyed seeing the planted bulb fields from the train window on the way, I imagined generations of my own people before me enjoying the fields in that landscape.

Going to church on Easter morning I walked up my street, the Prinzengracht, and over to the Singel, walking along central city canals all the way. On the city center street, the Spui, I entered a narrow passageway to come out at the Begijnhof where I would attend services at the English Reformed Church of Amsterdam.

The children on Amsterdam streets spoke a language I did not know. They came out of beautiful old attached houses that were architecturally strange to me. Yet the children's clothing and bicycles and the bakery goods and the jewelry in the shop windows were familiar.

I saw a couple under a window who looked just like the confident young man and woman I watched each morning from across the Prinzengracht as they rode off on their bikes to work—except this couple frowned at their maps, not knowing where to go. The couple's telltale open city maps and their American voices when they spoke revealed that they were among the thousands of Dutch Americans and other European Americans who visit Amsterdam during this season every year. They resemble the residents so very much in facial features, body, hair, and skin, and even in some aspects of culture like knowing and enjoying the foods and flowers. Yet, they are foreigners, foreigners every one, in not knowing their way around and not being at home. I was one of them, a foreigner struck happy at heart at my privilege of my short-term residence in my newfound land of maternal ancestry.

Inside the Begijnhof courtyard, I entered the now-familiar circle of fifteenth-, sixteenth-, and seventeenth-century houses, the first by the entry passage a wooden house built in 1470. Bountiful spring flowers surrounded the church and blossomed in the tiny front gardens of the houses—daffodils, hyacinths, grape hyacinths, pansies, bleeding hearts. It was a chilly day with a little wind, and the pink blossoms of the flowering cherry tree beyond the church blew in the wind, as did the heads of a dozen different varieties of daffodils in the churchyard. It reminded me of nothing so much as azalea-time in Shubuta and the masses of spring flowers around Janette Hudson's home there.

The Easter service in the Begijnhof church was conducted in English by the Scottish minister. His English dialect was familiar to me from my having Scots friends in my neighborhood when I lived in Cambridge, England. The form of the service, its prayers, and the Easter hymns sung were familiar to me from my childhood Methodism, a descendant denomination from English Protestantism. I listened to the familiar English of the Scotsman conducting the service, sang the familiar Easter hymns from my U.S. southern childhood, and read the familiar prayers from Protestant Christendom. I stumbled over "forgive us our debts," saying "forgive us our trespasses"—the Methodist way instead of the Presbyterian—in the Lord's Prayer, and remembered how, at my mother's funeral, I felt home free when my ailing father beside me began to mumble safely that same prayer at the right place in the service. The sun came out at one point in the service as we sang in the Begijnhof church, and it shone through the clear glass windows (Dutch, Reformed, after all) directly on the well-placed bouquet of golden lilies in the chancel.

In the church service, an infant girl was baptized, daughter of a Dutch father and a Chinese-ancestry mother from Singapore, wearing the christening gown worn by her grandfather, and the words were the same we had used in Boston and Minneapolis at the christening of our infants, Natasha and Stiles, no doubt the same words used for my brother and me when we were christened as infants.

I was happy that I had gone to the Begijnhof English-speaking church that Easter morning, a church founded as an English church in 1607 in the wave of English people who fled England to the Netherlands by a similar group to those who would settle in New England in the early years of the seventeenth century. I had gone searching for my maternal ancestry and found my U.S. national ancestry instead. As I walked home along the Spui and the Singel and the Prinzengracht, I imagined Dutch life in the past as my past, heard Dutch language on the street as a language with which I had a connection, imagined the houses and streets and waterways as ones with which I had ancestral memory.

"Mama's mama was all Dutch" became a parable of American ancestry to me, that ancestry of blends and mixes, conformities and contrasts, ethnicities and languages, religions and foodways, families and places that make up American cultures. It was my mother's mama's mama who was all Dutch, not me. I was a visiting American professor for a term when I attended the Begijnhof church one Easter, a foreigner. My passport says USA; my place of origin, the U.S. South; my precinct of citizenship, Minneapolis, Minnesota, in the U.S. Midwest; my relationships, international; my race and national origin, many splendored.

Chapter 2
Shubuta's History

> *The buildings [of the town] are quite proud in their false fronts, trying to be everything that two stories can be and a little bit more. . . . A child might have cut them off a cornflakes box and fastened them with two tabs, A and B.*
>
> —Garrison Keillor, *Lake Wobegon Days*

Florence Busby and I clambered down the steep bluff of the Chickasawhay River just beyond the cemetery to the narrow sandbar in order to see the site of the Choctaw village believed to have been there in the prehistory of Shubuta. Former mayor Busby and her across-the-street friend, Patsy Toney, had taken me for a tour of the town of Shubuta and its surrounding area a previous day, showing me commercial and business sites and residential neighborhoods in town and the churches and farms, forests and homes in communities near town. Florence had volunteered to go with me to the river and talk about its places of importance in town memory on this day.

She pointed out how the sandbar had been much larger when she was a girl and told how, on Sunday afternoons, Shubutans would take leisurely walks as families from their homes around town down to the sandbar. The sandbar was a favorite picnicking place at that time. Across the river now, a thick growth of trees is all that is visible.

The Choctaw village that established and named the place Shubuta is believed to have been on the east side of the river, the opposite side from where the present town stands, at the fork of the Chickasawhay River and Shubuta Creek. The Choctaw Shubutans appear to have lived there at least a few hundred years—a boat of theirs, carbon-dated at 300 years old, was brought out of the river nearby and identified in the late twentieth century. People also still find carved stone arrowheads in the ground at that site.[1]

A few white settlers came to live along the rivers and streams when Mississippi was still a territory before 1817 statehood. Families would come west and migrate up the rivers from the Gulf Coast and do hardscrabble farming in river and creek bottomland locations. The U.S. government made treaties with the local Indians in 1805 and 1830, the Treaty of Mount Dexter and the Treaty of Dancing Rabbit Creek; and by those treaties the lands around Shubuta became U.S. lands. In 1920, a government surveyor, George Dougharty, surveyed the land on the line between Mississippi and Alabama, land that took into its boundaries current Wayne County and Clarke County, the counties of Shubuta and nearby towns and rural communities.

In the 1830s, primarily in the coastal sections of South Carolina and Georgia, the federal government made available to potential settlers for 25 cents an acre the local lands around Shubuta acquired by the Treaty of Dancing Rabbit Creek. Adjacent lands only a mile or so away in one direction had been included in the land ceded in the 1805 Treaty of Mount Dexter, so individual white families and small groups of single men and families had bought land and settled there a bit earlier. This was territory on the Chickasawhay River and the Buckatunna Creek and other waterways south of Shubuta around Waynesboro. The earliest settlement was about twenty-five miles to the south at Winchester in 1827. The Powe plantation, the establishment of which preceded the settlement, was a part of the Winchester community, the ancestral home in the maternal line of Shubuta's white Hand family and black Powe family of which Cleo Powe Cooper was a descendant.

Thus began the land's acquisition by European Americans. After buying parcels of it from the federal government in South Carolina and Georgia, men gathered their families and servants, usually African American slaves, into wagon trains to make their treacherous journey to their new homes on the frontier. They had to cross Creek Indian territory, and their wagon trains were sometimes met with hostility and gunfire from the agitated Creeks. More than one wagon train suffered losses from Creek fighting, and many of the wagon train leaders entered into combat with the Native Americans. Among the people who arrived in the vicinity of Shubuta after having bought land in southern coastal states in the 1830s and traveled by wagons through the territory of the Creeks and eastern Georgia and on through Alabama were Evanses, Prices, Weemses, Pattons, Floyds, Coopers, and Hands.[2]

When there was first a U.S. settlement at Shubuta is unclear from historical records. In European exploration and trading times, and in territorial times, there is evidence of European trading posts, "stands" as the rough frontier inns were called, and missions among the local Choctaws. There are records of a French mission at "Youwannis" (Hiwannee) to the south, started in 1729 and lasting perhaps three decades. Former Clarke County Supervisor James Brewer described in an interview an eighteenth-century mission and school for Indian children at "Emmaeus" southeast of Shubuta, where there was a two-story log house with a dining hall and an outdoor kitchen and a split rail fence all around the property. Brewer said that he had been able to walk along the earthen remains of the buildings and fence. Just north of it was Jewel's Stand. Though he calls the place "Eewennans," this must be the Choctaw school to which white boy John Evans, as he wrote about it in his diary as an old man, was sent as the only white child after his family settled near Shubuta in the early 1830s, for Evans refers to nearby Jewel's Stand.[3]

By the 1840s and 1850s, there were sizable plantations in the area, notably the Lang Plantation in the community now called Langsdale, and the Horne Plantation in what is now Matherville. People who were to be town leaders in Shubuta in the twentieth century had settled and soon secured large landholdings north and northwest of Shubuta near what are now very small towns of Enterprise and Stonewall and the rural community DeSoto. In that period everyone depended on farming for their livelihood. There were many small farms, as well as the few big plantations along the rivers and creeks adjacent to Shubuta. Even the occasional doctor or lawyer came from a farm family, a large landholding one that had money enough to send a son away to a college or university or professional training school before he came back to practice in his community.

Some of the well-to-do planters began steamboat service on the river, and others started embryonic manufacturing plants for cotton cloth and cottonseed oil, around which rose settlement communities in Enterprise and Stonewall. Shubuta, however, came into its own with the arrival of the railroad. A post office was established in 1849. The M&O Railroad was begun and finished through Shubuta in 1855, some of it built by local slave labor. A roundhouse and shops for railroad mechanical service were built in Shubuta, making it a key location for switching the railroad cars and for railway track maintenance. The streets and lots for housing and businesses as they now stand were platted by the railroad company in the early 1850s, and all the town property deeds date from that railroad platting.

As the Civil War approached and Mississippi's secession from the Union was debated, white Shubutans took both sides of the secession question. However, once the war started, the Shubuta Rifles was the first unit in Clarke County to be mustered out for the Confederate Army.[4] The war hit Shubutans hard economically and socially, just as it did all southerners; but though the fighting and destruction of the war came as close as a few miles south of Quitman, the town itself was not ever under fire. Shubutan W. H. Patton as just a boy was a telegraph operator in Shubuta during the war; and he stayed on to work for the federal forces during the first years of Reconstruction.

In the fifteen-year period after the Civil War that is known as the Federal Reconstruction period, Shubuta may have stabilized faster than some equivalent towns in the South because it was not directly hit by the war and also because some other southern white people who were well-off had moved to Shubuta during the war to escape the effects of slave uprisings in other towns. Also, already established merchants like Morris Greenhood had remained in the town and no doubt helped rebuild the town's economy. Though the town was officially established by the State of Mississippi during this period, in 1867, there are no surviving minutes books of the town government, nor are there extant records of the town churches.

By the last decade of the nineteenth century, the railroad had been rebuilt and the importance of the railroad to the town's prosperity was again being felt. Shubuta once again became a trade center for both distant and near surrounding communities, this time the customers coming by trains as readily as by horse and buggy, wagons, and ox carts.

During the last years of the nineteenth century, Shubuta also started to become a boom town for the sawmilling industry. "Company houses," one of which still stands on a Shubuta street, were built for sawmill workers, and the Kaupp Lumber Company was established for large-scale timber cutting, hauling, and shipping out of Shubuta. This was followed by the accommodation of the railroad for timber shipment with what were called "dummy lines." These were temporary train tracks laid out into the woods where logging was being done so that trains could transport newly cut logs into town for shipment.

Shubuta's prosperity was probably highest in the first two decades of the twentieth century. During those years the virgin timber was rather thoroughly cut over. Newly invented automobiles came early to Shubuta, one of the Weems boys having the first one; and there was a car dealership in Shubuta before 1920. The town was still financially vigorous all through World War I, a war in which one of the doctors, J. A. McDevitt, served, and on through World War II, the war to which many of its sons went. It even fared better than most towns during the Depression, the Bank of Shubuta always remaining open.

With increasing numbers of cars, roads for faster travel became important in Shubuta as they did all over the country. Some roads were paved, and in the late 1930s building of the new federal Highway 45 through Shubuta was completed.

This plays out the thesis that the typical cycle of the lifeblood of a town comes with its transportation system, first the river, then the railroad, and by the 1930s the highway for the automobile. In Shubuta both the Choctaw village and the first white settlement were on the Chickasawhay River. When the railroad was built, it ran a little to the west of the river, and the town was designed and built in an orderly plan west of that to avoid flooding. When the highway came through, it too paralleled the river and the railroad tracks, and was more westerly still. Gradually, over the years, "town" moved west with the highway, so that today the thriving businesses and town services—the gasoline stations, the convenience store, the firehouse, one bank, and the new town post office—are all lined up along Highway 45.

For all the middle decades of the twentieth century, Shubuta was a town where nearly all the businesses were locally owned; where high-quality medical, dental, and legal services could be obtained; where most commercial services, farm and home equipment, supplies and services could be bought; and where food, clothing, and home heating fuel were available. A good deal of wealth was owned in the town. After slavery, the sharecropping system had been instituted on the farms around Shubuta and continued on past World War II, so most black people and some poor whites eked out a living as sharecroppers on the farms around Shubuta or worked in domestic or other services in town. Through the first two-thirds of the twentieth century the town had two public schools, one for black people on the far west side of town and one for white people on the far east side of town. Shubuta was a separate school district from the county, meaning there were no school buses, and few children went to school in Shubuta who did not live in town.

Gradually, by a process I call the urbanization of the small town, a concurrent development with highways and automobile transportation accelerated after World War II, and Shubuta began to be supplied with mass-produced products, foods, clothing, and equipment. After television's debut in the 1950s—"Boo" Hutto at the furniture store had the first TV set in Shubuta—Shubutans began to watch the same entertainment programs, the same advertising, and the same national news broadcasts as were watched nationwide. Alongside mass communication by the 1960s, much greater availability of fast travel was possible with more frequent use of air travel as well as long-distance train and automobile trips for Shubutans.

During the era of the civil rights movement Shubuta was modestly affected by its activity. Some local people were active on behalf of civil rights, and some outside workers came to Shubuta acting for civil rights the summer of 1965. There was only one civil rights march on Shubuta streets, late in the movement years, in 1967. However, when civil rights laws were passed, Shubuta changed, too. Shubuta institutions were desegregated by the 1970s. The schools in Shubuta had all closed in the name of consolidation. Therefore, other than government offices themselves, there were no longer any public gathering places or centers of focus in the town other than the post office. Stores on the street of town and the churches remained locations for informal communities to be established, and Shubuta continued as a stable center of population and of memory on through the twentieth century.

Shubuta's history is specific, though, so I will provide a little more detail of Shubuta's evolution in chronological order, starting with the Choctaws.

Shubuta Choctaws

Shubuta was probably a village of the Choctaw Indians for many generations before white people came to their river bluff location on the Chickasawhay River. A Choctaw settlement appears to have been on the east side of the river, for archaeologists from Louisiana State University are said to have found considerable evidence of a village there, and there is an earthen mound near the west side of the river believed to be a Choctaw burial place. It is still not uncommon to find carved stone arrowheads that give evidence to an earlier presence of Choctaws on those grounds.

The Choctaws were a kindred tribe to the Chickasaw Indians, and an origin myth of the two tribes holds that they were founded by brothers. (Another origin myth has them coming forth from the earth at a sacred site, the Nanih-Waiya, created by the Great Spirit, near Philadelphia, Mississippi.) The Chickasaws settled somewhat to the north of the Choctaws. The Choctaws were a forty-two-village nation in southeastern Mississippi, six of the villages being along the Chickasawhay River, one at Shubuta and a larger one at Hiwannee.

For my purposes, I am going to spell the nearby village name "Hiwannee" and refer to the early nineteenth century Choctaw chief as "Yowannee" throughout this work. In print and in lore there are several spellings of both the village name and the name of the most referenced Choctaw chief of the place that is now named "Hiwannee" as a contemporary rural community where once the Choctaw village stood. Because the first records seen by Europeans about this place were in French, "Youane" was the first spelling seen. On the earliest map of the area, dated 1771 and made by the explorer Bernard Romans, the place is called "Ewana." Other candidates, apparently corruptions of the Choctaw name, are "Yowanne" and "Hiowanni." It meant cutworm or caterpillar in the Choctaw language.

The Choctaws were a farming people and migrated in search of more arable land. They were also a peaceable people, in contrast with the Creeks who lived to their south and east and the Chickasaws to their north, fighting only when there was direct threat or attack upon them. The Choctaws had a highly developed system of government with a district governing council of chiefs, each village having a chief of its own and a village council. They had a strict legal code, punishing theft and murder most severely, and the chiefs met and discussed legal decisions and took actions together.[5]

The Native American people at Shubuta no doubt had their town at the fork of the river with Shubuta Creek and their burial mound stands today just beyond the Shubuta Cemetery, the burial place today as it has been since about 1867 for the white citizens of Shubuta. The word *Shubuta*, Choctaw for "smoky water" or "dusky water," was probably what the Choctaws called the dark, misty stream on which they made their home. On cool mornings even now one can see the mist rise from the black creek in light moist curls of vapor that remind one of smoke, and one can imagine the prehistorical Choctaws naming the creek and hence their settlement home for this natural mystery. The flowing water is yet today dark, veritably black in the deep pools of the stream.

Just as post–Civil War Shubuta is said to have been the largest town between Mobile and Meridian, Choctaw Hiwannee was the largest Indian village to the north of the Gulf Coast before the Chickasaw country north of present-day Meridian. In the time when native people alone inhabited the land, the Choctaws hunted, but they also planted. Corn, pumpkins, sweet potatoes, squash, melons, and beans were among their produce; and they traded with their neighboring villages. To do so, they designed and built roads, paths, or trails, running alongside the rivers and branching out in all directions from their riverside homes. Highway 45 today runs north to Chicago and south to Mobile, Alabama, near Shubuta along the trailway engineered by the local Choctaws. They were reputed not to use river transportation so much as the roads they built, though the carbon-dated three-hundred-year-old dugout canoe found in recent years in the Chickasawhay River near Shubuta[6] suggests that they were skilled builders of boats, too.

When the Choctaw lands just south of Shubuta were ceded to the U.S. government by the Treaty of Mount Dexter in 1805, the Choctaws were paid $500 for their holdings of 5 million acres in what is now southern Mississippi,[7] and the lands were open for sale and settlement to U.S. citizens at that time. However, the powerful Chief Yowannee of the Choctaws at Hiwannee refused to allow the government agents to come any closer to his people's location, thus saving their Red Bluff site about five miles downstream and that of the Shubuta people upstream from them for another twenty-five years. The meeting with the government he set at a legendary boundary red oak tree location said to be the site where the Chickasaw and Choctaw brothers shot an arrow facing the sun, so that, blinded by the light, they would set the boundary line between their territories with fairness and justice.

All of the remaining land, though, was taken by the Treaty of Dancing Rabbit Creek in 1830, and most of the Choctaws were expelled and moved to the reservation in Neshoba County near Philadelphia, Mississippi, or to the U.S. government's "new purchase" set aside for Native Americans, Oklahoma.

Choctaw Shubuta Memory: An Old Map, Earthen Mounds, and Corn-Grinding Stones

My husband collects antique maps of Cambridgeshire in England. Although I share his love of England's Cambridge and its county, my eyes glaze over at his excited discovery of the availability of yet one more expensive old map of yet one more version of what Cambridgeshire looked like to yet one more long-dead cartographer. I am not a collector. If I have one of something, that is enough, and I want my maps free to travelers at the state line and designed to give me directions for how to get somewhere.

Yet, maps I have found of Shubuta tell more of time and memory than I had thought I could know. The somewhere these maps take me is to an open past.

There is a map in the Wayne County Court House that verifies the handed-down oral accounts of the valor of Chief Yowannee during the Choctaws' resistance of the U.S. government's efforts to take over their land in 1805. When Chief Yowannee met the U.S. agents under the legendary boundary red oak tree and said, "Go south!"—in effect, "Stop! You may not proceed!"— he sent them back south and kept his people within the Choctaw territory by gerrymandering the Hiwannee district out of the U.S. control. Even today, the 1805 line on the recording map in the Wayne County Court House gives dramatic evidence. Where otherwise a straight line cuts across southern Mississippi marking northern limits of the Choctaw territory obtained by the government in 1805, the tooth-shaped Hiwannee land bites incisively southward into the government's region, still Choctaw by the chief's action.[8]

Though their town's name is Choctaw, no Shubuta citizens of today are identified as Choctaw. There are no Choctaws with tribal affiliation, personal self-identification, or conscious Native American ethnic practices in Shubuta. Shubutans are aware of the some three thousand Choctaws who live one hundred miles away on the Philadelphia Reservation, and many Shubuta people have seen dance programs and demonstration games of Choctaw stickball performed in traditional festive clothing by the Philadelphia Choctaws. Many have bought bead jewelry and pine needle baskets crafted by the members of the Philadelphia Reservation. From his service as a Methodist minister on their reservation, the Reverend Dr. Shaw Gaddy, the minister of the Shubuta United Methodist Church in the 1990s and beyond, knows the Choctaw language, a living language that is the first language in the homes of most of the Philadelphia Choctaws, and he knows much about Choctaw tradition and culture.

In Shubuta itself, though, there is little consciousness of the town's indebtedness to its Choctaw past. Shubutans, like all Americans, owe a debt to their town's native forebears for their conservation of nature, for their agricultural and building skills, for those staple foods like corn and sweet potatoes and squash. In Shubuta in particular, the built location of the town on the river bluff was first sited by the Choctaws, and the engineering of the roadways in their present locations was the doing of Choctaws. Even that main road, Highway 45, follows the trace of the Choctaw pathway from Shubuta to Mobile. The railroad before the highway had run close beside the rivers in much the way the Choctaws had made their riverside walkways.

For recovery of Shubuta's Choctaw memory, we must look to traces on the earth that are almost gone or to stone objects and stories that have changed as we have handled them. As with their roads and foods and words, we living people have used early Choctaws' knowledge to build our own. With their stories and the remains of their things, we breathe with them in our shared place.

Our tangible memory of Choctaw living comes in fragments of our experience. The day Guy Walker, the retired county surveyor, took me to the Wayne County Court House to see the 1805 map with the Hiwannee tooth bitten out of the U.S. government's land, he showed me a set of Choctaw cornmeal grinding stones.

The day Florence Busby and I went down to the Chickasawhay River through the heavy-hanging Spanish moss on the live oaks to the sandbar beyond Shubuta Cemetery, we saw the mound, now deep in the woods and beyond a monument to the Confederate dead, that is believed to be the Shubuta Choctaw burial place.

The day downriver near Hiwannee on the Chickasawhay when Keith Graham and I wandered over lands that his Kettler and our shared Graham ancestors had farmed, we waded through Carson and Mill Creeks to the remains of the solid virgin-pinewood gristmill that the homesteading Irishman James Graham had built on Mill Creek, gazed on the banks of the

Chickasawhay where steamboats were said to have brought passengers and the mail, and wandered among a new growth of trees on "the Kettler land" where slight rises and ridges in the earth with saplings growing from them are university-authenticated Choctaw sites.

On all these days we recollected Choctaw memory. It is a memory full of feeling—puzzlement, confusion, grief, pleasure, outrage, anger, appreciation, guilt—a memory filled with far more questions than answers, a memory that is profoundly American, a memory that is our own, one that belongs to all Americans, Native Americans, mixed Americans, black Americans, white Americans, us, peoples of the United States. It is each of ours, and a memory that is live, native, and Choctaw. It is a fragment of who we all are, our common truth.

Naming Shubuta

There is a story of how Shubuta got its name and that the name means "sour meal" in Choctaw that has been often told over the years. It appears in a booklet by upper-class Shubutan Frank Ledyard Walton, *Shubuta, On the Banks of the Chickasawhay River,* which was written in 1947 and was quite familiar to the local people. Florence Busby and I talked about the various accounts of how Shubuta was named and what it means as we climbed around the river bluff near the site of Choctaw Shubuta. She laughed her deep infectious laugh, and concluded, "It probably means 'smoky water' but I like the 'sour meal' story better."

Sour Meal

The Choctaw sour meal story is a myth of origin of Shubuta. There are several versions of it, and they do point to the reality that Choctaw people preceded white and black people living at Shubuta and to the fact of the town's name being from the Choctaw language. In a subtle fashion, perhaps these stories also establish in the telling by us white people over the generations a kind of unconscious sense of authority and superiority.

The Walton volume in which the sour meal stories are recounted is a civic boostering history book of the immediate post–World War II town and is also a boyhood memoir of its author. It is a privately published forty-eight-page booklet, the project of the cemetery association for the town's white people. We know from his middle name, Ledyard, that the writer is a member of one of the elite families of the town, for Ledyard is an early town leaders' name, along with Weems, Hand, Floyd, and Patton. Thus, the point of view is that of the town's privileged class. The records of the Shubuta Memorial Association, kept for many years by Robert C. Weems, were given to me by his eldest granddaughter, Mary Sue Mitchell. On the origin story, Walton writes that after settling on the riverbanks and harvesting a "bumper crop" at the end of the first year, the Shubuta band of Choctaws were preparing for their harvest festival. Walton writes,

> On a momentous night shortly thereafter, a sudden heavy rain soaked their supply of meal, causing it to sour. A howl and a yowl went up, such as only an angry band of Choctaws could raise, which made the bluff ring and the valley reverberate. In complete disgust and with much ado, they all with one accord shouted over and over, "Shubuta, Shubuta" to the thud of many stamping feet and wildly swinging arms and tomahawks. Over and over again, the raging band "tromped" and shouted "Shubuta, Shubuta," until exhausted at dawn, the camp finally fell asleep. In the Choctaw language, Shubuta means "sour meal." This old Legend of the Rain credits this episode to an era long before the coming of the white man.[9]

Walton goes on to write a version that is not an origin story for the name from the arrival of the Choctaws, but a more damaging and condescending story that buffoons the native people and submits them erroneously to the white people:

> Another Indian legend . . . dates the meaning of Shubuta to a much later period. The story states that an Indian had brought a sack of corn to the white settlement to be made into meal in the white man's mortar and pestle. This was a log set up in the ground just the right height to work over conveniently, having the top hollowed out to form a bowl. In this bowl the corn was placed and pounded to meal with the pestle, which was a piece of round wood, three or four feet long, made smaller in the

middle to give a good hand hold. The Indian had his corn pounded and started home but while walking a log across a creek, his feet slipped, upon which he exclaimed, "Shubuta," knowing that his meal was spoiled.[10]

The source of the kind of mortar and pestle described is not European but African. African Americans most likely introduced it to European Americans. Precontact Native Americans had their own grindstones for making meal.

The writer calls these stories legends, thus implying they are fanciful, but it is not clear whether he knows if the Choctaw "sour meal" thesis is historically accurate as the story of naming for the town. He does not show awareness of the linguistic evidence that the creek was probably named first with the Choctaw word meaning "smoky," *shoboti*. "Sour meal" would have been *bota shua,* since the adjective follows the noun in Choctaw.[11] Since tribal groups usually gave place-names from nature, names given at the beginning of their settlement rather than from human events that came some time after establishment of locations of communities, it makes sense that the village spot was first identified by its creekside place.

The selection and perpetuation of this story as a story of naming and a myth of origin for what is now the town of Shubuta has indirect meaning. While plenty of archaeological, historical, and mapping information show that there was a Choctaw village on the riverbanks near where Shubuta is now, and there is clear evidence that the name is Choctaw, the sour meal stories are not credible by linguistic or cultural evidence. The truth is that American Indians taught white people how to plant and harvest corn, not the other way around, and material evidence such as grinding stones shows that Choctaws were making cornmeal long before Europeans and European Americans came to their land. For example, Guy Walker, the retired county surveyor of Wayne County, Mississippi, showed me the set of ancient grinding stones, presumably Choctaw, that he collected in the vicinity of Shubuta.

Making a more straightforward historical connection between current white Shubutans and the Choctaws, James Johnston told me that his great-great-uncle Douglas Johnson (the *t* was inserted in the family name's spelling later) was one of the white men who went to Oklahoma with the Shubuta Indians, one who, as he said, "drove the Indians to Oklahoma in

1830. But he stayed out there," he said, "and married an Indian woman, had some children, and lived out there." There is a county in Oklahoma named Johnson County in his honor.[12]

Smoky Water

The entry for Shubuta in the careful 1941 county place-name study by Mary Frances Bass, *A Study of Place-Names of Clarke County, Mississippi*, says that Shubuta is "an incorporated town in B[eat] 2. Est. in 1853 when the M. & O. r.r. was built. Given the name of the creek. Shubuta, in some sense, may be said to be the successor of the old Indian village of Yowannee." Bass was off by two years on the date of establishment, which was proven to be 1855 in correspondence between Shubuta banker, insurance agent, and civic leader Robert C. Weems and the successor railroad company.[13]

The date of the railroad's completion has been much contested in the memory of Shubuta. However, a letter from Carl Fox, the general solicitor of the Gulf, Mobile, and Ohio Railroad Company, to Mr. Robert C. Weems, dated 15 November 1957, sets the definitive date from the railroad company's records: "Construction of the road was commenced at Mobile, and on 15 March 1855 the roadbed had been graded and the track laid to Quitman [north of Shubuta]. By 3 October 1855 the road had been completed to Enterprise."

Bass was right that the town in its organized plan was formed with the coming of the railroad; for that was the time when the town was platted into lots and streets for commercial and professional use and for residences surrounding the business district street next to the railroad. In the Clarke County Chancery Clerk's office today, the official registry and maps for land deeds in Shubuta all begin with this 1855 railroad platting.[14]

On the town's location, Bass was also right that Shubuta was the successor to an "old Indian village" on the Chickasawhay, but there was one at Shubuta as well as "Yowannee." Hiwannee is now a small rural community in Wayne County along Highway 45. Once it was the Choctaw village with the powerful chief who defied the U.S. surveyors and held onto his people's land. A century later Hiwannee was a thriving sawmill town of white and black people much like Shubuta; but by the end of the twentieth century, it was no place at all except a road sign, some houses, and a couple of churches along a gravel road off the highway.[15]

Telling about the location and naming of Shubuta Creek, Mary Frances Bass says:

> Formed in B[eat] 2 where Dry Creek and Hollicar Creek run together. Flows into Chickasawhay River near Shubuta. (C. Co. Soil Map, 1914). Comments on the name are: "Shubuta" is Choctaw *shoboti*, "smoky." It does not mean "sour meal" as some have erroneously reported. To speak of bad smelling meal a Choctaw would say *bota shua*, for the adjective in the Choctaw invariably follows the noun, never precedes it as in English.[16]

The name Shubuta, then, is a Native American name, Choctaw, and was there before the town and before the coming of the white and black people who would be called Americans. Shubuta resident, Methodist minister, and former Philadelphia Reservation clergy, the Reverend Shaw Gaddy, verifies linguistically from the spoken Choctaw language the grammar that Bass uses to demonstrate the meaning of the word *Shubuta* in Choctaw.

In its appearances on maps and in writing, there are many spellings of *Shubuta* and alternate pronunciations, as well. Janette Hudson told me that the earliest spelling she knew about was "Choboti." This is from the map in French that was the earliest map locating the Choctaw village. Country men in my childhood would call it "SHOE-booty" in humorous speech. Its local pronunciation is "Shuh-BOO-ta," but outsiders without a southern accent often mispronounce it "Shuh-BEW-ta." Whatever the variations of spelling and pronunciation, Shubuta appears to have been "Shubuta" for some centuries, not just decades.

Surveying the Land

One of the most exciting discoveries of my archival research about Shubuta was the state line surveyor's notes in the county archives in Waynesboro. It ranked in delight up there in the top five archive experiences for my project alongside Chip and Mary Sue Mitchell's showing me the contents of "Auntie's trunk"—Miss Mary Weems's—full of letters, speeches, souvenirs, and a travel diary; Syble Meeks's giving me copies of the Shubuta newspaper, the *Mississippi Messenger;* Guy Walker's taking me to the courthouse in Waynesboro to see the early map with the Choctaw tooth of Hiwannee land carved out of the 1805 treaty acquisition; and Cassandra Cameron's showing me the Phillips archive in the Shubuta Library. This source was another one in the Waynesboro court house shown to me by retired county surveyor Guy Walker, and it was the original surveyor's notes from 1820 for officially forming the boundary line between Mississippi and Alabama within a very few miles of Shubuta.

The U.S. government sent the surveyor to make the lines between Alabama and Mississippi just after the time of statehood, 1817. His colorful 1820 surveying notes tell much about the landscape, the vegetation, and the wildlife, the living conditions of the few white people there, and the personality of the surveyor, as well as the establishment of the state lines of demarcation, which he was paid to do by the state.[17]

"This mile is broken land, soil sandy, Timber [sic] chiefly, Pine, Oak, Chesnut [sic] and some Hickory, the bearing of the hills and vallies towards the Tombeehbe [sic—Tombigbee River]," wrote surveyor George Dougharty on 29 May 1820 in his field notes on the first day of surveying the line between Mississippi and Alabama just south of the funny tooth-shaped indentation on the map that Chief Yowannee held onto, at one point just one mile south today of the road sign announcing the entry to Shubuta.

Dougharty mentions the vegetation and the soil often, as if markers of permanence. He set a post at a "Red Oak," mentioned that the "First 45 chs [chain-lengths]" were "low wet pine land, thence higher and very bushy, soil 2nd quality, Timber Pine, Oak, Chesnut, Gum, etc." at his "8th mile south" entry. At the twenty-second mile south, he crosses a "big Red creek" that is "25 lks. wide, 5 feet deep, course SW" and comments "this creek has no swamp at this place with a high bank on the north side—a good sandy mill seat."

He locates people and roads as well as habitat. He crosses the "road from Winchester to St. Stephens" and sets posts "from the Old Mobile trading road." He mentions stopping at "Mr. Crane's mill"[18] and setting post number 8 in "Mr. Napell's field" and post number 6 one chain-length "South of Phillips' road. Poor flat pine land."[19] He reports going to Winchester to get provisions. Once he put two bottles of rum in to balance his load.

Dougharty apparently worked and camped with three or four men he hired locally. He writes in his notes that the chain man and the rod man could not read or write, so they would remember for a mile what they measured and tell it to the surveyor when they got together again. Dougharty took field notes through the day, but he would add things at night at the camp site.

He wrote that he finished the survey of the line on 19 July 1820 and set a large post on the corner of the Choctaw line.

Entries in the surveyor's field notes continue beginning 11 July 1823. Apparently, Dougharty has returned to the area to do further surveying for the government. On 17 July, he writes, "Bought a pack horse and some camp equipage. Contracted for a beef and meal provided the cows come up." He also hired some of his workers in Winchester. On 18 July, he writes, "Hired two more hands." Apparently, the cows did come up because he continues, "Killed a beef and sent to mill."

The next day, Sunday, 20 July, he writes, "This being the Sabbath day it was devoted to making mockersons, Leggins, Woutys &c &c &c [*sic*]."

Presumably, then, the provisions he was buying and the workers he was hiring were for further work. The next week he had setbacks on Wednesday and Thursday, 23 and 24 July. Wednesday he writes, "Here Roan Oak [his horse] got into a yellow jackets nest, threw the cook, Kilt his Knee, broke the Coffee pot, spilt the meal, ran away, and prevented my doing any more work." And Thursday, "Rain! Rain! Rain and no tent. Cooped up in a small Pine bark camp with a Yankee and 2 Runaway Georgians all great travelers and monstrous liars."

Entertaining as well as informative, the surveyor's notes give a quick glimpse of the landscape and conditions on the Shubuta frontier.

The equivalent records do not exist for Clarke County or for Shubuta itself because some of what is now Clarke County was a part of Wayne County when Dougharty did his survey of Wayne County in 1820. Also, a part of what is now Clarke County was still occupied by the Choctaws until the 1830 Treaty of Dancing Rabbit Creek. Even if there were surveyor's records after Clarke County was organized in 1833—after the Treaty of Dancing Rabbit Creek that yielded this portion of Choctaw land to the U.S. government— the records would have been in the county courthouse at Quitman, and that courthouse was burned with its records in it by Union general William Sherman's late Civil War raid, 14 February–5 March 1864. Only the land deed records were saved by being hidden in a swamp when the raid was imminent. Sherman's siege brought about total destruction of the town of Meridian, of the M&O Railroad, and all public buildings, roads, and bridges through Quitman and south to within ten miles of Shubuta.

Still, Wayne County's records are more than analogous, for Clarke County was not formed until thirteen years after the 1820 survey. The survey Dougharty did starts one or two miles distant from current Shubuta on the county line that is there because of the Choctaw boundary line that preceded it and moves fifteen or twenty miles' distance. Thus, Dougharty's notes record the people and the land that surrounded Shubuta, that drew in to Shubuta. To the north above Shubuta, it is the same kind of land on the same river to which diarist John Evans's father came as the first white male settler in the Choctaw Nation at that place called DeSoto, and he had great-great-grandsons in Shubuta.[20]

Missionaries, Traders, and Settlers on the Shubuta Frontier

Panthers, wild cats, bears, and wolves growled and howled in the "dense wilderness" in which, in 1832, John Evans's parents settled near the Chickasawhay River in the whereabouts of what is now Shubuta. In that vicinity were broad sandy river banks, high red bluffs, and tributaries that would later be called Carson Creek, Sand Creek, and various Mill Creeks for the white people's grist mills that the waters later powered for cornmeal grinding. There was also the creek that the Choctaws already called Shubuta, forking away from the Chickasawhay near the Choctaws' burial ground on its west bank across from their east-bank village.

The first Europeans on record to come to the vicinity of Shubuta were French missionaries and fur traders. There may have been Spaniards who explored the region before them, for there was a period of Spanish claim to the territory, but Spanish people's presence is not documented. Hiwannee Indians possibly saw the first white people of any in the region, since in 1729 French Catholic missionaries, Fathers Beaudoin and LeFevre, established a mission church among them and built a chapel and trading post. To devoutly Protestant, both white and black, Methodists and Baptists who dominate the area today, some of them fundamentalists without much experience with or knowledge of Catholics, it is a significant contrast that the first white Christians who lived there were Roman Catholics. Charles H. Cole IV writes in his local history of what he calls "The Chickasawhay Country" that Catholic missionaries and fur traders went out among the Creek and Choctaw Indians from Mobile soon after that town was established under the French flag in 1702. Among their missions and trading posts was one at Hiwannee begun in 1729. This is the first account of white residents in "The Chickasawhay Country."[21]

The mission priests at Hiwannee, Fathers Beaudoin and LeFevre, built a chapel, the foundations of which, Cole reports, have been traced. It was called Saint Bernadette's Catholic Church. Cole also tells of a diary by a French fur trader named Roulet in which the diarist writes about the Hiwannee mission, saying he found the "Indians friendly and eager to trade." Roulet describes the area around "Youwannis," his word for the village.[22]

The mission may have lasted more than thirty years, but there is no record of its ending, whether the Indians drove the French out, or whether the French left for other pursuits. There is simply evidence that it was abandoned sometime before the close of the French and Indian War of 1763. It was at this time that the land was claimed as British territory, what they called the Territory of British West Florida.

There are likely to have been other mission settlements or schools for the Choctaws in the region in the eighteenth and early nineteenth centuries, together with "stands," the innlike locations for rough lodging, food, rest, and provisions needed by the traveling explorers, fur traders, or other occasional French or English territorial or U.S. frontier travelers. One later stand on record near Shubuta was Jewel Stand, with a school for Choctaws beside it, built before the 1820 U.S. survey of the land. David Gage, a Presbyterian minister, and Moses Jewel, a teacher, from New York, built the school and the stand about a mile and a half from the Alabama line. Diarist John Evans wrote that the school was "for the purpose of teaching the Indians domestic habits."[23]

In the 1760s, a colony of Scots had settled along the Buckatunna Creek at a place they called Shiloh. They were a Gaelic-speaking group, and they farmed some plots of land within the forest, hunted and trapped animals, kept to themselves and prospered. Little was known about them to others in the area. A few other farming settlers came into the southern gulf-coastal territories after U.S. nationhood but the other early contact the Shubuta, Hiwannee, and other Chickasawhay River Choctaws had with whites was when settlers came to plow and plant the river bottoms after the 1805 and 1830 treaties.

The waterway the earlier white people had settled along in the area was Buckatunna Creek, southeast of Shubuta. European Americans may have come there as early as 1809, up the Chickasawhay from where it joins the Pascagoula River before that river empties into the Gulf of Mexico. The gorgeous white-sand beaches of today's Mississippi Gulf Coast are more than a hundred miles south of Shubuta. Some settlers traveled by river, floating their belongings, including farm animals, and the people in their groups by rafts and flatboats up the rivers. Some would stop at more southerly sites and then move up river in a few years.

Besides migrating from other isolated riverside posts and plantations of the first white settlers along the Pascagoula and Chickasawhay Rivers and Buckatunna Creek, the first whites got to Shubuta by at least three overland ways from the early 1800s through the 1830s. One was to come up from Mobile, Alabama, on what John Evans refers to in his memoir as the "old trade road" to Mobile, a major Choctaw route south. Another way was to come overland east to west along the Three-Chopped Way, also an Indian road, which went from Fort Stoddard in what became Alabama to the south to Natchez. The third was the Fort Saint Stevens to Natchez road, which crossed the Chickasawhay within a very few miles of Shubuta, as surveyor John Dougharty's 1820 notes testify.

Government agencies also were concerned about providing roads into the newly opened U.S. territory. The Mississippi Territory General Assembly, considering how settlers would come to the former Choctaw lands, in 1809 commissioned work "to open a road from the Pearl River where the present Choctaw boundary line crosses the same, the nearest and best way to the Chickasawhay River so as to interest some at or near the lower end of the Higawana [Hiwannee] Reserve."[24]

There was also interest in roadbuilding from the U.S. War Department for use in its military operations against the Indians, and it was that department that built the Tennessee Trace between June 1817 and January 1820 from Madison, Louisiana, to Muscle Shoals, Alabama, crossing present-day Clarke County, Mississippi.[25]

Testimonials of Shubutans like Aubrey Jones, the census records, the Hand family genealogy book, and John Evans's memoir all tell that many white ancestors of Shubutans were born in Georgia and coastal South Carolina,[26] so the Fort Saint Stevens to Natchez Road is a likely route for them to have traveled in ox carts and covered wagon trains and arrived in the Choctaw country in the Chickasawhay proximity. There they claimed their farmsteads, cleared the river bottoms and fields of land for farming along the creeks and branches around Shubuta. Nearest Shubuta, the European and African Americans came first to locations on the Chickasawhay River to the north at present-day Enterprise, Stonewall, and DeSoto, communities today eight and twelve miles away.

One of the earliest settler families who have descendants in Shubuta, the Powes, came in 1811 to Winchester, a no-longer-existing village that was twenty-five miles south in current Wayne County. The man who bought the land was William Powe and his wife was Harriet Elizabeth Marcia Pegues Powe. They and their eleven children and forty-six slaves came from the Chesterfield District of South Carolina and established a farm near what became settlements of Buckatunna and Winchester. They had to get a permit from the governor of Georgia and promise that they would travel peacefully through Creek Indian Nation territory on their journey. They rolled their goods in oaken hogshead barrels alongside the river as they traveled. Rather than a log cabin, as settlers were usually building on the frontier, Powe, using slave labor, oversaw construction of a three-story house with sawn and planed lumber and hand-carved molding and mantels.[27]

John Britton Hand moved with his family in 1820 from St. Stephens in Alabama "driving livestock along with them, as they moved some fifteen miles westward along the 'Three Chopped Way,' an Indian trail which ran along the ridges from St. Stephens to Natchez,"[28] a descendant writes in the Hand family genealogy book, *Handbook*. They moved to a farm they bought in Wayne County about seven miles from Shubuta. John Britton Hand bought more land around Matherville and on the Chickasawhay River from Enterprise to Stonewall and built a landing and ferry-crossing on the river known as Hand's Ferry. He built the first school for settler children in the western part of Clarke County and hired Irishman Jeremiah Hennessy to run it.

One of the families who came in 1830 from South Carolina was named Price and settled on land just north of Shubuta. The father, John A. Price, built the first bridge over the river on his land, the bridge that came to be known after the twentieth-century lynchings as the Hanging Bridge. Later, the family moved to a house in what is now town, a house that is one of the three pre–Civil War homes still standing and one that predates the Price family's 1830 arrival. This house on the northeast corner of North Street later served as both the home and mortuary business of Will Patton and sat across the street from the Shubuta twelve-grade school for white children. Now it is on the National Register of Historic Places as the Price-Patton-Pettis House.[29] The wagon train in which the Prices traveled from South Carolina included four extended families who were later to be known as among Shubuta's most prominent people, the Prices, Weemses, Pattons, and Floyds.[30]

Another early family of settlers coming originally from South Carolina to the Shubuta vicinity, James Johnston's ancestors, settled in Alabama before moving to Mississippi. The progenitor of the family in Shubuta, Arista Johnston, was born near Shubuta and moved back in 1869, after the Civil War. During the war he had lived as a child and teenager in Alabama. In Shubuta, he had two families of children, one with his first wife, Amelia Heidelberg, who died in 1873, and the second with his second wife, Mary A. McCoy. He farmed all his life and served in the Mississippi Legislature from 1900 to 1902. Johnston's ancestors were among the settlers who used river transportation to migrate into Alabama and Mississippi, bringing slaves with them. In a family history piece he writes of his forebears John Johnston and John Linden setting out from South Carolina to the Mississippi Territory around 1800 and coming to the Tombigbee River at Cotton Gin Port, "where they constructed a raft to move their negroes [sic] and goods down the river on. Having embarked on this raft their negroes and other plunder, the raft was started down the river, but it was soon wrecked and about 100 negroes were drowned."[31]

Colonel John H. Horne and his brother, Collins, came from Milledgeville, Georgia. Like the Powes, they settled in Winchester for a while but they came to Matherville in 1835. John Horne eventually owned a thousand acres and built a stately plantation house with a ballroom on the third floor. When the M&O Railroad came through, Colonel Horne built fifteen miles of the road from Winchester to Red Bluff, later named Hiwannee, and was paid with a large amount of M&O Railroad stock. At the time of the beginning of the Civil War, he owned more than nine hundred slaves.[32]

These plantation founders with large landholdings and numerous slaves were the exception rather than the usual, however. While the big plantation homes became the centers of the social, political, and economic life of the region, the majority of the white settlers were small landowners, who had no slaves or only a few slaves, and merely eked out a living from the land. Their homes, likewise, were very small, typically being two-room log buildings with dirt floors. A plantation might have outbuildings for a tannery to make shoes and leather farm goods; a blacksmith shop for shoeing horses and doing other metal work; a smokehouse for curing meats; corncribs and other storage sheds; barns and barnyards for horses, mules, oxen and cattle, pigs, and chickens; a cane mill for making syrup; perhaps a turpentine distillery; a creamery, perhaps set over a cool, flowing spring, for milk products; outdoor kitchens and wash houses. Many of the poorer farmers had no such buildings and equipment at all, or few of these things, but shared their small, clean-swept yards with their animals and quite literally lived off the land in the small spaces they had cleared for themselves in the midst of the extensive surrounding woodlands.

When the white people settled around Shubuta and began to farm, they were at first friendly and cooperative with the Choctaw people who were there, but the weight of U.S. government treaties and its program of "removal" of American Indians from their home places in combination with the European individualistic concept of personal, private ownership of the land, soon drove most of the Choctaw residents on the cruel walk to Oklahoma, or to the reservation at Philadelphia, Mississippi.

Cemeteries, Plantations, and Pre–Civil War Houses

On the outer edges of Shubuta, about equally distant from Highway 45 in the center of town, are two cemeteries. The Shubuta Cemetery on the east along the Chickasawhay River with its steep banks and Spanish moss–covered live oaks is where the white people are buried. On the west near where the paved roads turn to gravel is the Shubuta Davenport Cemetery, where black people are buried. Out in the country or near Enterprise and DeSoto there are family burial grounds from the nineteenth century of some families with descendants in Shubuta. These include the Bass and Everett Cemetery, the Gilmore Hill Cemetery, the Old Gavin Cemetery, the Pleasant Hill Cemetery, the Adams Chapel Cemetery, the King Cemetery, and the Enterprise Masonic Cemetery. The Masonic Cemetery at Enterprise has graves of both black and white people.[33]

Inside the town none of the churchyards holds a cemetery, though out in the country several churches whose communities are oriented to Shubuta as town have churchyard cemeteries. One of them is the Tribulation Baptist Church, a few miles west of Shubuta on the Eucutta road, whose members are African Americans. Another is the Geneva Presbyterian Church, a congregation of the white Southern Presbyterian denomination belonging to the villages of Matherville and Langsdale.

Matherville and Langsdale began as slave-operated plantation centers, in Matherville the plantation of John H. Horne, in Langsdale the plantation of Clem Lang. Lang seems to have been the bachelor son of an extended family who originally settled on the place around 1833: the 1840 Census of Slave Inhabitants of Clarke County lists a total of more than one hundred slaves owned by "the estate of W. A. Lang," Olivia Lang, Willis Lang, and Clement Lang.[34] By the time he seems to have been the plantation master at Langsdale a decade later, Clem Lang owned vast acreage and planted crops with slave labor. Slaves built for him the grand white-pillared plantation house, finished in 1859, that still stands today. The house is in the mansion style of antebellum houses familiar from Natchez and Vicksburg, the only one remaining in the immediate area of Shubuta. It cost $35,000.00 in addition to the slave labor when it was built. The plantation bell was molded from six hundred silver dollars.[35] Lang did not ever marry, and from developments unknown to future generations, relatives of his named Falconer took over the place and ran it after he returned to England. Reverse immigration was not uncommon in the nineteenth century, but the mystery of this one is atypical. It may be as simple as avoidance of the Civil War. However, there is local lore of romance about Clem Lang's departure and the connection in the tales of his having been a relative of the next-generation Archbishop of Canterbury who in 1936 crowned King Edward VIII of England, that king who later abdicated and became the Duke of Windsor.

The Horne Plantation at Matherville, with its similarly fine house, like the Lang House had typical plantation outbuildings, a school, storehouses, and a store, but the Horne house no longer stands. The Lang House, while no longer having slave houses, storehouses, or other outbuildings, was restored by the Cross family in the first half of the twentieth century, and Elsie Jones Cross and her husband, Robert, lived there for many years. Langsdale and Matherville's plantation places were agricultural centers for some decades, then villages each with a doctor, a school, a post office, and some country stores for some decades more. Matherville, in contrast with Langsdale, is still a small village with a country store, a church, and a row of houses. It had its own post office much longer than Langsdale did, and it had a one-room school for a number of years in the late twentieth century.

After some years of deterioration, the elegant Lang plantation house has been restored in recent years, its walls, pillars, and porches freshly painted and its grounds newly landscaped for gracious country living just as it was after Clem Lang's slaves built it; but no white people named Lang or Horne live in Matherville or Langsdale any longer, though Horne descendants are buried in the churchyard of the Geneva Presbyterian Church. Some black people named Lang, however, live on the country road near Langsdale.[36] Since the plantation black people followed the local convention of having the same name as the white owner's families, they may or may not have been related by blood. However, the 1840 Clarke County slave census, which lists black persons not by name but under the slave owners' names and by the categories of sex, age, and color, records all of Clement Lang's slaves as B for black under color, not M for mulatto. Thus, it is at least possible that the Lang Plantation owners did not participate in the widespread practice of miscegenation. (Enoch Hand, Samuel Howze, John Evans, William J. Howze, and Shadrach Hogan are among those local slaveowners who owned mulatto slaves.)[37]

Black people named Falconer and their descendants have continued to live in and near Shubuta. The best carpenter in Shubuta through the middle decades of the twentieth century was named Falconer, Mary McCarty's grandfather, heir no doubt to his slave ancestors' skill and experience with the Lang Plantation carpentry. Pearlie Mae Hozie, who was recognized in Shubuta as a black community leader in education and in civil rights through the last half of the twentieth century, was born a Falconer.[38]

1830s to 1850s Shubuta

It is unclear how much of a settlement of white people there was at Shubuta as the farming and plantation-owning settlers came in the 1830s and 1840s. A few houses in the current town or those building sites date to that time, one being the Hand house, now owned by Brevard Hand, that was built for himself by a white carpenter named Thompson in 1834. Also, a Jackson doctor, Charles Neill, told Florence Busby that he recollects being told that his grandfather was a doctor in Shubuta in 1834. However, such records or memories are limited.

The historical record is clear, though, in showing that a U.S. post office was established at Shubuta on 18 December 1849 with Benjamin Blakeney named as postmaster, indicating at least a population center there at that time large enough to warrant mail service.[39]

From the late 1830s through the early 1850s, the ancestors of Shubutans farmed along the Chickasawhay River and the creeks that ran into it. Some families owned large tracts of land and farmed with the work of slaves—the Clarke County Census of Slave Inhabitants dated 5 August 1850 lists only a dozen households that had twelve to twenty slaves, among them Levi Sumrall, Alex Gordon, John S. Howze, William J. Howze, John Evans, George Evans, and James M. Hand, and only the Langs (the estate of W. A. Lang, Olivia Lang, Willis Lang, and Clement Lang) having more than one hundred.[40] Matherville's Horne Plantation is not listed here because it was in Wayne County, but it was nearer to Shubuta than were many Clarke County locations. Other people lived and worked on modest landholdings. However, for all of them their primary means of both communication and transportation was the river. Also, the other people with whom they related were primarily from other riverside households from Winchester and Buckatunna south of them in Wayne County, and north to Enterprise, Stonewall, and DeSoto. The farmsteads and plantations were largely self-sufficient, growing staple corn, sugarcane, grapes, and other foods for the people and feed crops for their livestock. The farmers kept chickens and other fowl and cattle and hogs for their eggs, milk, cooking fat, soap-making, and meat. On the larger plantations, the owners retained blacksmiths, carpenters, leather tanners, cooks, and house workers among the slave population.

Men from around Shubuta carried their produce, largely cotton, to market as far as Mobile sometimes, taking it by river on flatboats, keelboats, and later steamboats. They also drove animals or hauled cotton, corn, smoked meat or other foods, or syrup, made from their sugarcane, on their wagons over the primitive roads. Such market trips could take months, and family stories abound of Shubuta area great-great-grandfathers who drove chickens or geese fifteen miles on foot to sell somewhere or who loaded their goods on a homemade raft when the river water was high enough only to have the raft sink a few miles downstream.

At Shubuta there was a port on the river, and also one at Hiwannee. When steamboats became available on the Chickasawhay, they ran from Enterprise to Mobile, carrying goods and the mail, their schedule dictated by the water height and planting and harvest seasons. One planter, New York–born Captain Thomas Jefferson Woolverton (1814–1867), who settled in Clarke County about 1844 and who built the plantation Millbrook on Jackson Creek near Stonewall, earned his title as a riverboat captain. He built a Greek Revival style manor house, was a very successful planter, cotton broker, and mercantile businessman, and owned and operated two steamboats on the Chickasawhay, the *Lancaster* and the *Ben Bolt*. When river conditions allowed, he hauled cotton downriver from Enterprise to Mobile and brought goods for the mercantile business back upriver with him. These would have been among the steamboats that stopped in the ports of Shubuta and Hiwannee.[41]

Shubuta became a documented U.S. State of Mississippi town, though still not chartered or incorporated, in 1855 when the Mobile and Ohio (M&O) Railroad went through and platted the streets around its center as lots for houses and commercial businesses. Shubuta went onto the map to stay with the coming of the railroad. In this period, all of the people farmed, whether on the large plantations or the many small, subsistence farms. Farming was what they came for, and farming was what all the black and white people did, nearly all the African Americans as slaves to their European American masters. When the railroad came, Shubutans could begin to think of traveling and sending their goods away on the rails on a reliable schedule rather than depend seasonally on the river or the deep-rutted muddy roads. The M&O Railroad built a roundhouse and shops at Shubuta, which meant that the economy was bolstered to support the workings of the railroad as well as the farms, and the town grew as a transportation and communications center, as well as a farming town.

Before the Civil War

When Moses Greenhood first came to Shubuta on the M&O Railroad train soon after 1855, he and other railroad passengers had to go two and a half miles from the Shubuta station to Wiley Rogers's place for lodging. This was presumably a private home that took lodgers. Greenhood soon opened the first store in town and became one of Shubuta's first businessmen. According to W. H. Patton, himself an important businessman later in that century and early in the next, the first 1850s business leaders in town were W. H. Cherry, J. B. Gates, Sam Meyer, D. C. Richards, Isaac Champenois, T. T. Howze, Dr. J. W. Avery, A. Carr, and Elijah Parker. There was a drugstore run by the doctor, D. M. Dunlap, as was usual at the time, and a hotel named the Parker House had opened by then.[42]

The reporter of this early information about the town, William Hinkle Patton, moved to the Shubuta vicinity with his parents, Sarah A. Hinkle Patton and James J. Patton in 1859 as a 9-year-old boy, the eldest of five children. James Patton was a planter. As talk of secession built up, the elder Patton opposed it strenuously, but like many others, he joined the Confederate war effort as soon as it began, joining Company E of the 37th Mississippi Regiment as an orderly sergeant; but he died in 1862 of typhoid pneumonia, contracted at camp at Columbus, Mississippi, leaving young William at age 12 to fend for the family. The boy had already moved to town as a kind of apprentice to Dr. Dunlap, who was postmaster as well as physician and pharmacist, and young Patton ran the post office, clerked in the drugstore, and lived in the Dunlap home, remembering Mrs. Dunlap as showing great kindness toward him. By the end of the war, Patton's mother and siblings had moved to town, and by the time he was 14, Patton had learned telegraphy and was supporting his mother and family by running the telegraph office for Shubuta and for the Confederate government war effort. He stayed on a few months after the war as telegraph operator for the Federal government.[43]

Shubuta and the Civil War

Everything about Shubuta's way of life, its economy, and race relations changed, as they did all over the United States, with the Civil War and its outcome of the defeat of the South and the end of slavery. Shubuta experienced its white sons going off to war as Confederate officers and soldiers. The Shubuta Rifles was the first Clarke County unit to go off on Confederate duty. The M&O Railroad going through Shubuta also played an important role in the war. During the war a Confederate newspaper, the *Weekly Southern Republic,* was published in Shubuta. I have only been able to find one issue of this newspaper, located in the Meridian Public Library, but it is vol. 4, no. 18, 1864, suggesting that the newspaper had been publishing since 1861, the first year of the war.[44]

Before secession and the formation of the Confederacy, some Shubutans, like James Patton, were worried over the prospect of war and opposed its coming. Some others were active warmongers, bragging they could "whip the Yankees before breakfast." Most men and women in the area were "ardent secessionists" in this "stormy time in our community," recollects Joshua M. Phillips in a document saved in the Phillips archive. His father, however, "was opposed to hasty action" and hoped that after his inauguration President Abraham Lincoln could bring about reconciliation. Joshua Phillips remembers from being a young boy in the early 1860s his father having heated arguments with a neighbor, both of them slaveholders, the neighbor wanting to whip 'em before breakfast and Phillips arguing to "wait until Lincoln takes his seat." The boy wondered why it took that man Lincoln such a long time to sit down.[45]

Still, both men joined the Confederate army like James Patton did when the war started. In fact, a number of Shubuta men had joined the Mississippi Militia before the war had begun, making it possible for the Shubuta Rifles to be ready for Confederate duty at the very beginning of what some southerners still call the War Between the States. This unit, which was a company of the 14th Regiment of the Infantry and was mustered out in Clarke

County on 28 March 1861, was led by Robert J. Lawrence, captain; George Anderson, first lieutenant; Everette M. Johnston, second lieutenant; and William B. Falconer, third lieutenant.[46]

The people of the surrounding area of Shubuta felt the war acutely. They suffered the disruptions of family life and farming and transportation that were felt in both the North and the South, and the war came so close to them that they feared becoming a war zone. The M&O Railroad was immediately taken over by the Confederate government, so Shubutans saw troops and supplies going through on the trains as they supported the war. They might have seen Confederate president Jefferson Davis travel through town on the M&O in October of 1863 when he went from Lauderdale Springs near Meridian, where he had visited his war-displaced brother, Joseph, and dying sister-in-law, on his way south to Mobile to inspect the troops there.[47]

Late in the war, from 14 February through 5 March of 1864, massive destruction came very close to Shubuta. In a foretaste of General Sherman's capture of Atlanta and march to the sea, Sherman's army destroyed everything in its reach in and around Meridian, coming very near, about ten miles, but not quite to, Shubuta, to a place just south of Quitman. Sherman's infantry soldiers failed to rendezvous with the cavalry in Meridian as planned, in February 1864, for a march toward Mobile or Selma. Angry that the cavalry had not arrived yet and that the Confederates had learned of his coming and escaped with all the military property and all the trains, engines, and cars of the railroads, General Sherman gave his men tools and orders for totally laying waste to Meridian. The soldiers destroyed the whole town and then tore up the railroad tracks and burned crossties, which were made of solid heart pine, bending the rails out of shape over those intensely hot pinewood fires. They destroyed culverts, trestles, and bridges over the waters. They burned buildings and ransacked houses and storehouses in their way, utterly ruining the railroad several miles in every direction from Meridian, including Quitman and south a little beyond Quitman. Sherman later claimed, "For five days, 10,000 men worked hard and with a will in that work of destruction, with axes, crowbars, sledges, clawbars, and with fire, and I have no hesitation in pronouncing the work as well done. Meridian, with its depots, storehouses, arsenal, hospitals, offices, hotels, and cantonments, no longer exists."[48]

Because Shubuta was not literally touched by the war, even though cannonballs were found a few miles away and the railroad was completely disrupted, some white people moved to Shubuta to escape war activity in other places, and everyone was subject to the wartime poverty that gripped the South as the war went on and all the people were sought, slaves and masters alike, in some kind of service to aid the Confederacy.

It is no wonder that an advertisement on 4 June 1864 in the *Weekly Southern Republic,* the newspaper of "An Independent South," published in Shubuta, asked on behalf of Major M. Merriwether "to hire ONE HUNDRED NEGOR LABORERS, Ten mule teams, 4 or 6 mules each, and ten yoke of OXEN, to get and haul TIMBER for the Railroad Bridge over Tombigbee River, near Demopolis. I also want to employ FIFTY CARPENTERS, White Men or Negroes, for the same work. I will pay liberal prices and furnish rations and quarters for the men. Signed W. P. Barker, Agent for A. L. Maxwell."[49]

Even so, in the *Weekly Southern Republic,* ordinary life is represented as continuing to go on, for along with the bridge builder's ad, the resolutions of the Congress of the Confederacy, and reports from battlefields, there were articles about dailiness of life, local elections, and church. Household hints and information about the rainfall are in the 4 June 1864 newspaper. Also, notices are posted for Clarke County elections in the coming October. In Beat 2, Shubuta's district, C. F. Goodwin and W. H. Cherry were candidates for constable. John S. Dabbs was running for reelection as county sheriff, and John Shanks was candidate for tax assessor. Divine services are announced for the next day, Sunday, at the Shubuta Methodist Church with its minister, the Reverend J. T. Heard, preaching.[50]

There are also two notices of runaway slaves being held in jails in other counties, one "a negro man calling himself PETER, and says he belongs to Jock Lock of Clarke County, Miss." Another, "calling himself LEWIS and says he belongs to John Horne of Clarke County," was described in this way: "said boy is about 25 years old, weighs about 175 pounds, and is five feet ten inches high. The owner is asked to come forward, prove jeopardy, pay charges and take him away."[51]

At the end of the Civil War, Shubuta experienced the liberation of its slaves and the homecomings of its defeated soldiers like the rest of the South. Joshua Phillips tells of his father, Captain W. C. Phillips, coming home "a mere shadow of his former self," having been in the siege of Vicksburg, after which he became ill and was hospitalized until the surrender. After his release, he walked most of the way home, getting a ride with a neighbor for some of the last miles of his way, but walked up the road to their house "under a scorching July sun," a part of a defeated army come home.[52]

After the Civil War

After the war Shubuta was possibly able to rebuild economically somewhat faster than places whose buildings and infrastructure had been demolished by the war, but rebuilding was still slow. Some formerly wealthy white families who moved to Shubuta to escape the war from other places, especially Alabama, people like Alexander Connor, later a judge, and his sisters and wards, the Case children, were able to assist in Shubuta's restoration.

Shubutans suffered in the recovery from the Civil War just as people all over the United States, particularly southerners, did as they found their lives, their economy, their culture, and their system of government forever changed. I was able to find no public records or reliable orally transmitted memories about Shubuta during the Reconstruction period of 1865–1876. However, by his own recollection, 14-year-old W. H. Patton continued to work as the Shubuta telegraph officer for the Federal government in 1865, during the first months of the period known by historians as Presidential Reconstruction, 1865–1867, as he had for the Confederate government at the end of the war.

Some southern white families in addition to the family of Alexander Connor, guardian of Annie Brevard, who became the teaching pioneer and mother of the Hand family, came to Shubuta during the war after slave uprisings or threats of Union encroachment. Others like Arista Johnston returned to settle near Shubuta right after the war. The U.S. Census of 1870 (discussed in chap. 1) shows numerous white households in Shubuta then who were Shubutans before the war, and only a few seem to have moved there after the war. The minister Josh T. Heard was still there, as was the merchant Morris Greenhood. Cooper and Champenois families, residents through the Civil War time, were still residents in 1870. In the town proper, the black people in the 1870 Census were only those who lived in and were servants in the households of white people.

On the farms, the agricultural sharecropping system was instituted not long after the Civil War, tying a few white people and most blacks into a new economic pattern of being beholden to a white landowner. Shubuta joined most of the nation over the next decades in instituting Jim Crow laws that provided racial segregation of public facilities and commercial properties where before the law had been silent on race.

The town itself got its charter of incorporation in 1866, which meant it was from the first Mississippi Reconstruction government. The form of government still in place in Shubuta was begun then, a system by which a mayor and five aldermen are elected at large, serve four-year terms, and make and supervise enforcement of laws for Shubuta. The Shubuta Female Academy was formed in 1867, joining the Shubuta Male Academy established at an earlier date. Thus, both the boys and the girls of Shubuta's white upper class received excellent education, though the 1870 Census shows that the vast majority of Shubuta's white people as well as black people were illiterate. (This is still true by the 1900 Census.) Following the 1870 School Law in Mississippi, Reconstruction legislation required public schools all over Mississippi, but the Minutes Books of the government in Shubuta from that time are lost. By the beginning of the twentieth century, however, town minutes show public funding provided for a school for white children and a school for black children, a system that probably began at some level in the 1870s.

The Hudson Drug Store was formed in 1868, one of the longest continuing businesses in town. In 1879, the daily *Mississippi Messenger* was begun, and it continued to be published until sometime in the 1930s. The *Messenger* covered national and international and political news, but it catered to the local, too. It would have a special sheet published when there was a death of someone of stature in Shubuta, for example. A Masonic Lodge was established in Shubuta, and the two churches for white people, the Shubuta Baptist Church and the Shubuta Methodist Church, thrived. Shubuta lawyers were well-known in the region in the late nineteenth century, and from among them, Daniel Webster Heidelberg served in the state legislature.

W. H. Patton, Shubuta's 14-year-old telegraph operator in the last year of the Civil War, became an eminent businessman, first serving the Adams Express Company as its agent in Shubuta for six years right after the war, then going into business for himself in a small store and eventually into a large store, Heslep and Patton, owned with his father-in-law and then on his own after Heslep's death. His "mercantile business," where everything from iron cookstoves to yard goods was sold, was the largest in Shubuta for half a century. He also owned a water-powered sawmill, a cotton gin, and a gristmill. He was a Baptist, a Mason, and for a time was a trustee of Mississippi College, the Baptist institution near Jackson. He served on Shubuta's town council as an alderman for many years, twice briefly as mayor, and he became a nationwide leader of anti-alcohol campaigns. He claimed to scratch off the ballot the name of any man running for public office who was known to imbibe alcohol, and for several years he worked for a Prohibition Party ticket for president and vice-president of the United States.[53]

An eightieth birthday party for W. H. Patton hosted by John J. Gonzales "of New York and Atlanta" took place in the Shubuta home of J. W. Poole, where a "sumptuous banquet" was served "due largely to the untiring efforts, as well as the efficiency of Mrs. Poole and her daughters." Former employees of Patton were present or sent letters to be read and an extensive program of speeches was given. One speaker, the Reverend L. E. Hall of Hattiesburg, said that since Patton had done so much for the state and the country, he was pleased to make "the long and tiring trip [from Hattiesburg] in order to join in honoring him." An impressive letter was read from Wayne C. Wheeler of Washington, D.C., "chief counsel of the Anti-Saloon League of America," praising Patton "for his persistent fight of more than 50 years in the temperance battle and for prohibition."[54]

Sawmilling Town

Around 1900, large sawmilling operations came to Shubuta, the first of them the Kaupp Lumber Company, followed by Brownlee Lumber Company by 1906. The best evidence for the rise and fall of the timber-cutting industry around Shubuta is a collection of town maps made by the Sanborn Fire Insurance Company in 1885, 1890, 1895, 1900, 1906, 1912, and 1926, copies of which are available in the Mississippi state library in Jackson. The 1900 Sanborn map of Shubuta shows no sawmill operations. Only the cotton gin and grist mill of A. P. Hand are shown on the east side of the railroad tracks; a turpentine shed, a stock pen, and a cottonseed warehouse, along with the passenger station, the freight depot, and the cotton platform, are beside the tracks on the other side.[55]

The 1906 map shows the Shubuta Oil Mill (the one founded by the "capitalists" in 1902) having replaced the A. P. Hand cotton gin and grist mill, the turpentine shed removed and additional railroad tracks off to the east. These tracks accommodate a large Kaupp Lumber Company operation on one side and Brownlee Lumber Company on the other. The new tracks are called the Shubuta and Southwestern Railroad, and "tramways" run off them in the Kaupp property to a tram platform beside "steam dry kilns," a planing mill, and lumber storage platforms in addition to several lumber piles and a lumber dock. Brownlee Lumber has a "cross arm factory" with an office, sheds, a woodworking shop, and a painting shop next to the ancillary railroad tracks. Farther down there is another small collection of buildings called the "Brownlee & Hazelton Handle Factory."[56]

By 1912, according to the map, the Kaupp Lumber Company is no longer there, but the Brownlee Lumber Company has lumber piles and platforms in all the space held six years before by both Kaupp and Brownlee.[57]

On the 1926 map, J. G. Brownlee Lumber Company is still recorded, but it occupies a much smaller space, and it is joined on the site by the Shubuta Electric Company and a planing mill, identified with "E. L. Wetherby, owner."[58]

It is clear, then, that the railroad and the sawmilling business in the early twentieth century made Shubuta a vigorously growing sawmill town where the virgin pine forests of the vicinity were cut and sawed and shipped away on the railroad for sale abroad. There was new prosperity in Shubuta from 1900 until about 1920 with sawmill jobs for some blacks and poor whites, and wealth for some owners of land and mills. In 1902 a bank had been formed, the Weemses' Bank of Shubuta, and cotton gins and a cottonseed oil mill joined the sawmilling businesses of the town.

The *Mississippi Messenger* figured prominently in Shubuta in the early twentieth century, and a millinery shop, a jewelry store, and later an automobile dealership joined the newspaper office, the drugstores, dry goods stores, hardware store, feed store, grocery stores, and doctors' and lawyers' offices on Eucutta Street. Shubuta's sons went off to World War I, and then the town experienced the exhilaration of the 1920s. Shubuta went through the Depression, though the Bank of Shubuta did not close. When World War II came, both black and white Shubutans fought in the war, and gravestones mark their deaths in the Tribulation Baptist Church cemetery, the graveyard of the Geneva Presbyterian Church, and both the Davenport Cemetery and the Shubuta Cemetery in town. Returning soldiers came back to a segregated South, but two decades later Shubuta experienced at least a mild version of the racial explosion that was to be the civil rights movement. Some daughters and sons of the town were civil rights activists, and after the civil rights laws were passed in the 1960s, Shubuta experienced desegregation. Like some other southern towns, Shubuta came to obedience to the new laws holding the memory of lawless violence in its past in the form of racist lynchings at least two different times in the memory of living townspeople. Its identity as a town, like so many U.S. southern towns, had changed shamefully when down in the deep woods and over the Chickasawhay River a mob of white men hanged some black people from a bridge known locally ever after as the Hanging Bridge, and the perpetrators from both 1917 and 1942 were neither caught nor punished, though their names are known by some people alive today.

Changes around Race

Many features of U.S. racial history, as well as U.S. economic history, political history, and social history, are verified in Shubuta history. "Color or race" is a category on the forms used by the U.S. census takers on the 1870, 1900, and 1910 census documents I examined, and color-words have been widely used to label race, which in turn is a linguistic invention that roughly equates "continent of origin" in the mixed population that has come to make up the United States. All the color-words except "white" for European Americans and "black" for African Americans have come to be seen as pejorative so that no polite person, not to mention serious scholar, would refer to Asians or Asian Americans as "yellow" or to Native Americans or indigenous inhabitants of North and South America as "red," as in "Red Indians." This, however, was the language still used in 1947 when *Shubuta* booklet author Frank L. Walton introduced the Shubuta Choctaws:

In the long ago, when the White man ruled one continent, the Yellow man another, and the Black man still another, the Red man ruled a vast world, much of which was unknown to him and all of which was unknown to the others. It was a paradise world, a Red man's heaven, for within its great borders, he found everything to make life worth living: climate, food, shelter, and space. To the Red man it was the Universe.[59]

Shubuta, like the rest of the United States before what is now called (with an attempt at linguistic neutrality) "contact" between Europeans and Native Americans, was a place inhabited by a settlement of an indigenous population.

On race, security, and tranquillity, Shubuta is Small Town, USA. This has its attendant emotional and mythic value. Novelist Rosellen Brown, author of *Civil Wars,* which has a Mississippi setting, and of *Before and After,* writes, in a *New York Times* article headlined "Paranoia on Main Street," about the change of mood in her summertime home of Peterborough, New Hampshire. Peterborough was where playwright Thornton Wilder lived and set his well-known theater work, *Our Town,* and Brown says that he represented the town "unchanged, [and used] the names of the nearest mountain and river and exemplified the community's peace, modesty, and common sense. ... This is a town where shopkeepers still walk fearlessly down Main Street carrying their bags of cash-register money to the bank . . . [and] where many people don't have keys to their front doors."[60]

The year of her writing, however, she notes that after the Oklahoma City Federal Building bombing, people are frightened of strangers, alarmed over young people using drugs, horrified by what she says "detonated the peace of the so-called Heartland on April 19 in the name of American values."[61]

The same could be said of Shubuta, where Thornton Wilder's play *Our Town* is remembered from its performance in nearby Waynesboro thirty-five years ago. Some of the people who live in Shubuta now acted in that production or attended its performance. As in Thornton Wilder's town, the people who live in Shubuta look at it with pride of place. They value their quiet riverside community and their sense of its long-term peacefulness. People who once lived there remember with nostalgia. A retired white Baptist minister writes, "I can still remember the old wooden school house and the day that I was allowed to visit and sit in the class with my brother there. I have been broken hearted each time one of the beautiful old homes has burned and have rejoiced to see both the Methodist and the Baptist churches kept in great condition. I still go to the cemetery, look at the headstones and let my mind review the wonderful memories of the people I loved." Yet, Shubuta people comment on getting keys for their never-before-locked doors, and a secure and strong woman living alone in Shubuta mentions having bought a gun and learning to fire it in case she needs to protect herself in her home.[62]

By contrast, Otis Bumpars sees the town as renewed after desegregation, and Cassandra Cameron and her generation of black Shubutans see themselves as having new potential after the national, legal, cultural, and intellectual changes around race after the civil rights movement era.

Small Town, USA, Shubuta is also unmistakably U.S. Southern Town; and the lasting historical factor that distinguishes it from other American ones is race—the fact of race, race ideology, racism, the legacy of slavery, and a class system both social and economic begotten by racial attitudes and behaviors.

Transportation, Population, and the Town

Shubuta's story and those of its people mirror the master narrative of U.S. history and also the muffled stories of many Americans of multi-America. One connecting link of those stories, one means of showing Shubuta's birth, growth, and life as a town with its several stages and several parts, is an account of the use and development of transportation systems.

Shubuta today looks like many another town in the U.S. countryside and along many federal and state highways. Main Street is a metaphor for a central place in an American town, the business district, the main crossroad, the main place of public activity. Shubuta has no Main Street by name, but in people's consciousness the one-block-long set of attached commercial buildings running from the railroad tracks to the highway is Main Street in Shubuta. It was called that by many people over several decades and believed to be that in imagination and memory by most. Many townspeople probably don't know its name as a street or think of it having a street name.

Rather, it is simply "town" or "downtown," as in "I am going to town now" or "I am going downtown to get the mail." Named Eucutta Street, it runs out of town toward the rural community named Eucutta near a stream called Eucutta Creek. It has been named that since the first mapping of the town by the railroad company.[63]

After white settlement, the first transportation system was by steamboats, which traveled up and down the Chickasawhay River in the middle years of the nineteenth century, carrying the mail, passengers, and goods. There were regular stops at Shubuta and Hiwannee on steamboats coming up from Mobile and down from Enterprise. Capt. Thomas Jefferson Woolverton's *Lancaster* and *Ben Bolt* went back and forth from Enterprise to Mobile when the river was full enough to bear river traffic.[64]

The next American transportation system that gave shape to Shubuta was the railroad. In the middle of the nineteenth century when railroads were crisscrossing the United States east and west, north and south, capturing the imagination of the American people along with the investments of entrepreneurs and the labors of new working classes of Americans, Shubuta was identified by the Mobile and Ohio Railroad Company as one of the towns through which its rails would run carrying people and products north from Mobile, as well as a center for its shops and roundhouse. After it was built and began running in 1855, the horse-and-buggy roads that had threaded over the prairie and through the woods *to* the river now went out in all directions *from* the railroad. What one might think of as "Greater Shubuta" today, including the rural communities that still call Shubuta "town" or are served by its post office, is made up of old settlement locations that were themselves small towns at the time of the coming of the railroad or were trading posts or plantations. Later some of them were sawmill towns that rose and fell, but the railroad and the dirt roads that networked Shubuta in Clarke County and northern Wayne County made up a "district" like a wheel of which Shubuta was the hub. There were to the east Langsdale, which had grown up around the Lang Plantation, and then Matherville, which had developed from around the Horne Plantation; Chapparel to the southeast; Hiwannee to the south; DeSoto and Enterprise to the north; and Eucutta to the northwest. Local trains went out to some of these communities, particularly for logging and sawmilling by the turn of the century; but most of their people in the last decades of the nineteenth century and the early twentieth came in to town in wagons or buggies or on horseback or mules once or twice a year on corduroy roads, taking several hours to make the journey. To all these people, which included my own family, Shubuta was their town as much as it was the hometown of the people on "Silk Stocking Row," or North Street of the wealthy inhabitants, and Eucutta Street in the town proper.

After the railroad, the next change came with cars. Elsie Jones Cross says the earliest automobile in Shubuta was in 1918,[65] but an ad in the *Mississippi Messenger* for a car dealership appears as early as 1918, as well.[66] Automobiles brought improved roads, and by the 1930s blacktop.

In the late 1930s, the town provided right-of-way for U.S. Highway 45 to be built through the town on a street intersecting Eucutta Street and called High Street on old maps.[67] Within a few short years of its construction "the highway" was Main Street. Until well after World War II, the stores remained intact and local, and trains ran regularly several times a day on the Gulf, Mobile, and Ohio Railroad (GM&O), the merged railroad company, showing Shubuta to be a vital and thriving independent community, prosperous on its own, but in communication and contact with its outside world.

In a 1933 piece written about Shubuta by Dr. Albert P. Hand for the Clarke County centennial celebration (and liberally adapted by somebody for a 1973 update), the businesses and professional offices in town, nearly all locally owned, are described thus:

> Here is the Ford Agency for the whole county, operated as Shubuta Motor Company by L. D. Patton; the well-equipped garages of J. R. Box, J. E. McLendon and Thad Fagan; the Gas and Oil Distribution of Otis Fagan; the saw-mills of Brownlee-Patterson and Walter Bonney; the Shubuta Tie and Timber Company of J. E. Toney; the oldest and most modern Drug Store in Southeast Mississippi, established in 1865 and owned by T. F. Hudson; the Bank of Shubuta, as strong as Gibraltar and some think impregnable, but absolutely safe; the headquarters of the Southern Bell Telephone for two counties, managed by T. B. George; two of the oldest mercantile establishments, G. S. Weems, Jr., and W. J. Patton; and if you become so unfortunate as to have need of W. J. Patton, he is the

best equipped, most experienced and silent-service undertaker, and his customers never kick; the up-to-date Jitney Jungle of Mrs. Patton and W. E. Calhoun; the well-stocked Johnston Mercantile Co., the grocery stores of A. T. Rogers, and Thames and J. P. Patton; E. A. Arrington who keeps an appetizing restaurant, and eats his own cooking; J. K. Pace, the up-to-date barber and presser; the cotton gin of Mayor Gillespie; the ice and ice-cream factory of T. M. and P. E. Spinks; the hardware and leather works of J. M. Nettles. That grand old young man, dean of the legal profession, Hon. D. W. Heidelberg; Senator and everything-else Wm. Edwards, who poses as a farmer, but is in reality a lawyer; the dental profession is ably represented by Dr. P. W. Johnston; the medical profession by Dr. J. A. McDevitt and Albert Hand; and a whole host of other bigger, better men and women.[68]

Still, by the 1930s change was in the air. The automobile and the highway played their roles in the fast movement of people and things to the next town and the next item on their own schedule. Soon, mass distribution of mass-produced products came to Shubuta like everywhere else. Eventually, today's warehouse stores, billboards, gas stations, and convenience stores lined Shubuta's main road just as they do others across the United States in cities and towns where they can be reached quickly in cars and trucks and delivery vans, or sped past on the highway with little notice even that there is a town there.

Today two blocks of the highway with the Shubuta Qwik Stop convenience store, the new post office building, one of the town's banks, gasoline service stations, a car wash, the fire station, the two century-old white churches, another convenience store, and some houses make up "Main Street." The highway is Main Street now.

At the present time, the Market Basket is the only grocery store in town, the Greer store, which opened early in the 1990s, having closed; and the Market Basket resembles more a country store from the past than it does a supermarket, selling local specialties like pork rinds and cracklings, lard and pails of molasses along with the milk and bread and bananas.

Some stores and businesses, the Town Hall, the medical clinic, the library, the hardware store, and the grocery store, the Market Basket, are still on Eucutta Street in the old commercial district. Some businesses even spill over across the highway intersection to the former residential area, namely, poignantly, the second bank in a converted mobile home on the lot where the Weems home was. Others of the Eucutta Street buildings like the old doctors' offices and most of the stores are boarded up, vacant, and one vacant lot is simply a junk yard. Cars line the streets when they are not zooming through on the highway, and Shubuta people stay in touch with the world on their computers, television sets, and telephone lines.

The Urbanization of the Small Town

While Shubuta at the start of the twenty-first century is, in some ways, a typical American small town, by the process I think of as "the urbanization of the small town" it is urban, too, in that its people participate in American mass culture in exactly the same manner as those in most cities and other towns in the United States. They do so through television viewing of the same programs seen in New York City or Seattle, buying country music or popular music records made in Nashville, driving cars made in Detroit or Japan like any other Americans, eating food processed in Minneapolis or grown in southern California or Mexico, using telephones and electricity and gas fuel services with nationwide standards and distribution, and being educated out of textbooks written for schoolchildren all over the United States. They often work for companies that buy and sell their goods overseas and are organized into a central bureaucratic management system in a single distant location, usually a U.S. city. Where once the businesses, the stores, the services, the schools, the churches, and other institutions were all local, often established, and usually run and owned within the town, now authority, focus, and activity are centered elsewhere, and the American small town has changed from being largely self-contained and local to being almost wholly connected to the region, the nation, and even the world. While it sometimes has character, quirky or intriguing personality, a fascinating history, and unique people, the town is no longer a distinct unit of American culture but rather only one piece in the network of places to live and drive to—or fly to—and to work and play and participate in humanity as American. The town of the past is gone. This is true of Shubuta as of most others.

Still, in the town, at the present time, the local means something. Townspeople know one another. You know who you are and where you came from in Shubuta, and other people from Shubuta know who you are and where you came from and who your people are. Where you came from is a *place* with moral and mythic value. Shubuta like many an American town, or, indeed, like many a village around the world, is a heart's crossroad; a location of earliest memory as well as present time; a bundle of emotional contradictions watered by a river in the shade of old oak trees and positioned by a railroad track, a few short lengths of streets, and a highway; and a subdivision of humanity placed on a spot of earth.

In the current urban world, a town is an analogue to a city neighborhood. Yet, it is not so entirely. The collective memory of a town is geological, geographic, and national, as well as peopled. The space it occupies and the contestations for its rule determine more for its people than city people know. A romantic attachment to the land is citified. In town, the land is just there, sometimes conquered and abused, owned, sometimes productive or beautiful, often loved, sometimes despised, but always there right on the edges of town to be reckoned with, fought over, drained, farmed, forested, pastured, cultivated, laid by, always remembered as the reason for being of the town.

The people of the town came to it from the land or for the land. About their being there, in these days we make moral judgments. Town "fathers" could be ruthless in their control, could be tyrants of their towns. Poor white people, as well as blacks, could be cowed by the limits of the local and oppressed by knowing no other place, no choice. Still, people knew each other, knew each other's names, knew the sick and dying and the newborn, knew troubles, and, if they cared, could help. It was not all bad, not all good, but knowing was a virtue. If patronizing, towns cared for their own. Towns had their class systems, as fast as any other. Shubuta was no different. Besides the castes of black and white, and beyond the memory of Choctaw, Shubuta had rich people, middle class, and poor. It had proud people, ambitious and adventurous. Its sons and daughters have traveled the world, its grandchildren live in many cities, many of them in high posts, both social and economic. Today's Shubutans are older people and poorer people, people not mobile for the most part. The descendants of nearly all the first-arriving white families have gone.

Coda on Memory

What the settlers found when they got to what is now Shubuta after the land had been surveyed there, besides the dense virgin forest, the abundant wildlife, and the plentiful water, was the remnant of a way of life disrupted by their coming. They also found a new start for themselves, new farmland to clear and plow and plant, new gardens to grow, "virgin land." It is a conflict we hold in our minds, a conflict in memory. Perhaps it was no conflict at all to the white settlers coming up the Pascagoula River, up the Buckatunna Creek and on up the Chickasawhay, or overland from South Carolina and Georgia along the Three-Chopped Way in oxen-pulled covered wagons to make new homes, new lives, new livings, to open new territory for themselves and their families.

The remnants that are left of all these people's lives tell us bits of all their stories. The chance remains of Choctaws in the region mingle with the bricks and bottles, the wooden mill posts, and the plants set in this place by descendants of African- and European-born people. These products of past labor meld with the residuum of citizens American-born. To these bits of leavings we add from our imagination and from our accumulated knowledge of U.S. and local and human history. Together they provide from a document or a story or a material object much that we can learn about the collective story of the town and interpretations of our memory. Some pieces of Shubuta's story can fit together around a transportation thesis of the development of the town. Others show us the economy, the government, schooling, lovemaking and childhood, food and pleasure, spirit and toil.

In the name of research, for my part in U.S. culture and history as well as for my sister- and fellow-Americans, I sought out and found a multitude of bits of Shubuta past. I looked long and hard in a hide-and-go-seek game with memory, and I caught past pieces for a moment and lifted them to the light. One by one, held up to the light of the warming sun, sometimes a beam of truth was what I saw in them, sometimes a glance of fancy, a glimmer of deceit, sometimes a shadow of sorrow or a sharp light of falsehood, a lie, though sometimes radiation of clear, bright joy, sometimes hatred, destruction, willful hurting, sometimes simple love, often only dailiness, routinized morning, noon, and night, always memory, revived, alive.

A map, a grinding stone, and some earthen mounds told me of Choctaw times. John Evans's diary and the 1820 state line surveyor's notes showed me a glimpse of frontier Shubuta. The coming of the railroad I finally understood from the Weems family letters. With transportation as my focus, I looked at the river traffic and the railroad and saw the Civil War conducted and concluded with the railroad's fiery demolition.

After the war, Reconstruction, and rebuilding, Shubuta saw the coming of the sawmills and, later, the automobile. Old newspapers and interview testimonial from James Johnston and from Elsie Jones Cross and the ads from the Shubuta newspaper brought the log woods and sawmills and the first automobiles back to the light of day. Finally, I moved to the coming of the highways in the 1930s and the orientation of the town gradually shifting along its commercial street from train depot to highway filling station and the bright-lighted billboard-posted American look of that highway-oriented town today.

Shubuta is a beautiful town, beautiful in memory, beautiful in its natural and material setting today. Shubuta is an ugly town, too, morally ugly, economically ugly, physically ugly. Ugly town, beautiful town, too.

TROPE 5: FLOWER GARDENS, QUILTS, AND CROCHET PIECES

Magnolia trees are everywhere around Shubuta. The botanically named *Magnolia grandiflora* are trees that grow to one hundred feet tall, have large stiff leaves with a shiny top surface, a rough brownish underside, and magnificent creamy white flowers, which are richly fragrant and can be twelve inches across. Approaching them from a distance when they stand among other trees, the flowers look like big white lights amid the green. Not usually used in Shubuta as cut flowers, for their petals quickly darken and fall and their smell is too strong for indoors, magnolia blossoms are omnipresent in Mississippi homes in art-and-craft forms of ceramics, oil paintings, watercolors, and photographs. The magnolia is the Mississippi state flower.

In Shubuta, some young magnolia trees were planted on the business block of Eucutta Street in recent years in the small park next to the medical clinic, sprucing up the appearance of the street. Many home gardens have an old magnolia tree among the pines and oaks in their long-ago landscaping designs as their owners extended their plantings to ornamental trees.

Fruit trees, too, abound in home gardens in and around Shubuta. Old gardens still have fig trees, and in August women make fig preserves from their bounty, along with peach preserves from the luscious peaches now more frequently bought from commercial orchards than homegrown. They make watermelon-rind pickles from watermelons that do still grow in gardens and patches on small Shubuta farms.

Pecan trees, too, are plentiful, sometimes one or two at a house, sometimes whole groves of them behind houses. When the pecan trees produce their sweet nuts in the autumn, the small, sweetest ones are from the volunteer trees, which have come up as shoots from the old trees. These make the best pecan pies, prepared by family recipes in memory or from cookbooks of all the local families. Occasional black walnut trees are still to be found, the rich meats of their nuts flavoring the finest homemade ice cream of the region.

In the spring white-flowering pear trees tower in the gardens, following the blossoming time of the low-branching pink flowers of peach trees. They follow the progression of the snowdrops, daffodils, azaleas, and lilies, blooming closer to the ground as spring advances. In the fall the pear trees' fruit ripens as the chrysanthemums' buds burst into petals, and pear preserves, too, are made in Shubuta kitchens. Some say out in the country from Shubuta one can tell where old houses stood in the woods and the clearings, when not even a foundation brick is to be seen, by the pear trees and rows of daffodils that come out and bloom in the early spring. All season long old roses bloom, and sometimes a thorny, viney rose gone wild can be seen at an old house site.

These domesticated trees on domesticated places were put there and cultivated for the most part by women. No racial segregation worked here. All the local women made their gardens. Seeking beauty and seeking the comforts of shade and food—who is to say which came first?—Shubuta women and their men of olden times saw that the fig trees and pear trees, oaks and magnolias, daffodils and roses were planted to last over the seasons of their lives, alongside the vegetables and watermelons and sugarcane they planted anew each year for their food and sweetening syrup. It was one of their arts, indistinguishable from their practical toil for maintaining their and their families' lives.

Likewise, the women worked with their needles in their homes in town and country. They made clothes for themselves, their children, and even their men, and then they dressed their beds and covered their furniture with the industry of their hands. Every family or home or cedar chest, or now, antique store or craft shop, has its share of small crocheted pieces—antimacassars for the backs and arms of their upholstered chairs, doilies and runners for their chests and dressers and dining room tables—and sometimes large ones like bedspreads or tablecloths made by family women, or women who had been paid to make them, the special, creative, artistic work, made after the basics were done. The same women, generation following generation, pieced together quilts from bits of scraps and worn-out or outgrown clothes, padded and lined them, and sat before quilting frames long winter hours quilting them, sometimes alone, sometimes in family groups or among neighbors. The quilts were their bedding, provision against winter night chill. After the essential quilts were made, then came the gifts: sisters quilting "Wedding Ring" and "Dresden Plate" and "Pineapple" designs for each other's hope chests for future marriages, old women quilting together to help out neighbors or friends or for pay, mothers and aunts quilting with daughters and nieces to teach them their craft.

Shubuta has had its share of invented beauty, lasting artistry of the everyday, crafted by its women in gardens, kitchens, and quilting frames.

TROPE 6: THE LANG HOUSE

The Lang House might have been the centerpiece of town had the railroad come through Langsdale instead of Shubuta in the 1850s. The Lang Plantation formed the center of community, and roads were cut out between it and other communities gathered around plantation houses and settlements in the middle years of the nineteenth century.

The U.S. mail found its way to Langsdale over the decades, as surely as it did to Shubuta and Hiwannee, DeSoto, Chapparel, and Matherville; and for many years in the mid-twentieth century Elsie Jones Cross was the postmistress for Langsdale in a post office out of a room in the mansion next to her kitchen.

Today the beautiful Lang House sits in solitary stately splendor on well-groomed expansive lawns on a little-traveled county road. Its freshly painted white pillars still reach two stories tall, and its antebellum facade is kept in good repair and beauty.

It serves as an icon of a former time.

Today a country house for pleasure and leisure, it once was an institution of cotton plantation order and productivity, a signature house of the Old South built by slave artisans and laborers, occupied by wealthy slave-owning planters and socialites, and surrounded by slave cabins of the black workers of the land. The agricultural institution changed with the war and new laws and successive ownership of the house from plantation to farm to leisure residence. The house remained on the land as fewer and fewer white and black people came and went from it until at last it stands alone.

It is a relic of memory.

Chapter 3
Church and School, Depot and Town Hall

> *Living with people at close range over many years, as both monastics and small-town people do, is much more difficult than wearing a hair shirt.*
> —Kathleen Norris, from *Dakota: A Spiritual Geography*

In Shubuta's lifetime as a town, its institutions of religion and education, transportation and government have not only fostered the economy of the place but also have provided the systems of meaning by which Shubutans have lived and tried to understand their lives. From the beginning of their contact with Native Americans, white people brought with them the institutions of church and school and with them tried to establish boundaries of ethics and values and frameworks for living. When the railroad came through, it brought not only a new means of transportation but also a new way of perceiving human life as less bounded, less restricted by location. Finally, with the formal establishment of government, new ideas about behaving toward one another as well as new means of making rules and laws came into being in Shubuta. In this chapter, I will explore these institutions of church and school, depot and town hall.

Shubuta Churches

Hanging around the Shubuta post office one May day in 1996, I met Shubutan Carol Mosely, who is a gospel singer. "I got to sing at the Jimmy Rodgers deal [festival that week in Meridian in memory of the country music singer]. I asked the Lord to let me sing and He did."

I asked her if she sang in churches, and she said, "Not just. I sing all over, in the street, everywhere."[1]

Another time I observed the bowed-head private prayer of a Shubuta woman in a restaurant at lunch time.

Again, I went into a home of a Baptist church member, and the picture Sallman's *Head of Christ,* a very popular devotional image of a hazel-eyed Jesus, was prominently hung on the wall. The woman repeated often that "the Lord has been good to me."

A kind of matter-of-fact Protestant Christian piety is a part of the everyday lives, the language, and the behavior of most Shubutans. It is a norm that most Shubutans would be surprised to think of as exclusive. Just as nobody who is publicly known to be Choctaw is any longer alive in Shubuta, there are no present-day people who are Jewish or Muslim. Yet, just as Choctaw names and objects still exist in Shubuta, so at least one Jewish name, Greenhood, is still embedded in the lasting name of a Shubuta site, Greenhood's Pond, named for the Shubuta merchant, Moses Greenhood, later Morris Greenhood, who owned the land and built the pond there after having arrived on the railroad soon after 1855 and established the first store in town. Likewise, there are no practicing Catholics in Shubuta today, though the first white residents of the area were the French Catholic priests who were missionaries to the Choctaws.

Still, the varieties of Protestantism itself in Shubuta are considerable. Personal behavior, the different forms Sunday worship takes, and even the church buildings themselves are key indicators of the differences of style and substance in U.S. Protestant Christian practice in Shubuta. In its Protestant variations, and to some extent in its almost unconscious assumption that its Protestant views are the national norm, Shubuta is microcosmic of the different sorts of Protestantism across the United States.

There are six church buildings inside the city limits of Shubuta. The congregation about which I was able to learn least on my research visits and sojourns is the Congregation Church of God. The church congregation is a black group whose denomination is announced by a fading hand-lettered sign on their partially painted concrete-block building, which has paint-peeling doors and a tower with a plain wooden cross rising into the glistening pine treetops surrounding it. The church building is across the street from Cleo Cooper's house on East Street, but when I have been at her house and asked her about it, Mrs. Cooper is cautious about discussing who goes to church there, saying only that they have very long meetings and that they are sometimes noisy in their gathering. She did tell me the church has about seventy members. She also mentioned that the minister worked at the Greer Supermarket. (The clergy in many of these small denominations, both black and white, are not college or seminary educated and work weekdays at other occupations than ministry.) None of my other interviewees, either black or white, even purported to know about the church, and I could not find the denomination listed in any published reference book. This reminded me how much researchers and interviewees alike are locked into the systems of economic class and race that, in a small southern town, churches signify more than any other institutions.[2]

Two other in-town churches that serve black congregations are the Saint Matthew Baptist Church and the New Mount Zion United Methodist Church. Mrs. Cooper's church is the Saint Matthew Baptist Church. Three churches have white congregations, the Shubuta United Methodist Church, which belongs to the same national church body as the New Mount Zion United Methodist Church; the Shubuta Baptist Church, which is a part of the Southern Baptist Convention; and the Assembly of God Church, the town's fastest-growing congregation and the group most recently moved into town from a former rural location.

The New Mount Zion Church is made up of the consolidation of three black Methodist former congregations, two of them from out in the country. That church has about one hundred members. Both Mary McCarty and Otis Bumpars are active members of it. Nearby there are still several rural churches that are oriented to Shubuta. The Tribulation Baptist Church, to which the black Carters and Camerons in Cassandra Cameron's family go, is out the Eucutta Road in the Beaver Dam community. It has a neatly kept white wooden building, its own churchyard, and a current membership of about thirty-five people. Other black churches with very small memberships are the Church of God in Christ out the river road toward Red Hill, the New Zion Baptist Church up Highway 45 to the north, and the Center Ridge Baptist Church and the Saint John's Methodist Church, both also north of town. Out beyond town on the Eucutta Road are small congregations of black people in the Sweet Pilgrim United Methodist Church, Coker's Chapel Methodist Church, and the Saint Mary Baptist Church. Cassandra Cameron mentioned that the biggest difference church members think about between Methodists and Baptists is that Methodists sprinkle for baptism, while the Baptists immerse. In her Baptist church, they now have a baptistery, but they once practiced immersion in the Chickasawhay River or the Shubuta Creek or Eucutta Creek as some of these smaller Baptist churches still do. In the nineteenth century, white Baptists in the town Shubuta Baptist Church baptized their new members in the Shubuta Creek or the Chickasawhay River, too, at well as at Cooper's Well, the well in the middle of the street of town, until they built their baptistery in their sanctuary in 1906.[3]

Other than the differences around baptism in the small black congregations, Cassandra Cameron says, denominations and congregations are similar and "everybody pitches in and goes to other churches for programs. Each church does have its own revival, but everybody takes food to dinner-on-the-ground at revival times—all the people from all the churches. The Methodists and Baptists—all go to all of the revivals. The preachers are friends of each other. Sometimes they are local, sometimes from Laurel or Jackson. The churches are all scripture based. Each church usually has a fall revival and a spring revival. Most churches have Sunday School. The Methodists have quite a bit of activity for youth."[4]

Some churches in the region have become defunct, the Pilgrim Methodist Church for white people in the Langsdale community being one of them. James Brewer remembers that his grandmother's funeral in 1936 was the last event for which the church was opened. He remembers with humor the family story of why the Brewers are Methodists. The family had been Baptists when they settled in the Langsdale community after coming from Charleston, South Carolina, in the 1840s, and his grandfather took his family to the Baptist church there.

> My great-granddaddy Brewer [says James Brewer] was bad about drinking, and the Brewers were Baptists and they went to church. When my granddaddy raised his family, he had them at church one Sunday over there, and my great-granddaddy came up riding the old mule that he had been plowing all week, drunk, and he wanted that mule to hear the preacher preach, so he rode him up to the window. All the churches were built up off the ground, you know, and had windows up kind of high, and you opened them when it was hot weather. He made that old

mule stick his head in the window so he could listen to the preacher. That embarrassed my daddy so that he got his family up and they joined the Liberty Methodist. That's the reason all us Brewers now are Methodists.[5]

Several rural churches around Shubuta have fared better than the closed Pilgrim Methodist Church because they have been endowed financially and also have had a few active local leading members who have kept the churches open and alive. The Geneva Presbyterian Church in Matherville is one such church: the Mathers family and others have supported it well. This was the church where Elsie Jones Cross and Erma Gay Mathers, postmistresses for Matherville and Langsdale, shared their long friendship over all their married lives; and its steepled white-frame building with its old purple and golden stained-glass windows was where both their bodies were brought back for their funerals. In 1993 Erma Mathers's body came from Biloxi, Mississippi, where she had been in a nursing home near her daughter, Martha Rose; and in 1999, when she died at 103, Elsie Cross was brought back from Tuscaloosa, Alabama, where she had been in a nursing home near her daughter, Elizabeth.

In town the Shubuta Methodist Church is also well endowed. Otherwise, it, too, might close. Its minister, Dr. Gaddy, fits its history and expectation of high levels of education, theological sophistication, and liturgical formality, since he is Edinburgh-educated. It would be unthinkable for this church to be served by a minister who was not college- and theological-seminary-educated. Dr. Gaddy also enjoys wearing "high church" clerical robes fitting to the church seasons and conducting a formal liturgy according to the *Methodist Book of Worship* and *The Methodist Hymnal*. However, he is elderly and has been retired from active ministry for many years. The attendance at the services most Sundays is eight to twelve people. Historically, however, this church has been the church of many of the town's social, business, and professional leaders, and for at least a century and a quarter regular church attendance and church support were among its members' routinized behaviors. Skilled and trained musicians—women and men with "cultured voices," as an earlier era's label for trained singers of classical music identified them, "cultured people" that they were—and professional piano and organ keyboard artists attended this church and provided music for its services. Many of its lay members for well over a century were, like Dr. Albert Hand, educated at Methodist-related Millsaps College in Jackson, believed by many to be the most intellectually stimulating and politically liberal college in the state, as well as church sponsored.

The previous Shubuta Methodist clergy, too, were learned men, college and seminary graduates, many having attended Millsaps College and Emory University's School of Theology. They usually had a more liturgically formal order of worship on Sunday mornings than the Baptists or the country churches had, and the hymns and other music for the services were classical and aesthetically complex, usually drawn from the official hymnal of the national church, *The Methodist Hymnal*. The church benefitted greatly from the denomination's connectional polity, that is, church governance from a national and conference level rather than from a congregational one. This means that the clergy is appointed by the conference's bishop rather than chosen by the individual church, and the standards of education and licensing for the clergy, as well and rules and policy for the denomination, are determined in the national church. For many decades, the ministers from the Shubuta Methodist Church and the Shubuta Baptist Church, which also had an educated clergy, along with the town's lawyers, doctors, and teachers were respected and active as the intellectual leaders of the town.

The Saint Matthew Baptist Church is one of the central institutions for Shubuta's African Americans. On one of my Shubuta visits Cleo Powe Cooper showed me around its church building with the enjoyment of the leading member of the congregation that she is. As she let us in with the key she had gotten from its keeper, she talked of the good new solid wood pews with their blue velvet upholstery we were seeing. She showed me the handsome matching pulpit furniture and carpeting.

"We be proud of 'ouver' church," she said. She gave me a full tour of the whole building, which has a series of rooms behind the chancel and folding chairs for the choir. The pastor's study had bare walls, but a one-volume concordance sat on his desk. The walls of the Sunday School rooms were filled with pictures, decorative hangings, posters, and artworks. The room for the smallest children had a small African cloth wall hanging and also a cardboard poster showing the tribes of Israel by descent through their mothers: Leah, Rachael.

In the fellowship hall with its dining tables and chairs were posters for each day of Kwanzaa, the African American cultural festival observed from December 26 until January 1. Mrs. Cooper said they had had a good celebration of those days. There was a collage poster of faces of prominent contemporary and twentieth-century African Americans—Jesse Jackson, Oprah Winfrey, Hank Aaron, Martin Luther King Jr. Another poster in a neat hand lettering named African American "firsts"—governor, Supreme Court justice, and other state and federal government officers.

The liveliness and contemporary focus of the congregation is signaled by their building and its materials. Their contemporaneity is readily apparent in their celebration of Kwanzaa in keeping with many other African American communities, churches, and other groups. The poster teaching young children the female line of the tribes of Israel is correspondent with the newest of feminist theology. Yet, their beautiful worship space with its new furnishings and their pastor's study with its biblical focus maintain what appears to be a vigor in their traditional Christianity, as well.

Church Members and Church History

On my excursions of learning about Shubuta, in addition to Cleo Powe Cooper's having shown me the Saint Matthew Baptist Church, Cassandra Cameron showed me her church building and its cemetery at the Tribulation Baptist Church; Linda McInnis, the Shubuta Baptist Church's historian since 1964, gave me a tour of the building and a look at the records and keepsakes of her church, including the marriage registry of services done by the Reverend Joshua M. Phillips; and Nerva McCaskey showed me Shubuta United Methodist Church records, archives, and silver goblets and serving pieces kept in a vault at the bank. The other United Methodist Church in town, the New Mount Zion Church, was discussed with me by its members Otis Bumpars and Mary McCarty in their interviews. From the Assembly of God Church, the congregation's historian gave me long notes and papers from the group's history.

Historically in little southern towns, the Baptists and the Methodists have dominated; and there have been, since after the Civil War, black congregations and white congregations of each in many such towns. Before the Civil War in Shubuta, Methodist Church records show slave members. Sometimes in somewhat larger towns with socially prominent white people, a more formal and highly liturgical church, such as an Episcopal Church, will be there, and often a Presbyterian church within mainline Protestantism will join or replace the Baptist or Methodist ones. These denominations are English and Scots in their origin, the church affinities brought west by the white people of English and Scots ancestry who came from the Carolinas and Georgia to settle in southern Mississippi in the 1830s and 1840s. Methodism is an eighteenth-century breakaway from the Church of England from which the Episcopal Church is a direct descendant, and several forms of Baptist churches are descendants of Scotsman John Knox's church or of New England breakaway churches from American Congregationalism.

In the twentieth century, southern country white people and less mainstream people have formed Assemblies of God, churches of a denomination founded in 1914 in Hot Springs, Arkansas,[6] which is pentecostal, fundamentalist, and practices spiritual healing and glossolalia. In additional to the black Baptist and Methodist churches that grew out of the national denominations their ancestors worshiped in with their slave masters and also black forms of Congregationalism, black Christians in small southern towns have some blacks-only denominations. In the South, these include the Church of God in Christ, the African Methodist Zion Church, and African Methodist Episcopal Church that are more evangelical, informal, and verbally expressive; but blacks do not tend to adopt the more rigidly dogmatic positions of fundamentalism that some white people and white churches do. Song and storytelling and exuberantly joyful sound are more characteristic of black churches lower on the social scale, while rigid pietism and literal beliefs in words, scripture, and dictums are more characteristic of white churches of less educated people.

In Shubuta, the largest number of black people participate in the New Mount Zion United Methodist Church, an all-black congregation that is a member of the same national denomination and the same Mississippi state conference as the Shubuta United Methodist Church since the consolidation of the racially segregated parts of that national church. They have a neat brick building, built in the 1970s.

The Shubuta Baptist Church was historically the congregation of many town government and business founders and owners in Shubuta, but also more comfortably the church home to the middle class. Today it is the second-fastest-growing congregation in the town. New members come both from people who move into town from the country or other places and from people who move up socially from the Assembly of God. Both are still all-white.

Shubuta's Sources of Meaning and Values

In Shubuta as in most of the United States at large, the source of most unwritten, unstated codes of conduct and meaning from its earliest national and territorial times is Protestant Christianity. While this once meant church attendance, and by the mid-nineteenth century Sunday School lessons, culturally it is something more basic than misdeeds persons do. Shubutans, like some other Americans, might label as "unchristian" or in conflict with biblical morality certain actions or events. This frame of reference is even more basic than the Ten Commandments, which Shubutans are likely to see as effective rules for personal and social conduct, rules superceded by the Golden Rule from Jesus, "Do unto others as you would have others do unto you." This rudimentary American tenet is Protestant in its source, though fully and uniquely American in its conceptual interpretation by the twenty-first century. The Ten Commandments are shared with the major world Abrahamic religions: Judaism, Islam, and Christianity, and Jesus's teachings are shared with all branches of Christianity: Catholic, Orthodox, and Protestant. However, the pervasive American belief in individualism originated with the roots of the Protestant Reformation. It took hold in Christian psyches in the German Reformation and was conveyed around the world by the Protestant intelligentsia and the faithful members alike. In the eighteenth century, that core Reformation tenet of individualism came to be the idea on which whole political cultures were based, and democracy came to be the principle of government that formed the genesis of the United States.

Along with the Protestant religiousness that individualism spawned—the priesthood of all believers, which means the intellectual and spiritual authority of the individual—individualism's child was political democracy: one citizen/one vote. The political authority of the individual to choose and to act was embedded in the founding documents of the U.S. government, and thus both individualism and democracy are hallowed as principles in the United States in a uniquely quasi-religious way. While transformative of the European-influenced world from the notion of governance of church and state by powers external in their authority to self-governance and shared governance by "the people," the idea of individualism has an underbelly of extremism as well. This extremism of the concept of individualism breeds self-importance, self-aggrandizement, narrow-mindedness, social fragmentation, and intolerance when the individual is emphasized at the social cost of the community. It is the same in Shubuta as in other places in the United States.

The earliest of the traders, explorers, missionaries and settlers brought forms of European American religions with them, and they changed over time to fit the circumstance and desires of the times. Shubuta as a town has maintained a centrality of religion, specifically, in the twentieth century, of Protestant Christianity, to its cultural and social identity. Some of the forms of expression and practice have also changed with the times, but the presence of religion as dominant in Shubuta society has remained a constant.

Education in Shubuta

Education, like religion, has been significant throughout Shubuta's life as a town. The missionaries who came to the Chickasawhay country in the early nineteenth century set up a school for the Choctaws, which the young white boy John Evans attended. Today both white people and black people express regret that there is no local school. They say that the community organized itself around the school, and now there is no focal point for community. Down through two-thirds of the twentieth century, these were separate black and white communities, but they gathered around the two public schools to which most families sent their children. Today a few white children are sent to the private academies in Waynesboro and Heidelberg that were formed after desegregation, but nearly all Shubuta children, white and black, ride the yellow school buses to Quitman together where they all go to school in the public county consolidated K–12 schools.

Shubuta's history of a high level of education available to wealthy families' children, including girls, is a proud one. It made other Shubutans aspire to enter that educated class.

Dr. Albert Hand's mother, Annie Case Hand, was a teacher. It was young Annie who at 10 studied after school at the boys school after she and her brothers arrived in Shubuta in 1864 during the Civil War as wards of their bachelor uncle; and no doubt she was a star pupil when in 1867 the Shubuta Female Academy was established alongside the Shubuta Male Academy. This is the elderly woman whose "Green Corn with Chicken" recipe appeared in the 1925 *P.T.A. Cook Book,* she by then supporting the Parent-Teacher Association of her grandchildren's excellent public school in Shubuta. Annie Hand was also mother of Caroline Hand, who was celebrated for living beyond 100 years old as a productive Shubuta citizen, who was a college graduate of Mississippi State College for Women, and a teacher of Shubuta's white third and fourth graders in public school for four decades. Caroline Hand never married. She worked as a receptionist in her brother's medical office for many years after her retirement as a teacher, the office that had been their father's. Dr. Albert Hand was given Powe as his middle name, the name of his Hand grandmother's Winchester family. It is at least in part a tribute to his mother that Annie Hand's son Albert was the highest scorer ever on the Millsaps College entrance exam and was both intellectual mentor and beloved doctor of all the black and white "girlies," men, and children he treated indiscriminately in his medical clinic. There were two other sons, equally well educated and distinguished, who did not remain in Shubuta: James, a civil engineer who worked for the Mississippi Highway Department, and Charles Connor Hand, the lawyer in Mobile who was given as his middle name his mother's childhood guardian's family name. Her grandson, Brevard, now owns and has restored the antebellum home she brought to her marriage as a legacy from her bachelor uncle who reared her, which she and her husband in turn left to their daughter, Caroline, and "Miss Caroline" gave to Brevard.

Annie Case Hand's life is an example of the high value placed on education and the consequences it can have for a whole community

Frontier Shubuta had had one-room schoolhouses on plantation sites when planter parents saw the need for educating their own children and hired teachers. One-room schools continued in rural communities right down to the 1950s, when there was one in Matherville supported by public funds so that the village children could walk to school and not have to ride a school bus away from home.

In 1870 and again in the early twentieth century, Mississippi state laws required each community to provide public schools for their children. Shubuta complied with these laws, but the schools for white children were much more generously supported than those for blacks. For a while Shubuta had a Rosenwald School, a privately financed experimental school for black children supported in a number of communities in the early years of the twentieth century, but its memory is now gone from the town. Through several decades of the twentieth century, the public schools in Shubuta, the one for white children on the east side of town and the one for black children on the west side of town, were run by the town as a school district. This meant, for the most part, that country children did not come in to Shubuta to school unless they boarded with relatives in town; and it meant that everybody walked to school. For the black children, for most of this time, it meant only eight grades of education and a short school year of less than eight months, while the public school for the white children had twelve grades and a nine-month calendar. In town this meant that, while the children and their parents did not mix racially around school, the whites did mix across social class lines in school and around school activities with the children and grandchildren of "Shubuta's capitalists" and "the cultured people" mixing with the middle class and poor white people who lived in town. Likewise, the children and grandchildren of the former slaves, the farm workers and maids and the skilled workers and educated black people, mixed with each other, too. This was changed with school consolidations that brought country people into town and changed again with desegregation that brought together schooling for blacks and whites.

The stratification, both social and racial, that once separated Shubutans from each other began to break through education in the 1970s when black and white children were bused together to Quitman to school.

The Railroad

Another story of development with great influence in the formation of Shubuta is that of the railroad. The railroad, like the school, was all but gone by the 1990s when I returned to Shubuta for my research. Still, the Mobile and Ohio Railroad was a major influence in the organization of the town of Shubuta after 1855. Its history, too, is fascinating.

In the 1990s train whistles still blew as freight trains went through town in Shubuta, but none of them came from a passenger train. Train cars for lumber or logs sometimes loaded in Shubuta, but some trains just passed through. From the sidewalk of town one February day in 1990, I heard a train whistle and stopped and listened with the ears of memory, loving the sound of the train, and I saw a freight train with only four cars of lumber passing through. By the end of the decade, trains ran only twice daily in Shubuta and had cars saying "MidSouth," transporting freight, logs, and lumber. Anyone who was a child in a town where trains ran through on their rails will thrill to the sound of a train whistle and pause to listen for memory, perhaps, in recognition, respect, and yearning; but the railroad has diminished as a major form of transportation in the United States.

The depot, the architecturally handsome train station that sat by the tracks for many decades, was moved to the center of the town park in the 1950s and used as a community house. As the twenty-first century goes forward, the building is still there, unused, and it sags to one side with unkempt vines growing up one side of it. The park and the depot building show the change in the times from when Mary V. Weems, according to the town Minutes Books, was paid $2.00 a month for park upkeep, and Cleo Cooper's husband, John, as porter, bustled about the platforms of the train station getting people on and off the four trains a day that traveled through Shubuta.

Yet the town of Shubuta as we know it depended on the railroad for its shape. In 1855, though a post office and a settlement of some sort were in place to serve the surrounding farming communities, the town, as it became and now is, was imagined, carved up, and set out by the M&O Railroad Company. In the competition north and south for linking railways and railroad transportation, the Mobile-based Mobile and Ohio Railroad won the struggle with a New Orleans–based company to connect the Gulf coast with Chicago by rail and was incorporated 4 February 1848. The M&O line would run from Mobile to a Kentucky location on the Ohio River, and a Chicago company, the Illinois Central Railroad Company, would meet it, building south from Chicago. The M&O received "land grant" support through an act of Congress in 1850, through which Mississippi gave the railroad company 737,130 acres of land. The M&O Railroad set out its "right of way" for the railroad and then sold parcels of the land to buyers willing to build and to supply materials and labor for the railroad's completion. There were workers who started in Mobile clearing the land and laying the road beds and tracks for the M&O, and many sections were built by the farmers along its way making use of slave labor for the work. John Horne of Matherville, for example, built the railroad from Winchester to Hiwannee with the labor of slaves from his plantation. The railway company's historian comments that it "was a slow business, when cuts and fills were made with picks, shovels and wheelbarrows."[7]

Construction was begun in Mobile and by 15 March 1855, "the roadbed had been graded and the track laid to Quitman [north of Shubuta]. By October 3, 1855, the road had been completed to Enterprise," according to Carl Fox, the general solicitor of the Gulf, Mobile, and Ohio Railroad Company ["Gulf" was added in a company merger] in the 1957 letter to R. C. Weems. There was a roundhouse at Shubuta for storage and switching of trains, making Shubuta a hub for the trains, and Shubuta was planned as a town radiating out from the railroad tracks. Florence Busby's house, for example, sits a few lots east of the railroad tracks on a site where in the early twentieth century the Poole Hotel sat. Before the hotel, a home of the Floyd family active in business leadership had sat on that lot, but the property was first bought from the railroad company by Robert W. Miller and Flora Jane Miller before they sold it to Mary J. Parker on 18 April 1857. Among other Shubuta lot owners obtaining their land in the 1850s from the railroad were James M. Seale, W. H. Waltman, W. H. Cherry, and A. H. Ryan.[8]

The first lots were sold from those platted and arranged by the railroad company in 1856. In the chancery clerk's office in the county seat of Quitman, all the deeds for lots in the town begin with the plats from the 1855 survey.

The railroad was completed its full distance from Mobile to Chicago on 22 April 1862, the company financially secure and the "rolling stock" ample to meet all the requirements of its extensive business—just in time for the Civil War.

The Confederacy commandeered the railroad for its use in transporting army men and supplies. The Confederate government issued bonds to the railroad company, which also held state of Alabama bonds and "fifty negroes

[sic]," all of which monetary value the company lost at the end of the war. Their bridges, warehouses, trestlework, and rails were destroyed along a 184-mile strip starting in Tennessee. In 1864 when General Sherman's men raided Meridian, they destroyed everything owned by the railroad—within 48 miles they took out bridges, trestlework, water stations, and warehouses and destroyed rails and fastenings 21 miles farther. This destruction came to within a few miles of Shubuta but did not reach the town itself. At the end of the war the company was reduced to one-quarter of its rolling stock and had neither tools nor materials to repair it.

Because of the roundhouse and shops and the intact rails in Shubuta itself, as well as the town buildings still standing, Shubuta was able to recover use of the railroad faster than many places, and by the end of the century when the railroad was fully rebuilt and operational, Shubuta was again a transportation center in the region.

From about 1898 to the Great Depression beginning in 1929, the railroad was the chief means of transportation for commerce and travel and was central to business in Shubuta's economy. It transported passengers and carried freight and livestock, but, most significant, it carried logs and lumber for the growing sawmilling business in Shubuta. In addition to the major Mobile to St. Louis line, trains went out to little communities to pick up logs and even people and brought them into Shubuta. Aubrey Jones remembered that his mother would take the train from their home out in the country in the Red Hill community into Shubuta to shop when he was a boy, going in with the train in the morning and coming back on the afternoon train. Trains even went out into the log woods themselves. What were called "dummy lines" were sometimes built, tracks that just went into the woods far enough for the men to haul out the logs they were cutting at the time. The need for this much transport of wood ended by the time of the Depression when the big sawmilling companies had left, though some woodcutting and hauling and railroad transport continued on through the decades until today.

After the Depression and the merger of the railroad company to become the Gulf, Mobile, and Ohio, from sometime in the late 1930s through the 1950s, more attention was drawn to the passenger service on the trains through Shubuta. One of the trains was named "The Rebel," and passenger trains were scheduled through town four times a day. These trains ran from 1935 to 1954 and "had a combination motor, mail and baggage car: two reclining seat coaches, one of which was picked up in the morning at Jackson, Mississippi, for the trip to New Orleans and returned each night, and a combination sleeper-observation car" plus a buffet car for meals. "The Rebel" was the train Shubutan Edith Jones worked on as a young adult in the 1950s in her glamorous job as a train hostess.[9]

Cleo Powe Cooper's husband, John, worked at the depot as a station porter, managing the goods and baggage that went and came on the trains. He was the only black person who worked at the Shubuta depot at that time, but the railroads gave new job opportunities to black people in some lines of work. Otis Bumpars spent a period of time doing roadwork for the railroad.

When passenger trains no longer stopped in Shubuta sometime in the 1970s, those jobs and the town's sense of identity with the railroad ceased to be. New transportation, the automobile, and its roads, the highway, became dominant, and another chapter in the way of life of the town ended.

Town Government

The Shubuta town government is well established, and the citizens seem to find it satisfactory. The Town Hall building was formerly the Bank of Shubuta building, a graceful, two-story brick building on the corner of Eucutta Street across from the far more ordinary concrete-block structure that is the town library. East of the Town Hall is the railroad and woodyard. Libby Owen is the town clerk, and Clyde Brown, elected in 1993, is the mayor and also manager of the Toney woodyard operation next to the railroad. Both the town clerk and the mayor jobs are part time.

Once when Clyde Brown was sick and out of the office, former mayor Randy Waller substituted for him. When Waller became ill, too, the town's business had to be carried on by woodyard owner R. L. Toney, laughingly called "our assistant mayor" by the staff in the office. Clyde Brown is the first black person to hold the office of mayor, just as Waller, who served from 1985 to 1993, was the first person who had moved in from out in the country, the Chapparel community, to be elected mayor. Florence Busby, mayor from 1968 to 1973 and 1977 to 1985, was the first woman, and Aubrey Jones, the first middle-class mayor when he was elected in 1937. Before Jones, the mayors had all been wealthy white Shubuta men like those from R. L. Toney's family, though most of them earlier arrivals in town than the Toneys: for example, William H. Patton, who served from 1905 to 1906 and again from 1908 to 1910; Arista Johnston, grandfather of retired postmaster James Johnston, mayor 1907–1908; John P. Spinks, mayor 1911–1925; and H. B. Gillespie, who served 1926–1927 and again 1929–1936.[10]

The town clerk is really the officer who handles the town's daily business and management, rather like a city manager in an urban setting. Libby Owen, the town clerk in the 1990s up until the present, is in her office from 8:00 a.m. until noon every day, and she oversees all the town's business, collects taxes and payment of fines, keeps the minutes books and ordinance books of the town government, sets up the meetings of the Board of Mayor and Aldermen, for the town attorney, and for the mayor in his role as town judge. She works with a deputy clerk, Diane Turner, as well as with the mayor in her office. Owen is white and Turner is black.

In 1997 at the time of my interview, the aldermen serving with Mayor Clyde Brown were Charles McFarland, Robert McFarland, John W. Barry, Yancy Taylor, and Jeanie S. McDonald. The officers are elected to four-year terms, and Brown has now been elected three times after having served as mayor pro tem the last two years of Randy Waller's term. All of these officers, mayor and aldermen, were reelected in the 2001 election.[11]

An important additional role the Shubuta mayor plays is board member of the Chickasawhay Natural Gas District, the gas board serving Quitman, Shubuta, and Waynesboro, with headquarters in the same building as the Shubuta Town Hall. Each mayor is paid a monthly stipend for gas board service, and its location in Shubuta is important to both the town's economy and its government. This utility was set up by the Mississippi legislature at the behest of then-mayor of Shubuta George Busby, Florence's husband, and must comply with the municipal laws of the state as it serves the three towns.

Shubuta has a municipal court with an appointed judge, who has to be an attorney. The mayor hears complaints and oversees the gas district business, but the municipal court judge handles court business. The municipal judge is Jim Potuk, who also serves Quitman in the same capacity. He hears cases of simple assaults, traffic violations, and driving-under-the-influence-of-alcohol cases. Only simple felonies are heard in the Shubuta court: misdemeanors go to Quitman to be heard by a grand jury in the county court.

The police chief is appointed by the town, and James Everett, formerly of Laurel, was serving in this full-time job at the time of my interview at the Town Hall. There was a part-time assistant police officer. At the end of 2001, Everett had retired and there was no police chief.

When I visited with Libby Owen in her office in 1997, I asked her what the city's responsibilities are. She listed them off: tax personal and real property in the town. "People also pay county taxes, too. School tax all goes to Quitman." She continued the list: overseeing the utilities of which the water department is Shubuta's, the gas the tri-city gas board's, electricity private and statewide through the Mississippi Power Company. The town is responsible for streets, street lights, and street cleaning. The church buildings are not taxable, but the medical clinic building is. The medical clinic is a private, not-for-profit federal-government-generated office. The mayor always serves on the board for it. Florence Busby deserves a lot of credit for getting the medical clinic, Libby Owen says: "as mayor she took responsibility for getting that clinic. She did a lot for Shubuta, getting grant money, money for sewers, HUD money."

The Shubuta Public Library is included in the town's budget, but it is a county agency and the county maintains and owns its building and pays to operate it. The town of Shubuta pays the librarian's salary and travel expenses and for the magazine subscriptions for the library.

Just then the chief of police, James Everett, came in, wearing his gun and a walkie talkie, but a big, casual smile on his face. Libby Owen introduced me to him and told me he had been in Shubuta as police chief for seven years. I asked him what he liked about Shubuta, and he replied, "Everybody always has a smile. Black or white, poor or whatever—people all help out. Yesterday a man got sick before day, and there were thirty people there to help him before the police got there."

That summed up Shubuta's government in the 1990s. While its jurisdiction has shrunk, no longer covering schools, the full supplying of the town's utilities, adjudicating legal disputes, nor the licensing of its businesses, its community connectedness has expanded across all the lines of gender, race, and wealth. It summed up Shubuta's culture, too.

TROPE 7: THE HANGING BRIDGE

The road out of Shubuta that leads to the Hanging Bridge is a red-dirt road where tire tracks after rain hold rivulets of muddy red water. Running beneath the bridge, the Chickasawhay River is roiled and churned brown by storms or at floodtimes, and is a tranquil clear black liquid mirror on bright days, summer or winter. Looking from high above the river on the metal and wooden bridge, one sees a sandbar glistening yellow in a graceful curve on the shore below. Dense trees grow very near both sides of the riverbanks, breathtakingly green in springtime, yellow and golden and russet in autumn. Not a human sign is visible, save the bridge, when one looks upstream or downstream at the flowing, curving river. Only nature, seemingly pristine, seemingly glorious, is in view in the river's meld of earth, air, water, and sunshine.

Standing on the bridge in friendly human company, one can imagine the riches of wildlife in the woods: white-tailed deer, wild turkeys, brown squirrels, and hopping rabbits; the abundance of fishes swimming below in the Chickasawhay: catfish and eels and bream and schools of minnows; and the stars shining over it on clear, dark, and clean subtropical nights. One can think of the decades, maybe centuries, of the pleasures of hunting and fishing in these woods and on this river, of the sustenance of people fed by them, and of the courageous joy of people sleeping under the stars in their camps of rough leisure or of hardscrabble establishment of home by the river.

The Hanging Bridge is said to have been built by John A. Price not long after 1830 on land he newly owned, as the first bridge near Shubuta over the Chickasawhay.[1] By the twentieth century, it was one of several crossings over the river not far from Shubuta with names only predicting the roads' relationship between the town and the river: the "upper river bridge" it was called. But when one night in 1917 some white men, with no murder trial and no sanctioning by law, hanged five black people they accused of murder from the bridge's bars, the bridge was named.

There was another lynching in 1942; this time two young teenaged black boys were hanged from the bridge by a lawless group of white men. Nobody was ever legally accused, tried, blamed, or held responsible for those hangings.

White children growing up in Shubuta after the 1940s were not taught the story of the bridge's naming. The bridge was referenced in the same tone of voice as "Highway 45" or "the road out to Chapparel," matter-of-factly, so, as much as any white people thought about it, it meant something like "suspension" or "swinging between banks."

Black children, though, were taught how the bridge got its name, but for many years, it was not something anyone in Shubuta's black community dared say aloud to anyone else.

TROPE 8: THE PHILLIPS ARCHIVE

The scrapbook, photographs, school programs, diplomas, and other bits of paper that make up the Phillips Archive in the Shubuta Public Library tell the story of Shubuta writer and pioneer teacher Georgia Dees Phillips; her husband, Baptist minister the Reverend Joshua M. Phillips; and their children, music teacher Annie Laura Phillips and businessman Oscar Phillips.

A scrapbook clipping dated 14 August 1878 reads:

> Yesterday at Hepsibah church Eld[er] Joshua M. Phillips was united in marriage to our esteemed friend, Miss Georgia Dees, of this place. Rarely indeed are two youthful hearts so pure and so entirely suited to one another, bound together by the silken cord of the church. May white-winged angels of love and peace ever be near them.[1]

Another clipping about the wedding identifies Joshua Phillips as the pastor of the Shubuta Baptist Church and as "a young man of decided talent and bids fair to become one of the leading ministers of his denomination." Georgia Dees is called "a woman of gentle christian [sic] character and cultured mind."[2]

Joshua Phillips's life is an example of how the civic and the religious blended in Shubuta for many years as it did in much of the South and other parts of the United States. Phillips was a Baptist minister, grew up in and lived out his life in the Shubuta Baptist Church. Yet, he was frequently called on to speak at public events, and at the time of his wife's death in December of 1937, his U.S. representative, Ross A. Collins, sent him a condolence letter on congressional stationery. Congressman Collins's letter, which could have been written by a minister given the religious expression of it, said, "God in His own plan will soon have all of us to understand the working of His will and that He is at the helm of all our earthly affairs."[3]

Phillips was pastor of the Shubuta Baptist Church for some periods of time, but more important, he and Georgia Dees Phillips made their home Shubuta for their lifetimes, Shubuta or its surrounding area having been their childhood home as well. They must have felt great security in being at home in their town. Georgia Dees Phillips is listed in a state library file on

Shubuta as a "pioneer teacher." She also wrote for the *Mississippi Messenger*, and once when she had been ill and sent an obituary to be published, the editor published her letter about her illness as well with an editorial comment, "Note: Mighty glad Mrs. Phillips is improving; for no finer spirit blesses our country."[4]

The Phillips's daughter, Annie Laura, was the Shubuta Public School music and piano teacher in the white school from 1916 to 1939, and their son, Oscar, went into business with Shubuta's Brownlee Lumber Company. He ran the commissary for the lumber company for a while in his early manhood and later owned the Phillips Mercantile Company.

Georgia Dees Phillips and Oscar Phillips made the scrapbook now in the Shubuta Public Library for Joshua Phillips's eightieth birthday. Thus, preserved in this family memento is a sense of the character of the man, as well as the affection of the family. It also suggests a striking representation of the values held and the expectations affirmed by Shubuta's white leadership class, which are often Baptist religiously, and socially and historically conventional and conservative.

Most of the clippings in the Phillips scrapbook are not dated, but they span the time from the 1902 founding of the bank at least until after the 1932 death of former Mississippi senator John Sharp Williams and the 1933 Clarke County centennial. Included in it are local Shubuta material, Baptist church convention news and religious devotional material, a little political material from state politics like the picture and obituary of Williams, who was admired for his moderate stand on rebuilding state governments, as well as clippings that feature Joshua Phillips himself in some public event.

One such ceremony recorded in a clipping serves to illustrate the civic respect accorded to Phillips along with his stature as a religious leader.

In September of 1933, a centennial pageant for Clarke County was presented in Quitman in the Terral-Dabbs Park, according to the newspaper clipping. Different communities from the county produced scenes—the one from Shubuta was on the Civil War and was directed by Miss Sarah Weems. The platform for public speeches for the day was occupied by the district attorney, the school superintendent, and other dignitaries along with Phillips, but the only one given a full sentence is Phillips: "The Rev. J. M. Phillips of Shubuta, opened and closed the meeting with prayer. The

Rev. Mr. Phillips is a native of Shubuta, Clarke County, and has been in the ministry sixty years."[5]

This was the man who as a boy heard his thoughtful father argue against secession and civil war, but to wait for Lincoln to take his seat, the boy who thought it took a long time for that man Lincoln to sit down, the boy who admired his father and believed his slave-holding father was good to his slaves. This was the man who as a young man quickly became a Baptist minister and received the education and ordination that established him as an intellectual and spiritual leader of his community and who married a woman who was his peer in social class, education, and "culture." He was a popular speaker at public events, saying the prayers at government-sponsored celebrations, giving speeches at decade birthday parties of other men of means or influence in his community, and performing the baptisms, funerals, and weddings for a large population of Baptists in his community. Elsie Jones Cross and Robert Cross chose him for the officiant for their wedding ceremony in the Jones home—the daughter, Annie Laura, played the piano—before the Cross newlyweds went to live at the Lang House on the Lang Plantation. One clipping in the scrapbook, also from 1933, tells of the Phillips couple attending a fiftieth wedding anniversary celebration of a man and woman whose wedding ceremony Joshua Phillips had conducted in 1883. The fusion of values from Baptist piety with social, cultural, and economic class values was complete for Joshua Phillips and Georgia Dees Phillips. The Phillipses were among Shubuta's "cultured people." That meant their education, artistry, religion, and public participation were parts of an unquestioned whole, and that participation placed them in the decision-making and office-holding group of their town.

Their archival record, given to the town library by their granddaughter, Helen, shows the mesh of Baptist religion, civic authority, and cultural custom of their time.

Chapter 4

Documents: Shubuta Memory in Maps, Pictures, Letters, and Buildings

> *'Tis a gift to be simple,*
> *'Tis a gift to be free,*
> *'Tis a gift to come down*
> *Where you ought to be.*
>
> —Shaker song

In Shubuta in the mid-1990s, people would stand around in the parking lot of the Greer Supermarket on the northeast corner of the intersection of Highway 45 and Eucutta Street, drinking Dr Pepper and Coca-Cola from cans, spitting chewing tobacco, and talking. An observer in an automobile going through the town's single stoplight at the crossing of Highway 45 and Eucutta Street would notice that most of the people were black, though whites and blacks talked with one another and interacted, smiled, laughed, and teased, as they came and went from their pickup trucks and air-conditioned automobiles parked in the store's parking lot. In the supermarket, some of the checkout clerks and supervisors were black and some were white. The Greer store in Shubuta was not locally owned, but was the first chain store to have come to Shubuta after a Jitney Jungle was there briefly in the 1930s. It was housed in a warehouse-style box building and had rows of aisles of groceries, housewares, breads, and produce like hundreds of thousands of other food stores all over the United States along the highways and in shopping centers.

Inside the building, at tables in a fast-food grill, black and white people sat down together at adjacent tables or with one another, and black and white children, schoolmates and friends, chased one another in the aisles, giggling in delightful play until their mothers good-naturedly stopped them.

As recently as 1965, such relaxed and easy public mixing of black and white people was out of the question. This Shubuta story of racial harmony contrasts with what a then-19-year-old white civil rights movement worker recruited to come to Shubuta for the summer of 1965 from the University of Wisconsin at Madison experienced. He remembers that he had no conversations at all with white Shubutans and he and the other nonsoutherners experienced the town as both so like and so alien to their previous experience as Americans. He says,

> what struck me most was how Mississippi was so familiar—it had stop signs and other signs of America, and yet it was so different. . . . I don't remember any socializing between whites and blacks. My sense was that blacks stayed in the black community. . . . I remember that in Shubuta the white streets were paved and had sidewalks and sewer lines, while the black community had dirt roads and drainage ditches, and no lights or sidewalks.[1]

The former civil rights movement worker also wrote, "Your letter brought back the 'Hanging Bridge.' I'll tell you that bridge scared the hell out of me."[2]

By the end of the 1990s, the Greer store was a vacant building and the stoplight had been replaced by stop signs on Eucutta Street on each side of the intersection with Highway 45. The new four-lane highway being built is bypassing Shubuta. Still, the two-lane highway through town is effectively Shubuta's Main Street at the present time, and that crossroad with Eucutta Street still the central compass point of town. Over the century and a half since the coming of the railroad, town center has moved up a block from the railway depot. On this main intersection of "Main Street," opposite the now-empty Greer store, is the late-nineteenth-century Shubuta Baptist Church building, the immaculately kept white wooden building that resembles many another church building in New England town squares, in midwestern neighborhoods, or on southern street corners. This church houses the congregation of white people in Shubuta that belongs to the Southern Baptist Convention. At Christmastime the church has a life-sized manger scene with Mary and Joseph and Baby Jesus displayed beside the church near the street. No one objects. Still a town of devout churchgoers, most of Shubuta's people attend church on Sunday mornings and are favorable toward Christian imagery, but unlike the Greer store shopping and restaurant seating, black and white Shubutans do not attend church together. Church is the last bastion of racial segregation in some places in the South, including Shubuta.

At the intersection of Highway 45, across Eucutta Street from the Shubuta Baptist Church, is the parsonage, the home provided by the church for the minister of the Baptist Church. This fine old house has long been the home of some of Shubuta's leading citizens. While this house is not one of the three houses in the town listed on the National Register of Historic Places, it is similar to the houses on "Silk Stocking Row," where the town's white founding families lived on the other side of "downtown." One Silk Stocking Row house is the restored Hand family house and Stovall house complex of Brevard and Allison Hand. The white Methodist minister lives in one. Most of the houses are still well cared for. One of them has been bought by a black family.[3]

On the fourth corner of the Highway 45 intersection, opposite the Greer store site and thus to the south, is the building occupied for many years by the Busby electrical supplies shop and the post office. Until April of 1999 when the new post office building was opened on the highway less than a block away, all of Shubuta's inhabitants got their mail from post office boxes in this building, as they do now in the new building. There is no house-to-house or street delivery of mail in the town, so that every morning after the mail truck comes, shopkeepers and residents converge on the post office; and Shubutans converse familiarly as they work the combination locks on their mailboxes and get out their letters and magazines and advertising flyers.

Documenting What One Already Knows

Since I knew Shubuta as the town one learns emotionally and unreflectively as one's first home, when I decided to write a book about Shubuta as a scholar of American life, I sought documents of Shubuta culture and history from people and libraries. However, when I asked for stories, people gave me the same materials over and over again: the 1947 *Shubuta* booklet and the article from the Clarke County newspaper about Shubuta at the time of the U.S. bicentennial. As I learned more and as Shubuta people understood better what I wanted, my questions became more specific, and Shubuta people voluntarily began to contribute sources that slowly gave me information to fill in the open spaces, to shape and shade and lighten and color the picture of Shubuta I was working to create. These documents taught me to see with an understanding much richer and more complex than my childhood knowledge from memory could allow me.

R. L. Toney brought me a photograph of a tombstone for the minister Joshua Heard, which he believes settles the argument over the founding date of the Shubuta Methodist Church, a disagreement in which some of the more highly educated families, who relied on historical ecclesiastical records for their data, maintained was 1857 and Aubrey Jones and the people he dubbed the middle-class Shubutans, who believed the oral tradition, insisted was 1840, when in a grape arbor his great-grandfather Samuel Jones founded the church. (I did not find a definitive answer to this question, but by 1999 the church building was designated a national treasure and listed on the National Register of Historic Places with the founding date given as 1843 on one plaque and 1840 on another one, both placed in the front entry of the building.)

Additional documents came from Janette Hudson, who in that first of my townspeople interviews showed me her copies of town maps made by the Sanborn Fire Insurance Company in the late nineteenth and early twentieth centuries. In Jackson, at the Mississippi State Department of Archives and History Library, I got my own copies of the maps from microfilm, and studying them led me to go to the Clarke County Chancery Clerk's office in Quitman to study the lot maps, which have deeds and wills attached to them, and to get copies of these county maps. I learned from the county files that the post office space on Eucutta Street was rented from a private individual who lived in Waynesboro, and I read Dr. Albert Hand's will with instructions for leaving a parcel of seventeen acres to his four children, his sister Caroline's will with the same four younger-generation Hands as her heirs, and the deed giving a parcel of land to Fred Edwin Stanley by his parents. I saw many other lot deeds and designations for the businesses in town.

Along with bringing me a shoebox full of camellias one winter day, Patsy Toney brought me correct information about her family's business, and she gave me addresses and phone numbers of people she worked with on the medical board that supported the government-provided clinic in Shubuta.

In the first and the last of my interviews, dated 1989 and 1999 respectively, interviewees talked about their churches and the church's centrality in their lives and they talked about education and its value to them and their families, leading me to recognize that however much scholars claim that secularity is dominant in American society, in Shubuta several versions of Christianity are alive and well and central to Shubuta's people. I learned that Shubutans believe, in addition to their religion, that education is the key to both public success and a good life. They lament the loss of local schools and believe that their town is diminished by that loss.

Other documents were given to me by Nerva McCaskey, who took me to the Shubuta bank, showed me its treasury, and gave me pictures and newspaper clippings from the bank's archive. Much later, visiting with Mary Virginia "Gin" Weems French on Fox Island near Tacoma, Washington, who worked in the bank all of 1937 when her aunts Mary and Sarah were on their trip around the world, I was shown family pictures of Gin's Weems grandparents. She offered me the familiar *Shubuta* booklet and the family pictures and papers.

After the *Shubuta* booklet that many people put into my hands, the next documents I was shown were in a glass case in the little Shubuta public library. Librarian Cassandra Cameron showed them to me on my first visit to her and explained that they had been given to the library by Miss Helen Phillips, a Shubutan as a child and then an elderly woman living in Meridian. These included pictures and program flyers, copies of some letters, and the splendid scrapbook from the Phillips family.

Church members took me into their church buildings and cemeteries, Cassandra Cameron taking me around the Tribulation Baptist Church and its cemetery, Cleo Powe Cooper showing me the Saint Matthew Baptist Church, and Linda McInnis giving me a look around the Shubuta Baptist Church. Florence Busby took me out to see the Hanging Bridge; showed me the sites in the town where the utilities and services she had presided over as mayor were operated; and took me to the places along the river and its sandbars where old-timers had picnicked near the Shubuta Cemetery, the Confederate statue, and the Choctaw burial mound. Libby Owen, the town clerk, showed me through Town Hall and the mayor's office and the aldermen's meeting room and gave me access to the town Minutes Books. Syble Meeks walked with me through the businesses in town where her father's shoe-repair shop had long been a gathering place, and Mary McCarty reminded me that black people in her Shubuta childhood "had back street," which had a cafe and a barber shop "run by the Dunbars" that served black people, who were not served on "front street." (McCarty pointed out, though, that in the 1940s and 1950s Drs. Hand and McDevitt "had a single waiting room" serving both white and black patients, and that the white undertaker, Will Patton, did funerals for both black and white people.)

In the state historical library in Jackson I found, in addition to the microfilmed maps, a clippings file on Shubuta, as well as microfilm of all U.S. Census data more than seventy-two years old, that which is by law available to users. I studied the census sheets available for Shubuta for the decades from 1870 through 1920 and learned of the slave census available on microfilm in the East Mississippi Regional Library in Quitman. At that library, I was shown what may have been the earliest extant diary of a local white resident, that of John H. Evans.

These sources, the people who gave them to me, and my interviews, my own photographs and visits, gave me a knowledge base from which I was gradually able to learn about Shubuta in this new way. All of the documents helped me, but some of them carry representative value, not only for Shubuta, but for U.S. cultural history as well. The samples I will lift up in this chapter and from which I will narrate their stories I think of as case studies of American history from Shubuta's past. They are John Evans's diary of frontier Shubuta, Georgia Dees Phillips's manuscript about slavery and the Civil War, the Shubuta town Minutes Books' record of Jim Crow laws, a printed program from a 1914 county fair, the 1928 travel diary of Annie Ruth Johnston from "Auntie's trunk," letters and pictures from 1965 Shubuta civil rights movement worker John Cumbler, and the painted-over sign on the Hanging Bridge.

Diaries, Letters and Laws: The 1830s Banishment of Native Americans

A case study of the 1830s American racial conflict known as Removal, the banishment of Native Americans from their lands to reservations and to Oklahoma, can be found in the diary of an old man from the Shubuta area, "Reminiscences of Olden Times" by John H. Evans. A photocopied typescript of the manuscript is in the East Mississippi Regional Library in Quitman and is undated, though textual evidence places it in the 1890s, the writer calling himself an "old timer" and says he "was born in Wayne County, November 15th, 1824, and [has] resided in Clarke County for the past sixty-nine years."[4]

Evans says his was among the first white families to settle in Clarke County, after the U.S.-Choctaw treaties opened up that territory to U.S. government sales. To be precise, he says "his father," but logic suggests that women and children were involved, too, in order for him to have been born there. His Evans grandfather and two uncles, he says, again naming the patrilineal order but using the word *families,* and "six other families" traveled by wagons from the Chesterfield district of South Carolina to settle in Mississippi. He documents his family's wagon train journey, made in 1809 in what he calls a colony of settlers on their way to Mississippi from South Carolina, and tells of the white people's encounters with Indians. Once on their way, they were required by Indians to stop and pay a toll at a bridge set up over a stream. Once a Native American man seizes a gun owned by one of the traveling colonists and a tussle results between a long line of Indians and a long line of whites before the white commander of the group orders his men to let go and the Indian man runs off in the woods with the gun as his booty. Evans writes of the men of his family forming a militia to fight the Indians and gives a graphic account of a white militiaman splitting open the head of a Native American in one-to-one combat. He writes of the local Choctaws welcoming the white settlers when they first arrive and tells a long and moving story from a later time of an Indian man, knowledgeable of the local woods and rivers, who searches for and finds a lost white child who had wandered away from her settlement home. He tells of the establishment of a school for the Indian children by the European Americans and testified that he was the first white child to attend the school. His friends and playmates were Indian children, among them, "boys named Lewis, Frank, Tom and George," so when those children were required to leave with their parents, he writes of a tearful farewell: "in the spring of 1834 . . . the first group of Indians [were moved] to their place of rendezvous at Muckalresha, old town in Nesholia [Neshoba] Co., . . . for their transportation to their new homes west of the Mississippi River."[5]

He writes that the movement of the Indians took four years, so it was 1838 before most of them would go. He noticed in the first group that some of them "refused to put their plunder [crossed out and replaced with *baggage*] in the wagons with the others." These people who would not put their belongings with the other Choctaws ran away and hid "in the Oaktuppa swamp, while quite a number of others came back to their old camping grounds and wept bitterly, for they should never again return.... [M]y playmates came back to bid me a last farewell; after which they returned to their emigrating party."[6]

Thus it was that this first white child who had gone to a mission school established for the Choctaws in the "Chickasawhay Country" no longer had any Choctaw schoolmates and playmates in his community. From this document I learned the local human story in Shubuta of adults and children alike experiencing the heartbreak and disruption brought about by what American history calls Removal.

Plantation Slaves and Masters

After Removal and prior to the Civil War, there were still small communities of Choctaws around and some Choctaw families in the vicinity down through the 1930s, though the dominant late-nineteenth- and early-twentieth-century population in terms of numbers might have been about equally divided black and white. In the town and on small farms near Shubuta before the Civil War, white individuals and families had only one or a few slaves, and many white households had none. Still, with the large numbers of slaves on a few plantations, there were likely to have been almost as many black people in slavery as there were other people in the area.

The work of the slaves in large measure was farm labor, with children, women, and men all working on planting and picking and tediously separating tight-growing cotton from its seed, and also at planting and "pulling" corn and shucking and shelling it by hand when it was "brought in," as well as at the plowing, planting, and harvesting of other crops like hay for animal feed and peanuts, sweet potatoes, sugarcane, turnips, and collards and other green vegetables for the people to eat.

Some male slaves also learned to be tanners, wheelwrights, blacksmiths, and carpenters for upkeep of the plantation buildings and fences where they lived or to do work the masters shared with or sold to other white people. Other black men were gardeners for the households or drivers for the wagons and carriages or butlers for the master's domestic life. These slaves were typically treated, fed, and clothed better than the "field hands" and therefore were sometimes resented by them.

Female slaves learned early how to cook and preserve foods and bake, do laundry by hand, clean and do housekeeping, so that some of them were assigned to be cooks and maids to master households.[7]

Around Shubuta, there seem to have been no slave uprisings, at least none has been documented, though there were runaway slaves documented in the *Weekly Southern Republic* during the Civil War. There was also little mobility of the slaves, it appears, before and during the Civil War.

One of the original documents in the Phillips Archive in the Shubuta Public Library illustrates the local Shubuta customs under slavery, customs that seem consistent with the stringent Mississippi state law, the Slave Codes. It is a four-page letter-style manuscript of reminiscences recorded by a Confederate soldier's son and it provides a view (that of a slave-owning white family) of the slave and master system and the Civil War in Shubuta. The Reverend J. M. Phillips, as an old man in 1932, provides in it an account of the son's remembrance of his landowner and Confederate soldier father, Captain W. C. Phillips, and his relationship with his slaves just before the Civil War. In the process, he reveals something of how slavery operated around Shubuta. The younger Phillips remembers, "After the fall of Vicksburg one of Sherman's raids came within ten miles of the old home [four miles north of Shubuta on Highway 45]. They burned the court house at Quitman, the county seat, and the railroad bridge across the Chickasahay [sic] River near there."[8]

Of the family's slaves, he writes in remembrance that they remained loyal to his family throughout the Civil War. There were "two men and some women and children" and even though Captain Phillips was away at war, "with the two men leading, they planted and cultivated and gathered the crops as diligently as if my father had been home."[9]

The men slaves on Captain Phillips's farm were married to slave women on neighboring farms, and they had children there. The reminiscence reports that the two men were allowed by their master to spend Wednesday nights and from Saturday night through Sunday night with their wives and children. Remembering what he saw as his father's generosity, Phillips says,

He also gave them a piece of land to cultivate, and every Saturday afternoon they were given the opportunity with the use of the horses, harnesses, and plows to work and make something extra for themselves. Of course he fed and clothed them well besides. They did not take advantage of their master's absence, but adhered strictly to his rules while he was away.[10]

The Slave Codes of Mississippi required any slave who left the master's place to have written permission for his or her going, a "pass" giving the exact destination and the exact times of departure and return. The Slave Codes also strictly prohibited slaves being taught to read or write so that they could not write passes for themselves or otherwise communicate by the written word. They also established and enforced a patrol of slaves, requiring all able-bodied white men of each county to serve a period of time each year patrolling the area for runaway or fugitive slaves by means of assuming postings and patrol duty around the county and demanding to see the passes of each traveling slave person.[11] Phillips writes,

> The negroes [sic] of the county were very much afraid of the patrol stationed at various places to see that they did not stray far from their quarters either day or night without permission. The "pass," which they always had to carry, was usually limited to 10 o'clock at night and if one stayed over time and was caught he suffered the consequences.[12]

Phillips says his father's slaves always were given the "passes" and always returned home within their limits. He does, however, remember a song sung in the voice of the slaves who nearly missed getting home in time:

> I run, I run, I run my best,
> I run myself in a hornet's nest.
> Oh run, nigger, run, the patrol will git you,
> Run, nigger, run, it's almost day.[13]

Jim Crow Laws

The official Minutes Books of Shubuta's Board of Mayor and Aldermen are probably typical records of a well-organized and orderly small-town government making its laws. Town ordinances include regulations on carrying weapons, taxation, the height of the sidewalk, the upkeep on the town's artesian well, the payment of a sanitation worker to clean out the inhabitants' "closets," presumably their outdoor toilets, and other matters of town governance. One document provides an illustration of the workings of Jim Crow laws all over the country. These were the laws legalizing separation of black and white people in public accommodations, commerce, travel, and assembly that were passed in the last decades of the nineteenth century and the first of the twentieth. This particular document is the law pertaining to Shubuta's depot and its grounds around the railroad, but there are several similar laws in the Shubuta town government minutes. In this one from 1910, the town government establishes segregation around the railroad station and tracks:

> Be it ordained by the Mayor and Board of Aldermen of the Town of Shubuta, ...
>
> Sec. 1. That the part of the station ground lying adjacent to and north of the waiting room set apart by the Mobile and Ohio Railroad Co. for Negroes at said depot or station are hereby set apart to the negroes, and that part of said grounds lying adjacent to and north and east of the white waiting room at said depot are set apart to the white people.[14]

Section 2 goes on to forbid any white person from "waiting or loitering" in the part set apart "to the Negroes" and any "negroe" [sic] is forbidden from standing or loitering in the white people's space. The exception is spelled out only "for the purpose of examining the bulletin board and for the purpose of getting on the trains and across the same when getting off the trains."[15]

This is an example of the Jim Crow laws that enforced separation of the races in full detail until federal civil rights laws of the 1960s superceded them and brought about legal desegregation.

A Program for a 1914 County Fair

Prosperity in Shubuta after the large sawmilling operations came in the early years of the twentieth century is readily documented by a program for the "First Annual Fair" of the "Clarke-Wayne Fair Association" held in Shubuta

3, 4, 5, and 6 November 1914. Aubrey Jones gave me a copy of this program bulletin from among his extensive Shubuta personal archives. He said he remembered seeing an airplane for the first time at the fair, when he was a boy.

Horse races were the main attractions of the fair, and the horse shows were held in the evening with a $1,500.00 purse for the winners. There were prize competitions for other livestock, including sheep and goats as well as cattle—Jersey, Aberdeen Angus, Hereford, Polled Durham, or Shorthorn—and many varieties of hogs: Poland China, Berkshire, or Duroc Jersey.[16]

There was a Women's Building, an Agriculture Building, and a Poultry Building. The program says that the racetrack had been "resurfaced with clay," and that there were "new stables and pens" with "permanent roofs on all buildings."[17]

Tuesday, 3 November, the fair's first day, was Children's Day, when all schoolchildren under 12 years old were admitted without charge. The second day of the fair was Old Soldiers' Day, when "ex-soldiers of the Confederacy and of the United States will be admitted free." Every day the Metropolitan Carnival Company was on the program with "fourteen side shows, new and up-to-date. Ferris wheel, ocean wave, merry go round. Two free attractions daily. Two brass band concerts daily."[18]

All of the mercantile companies in town have ads in the program, W. L. Weems offering "Rust Proof Corsets," the Phillips Mercantile Company selling boys' suits for ages 6 to 18 years, and Patton Brothers offering "Walkover Shoes" and "No Name Hats," and the One Price Cash Store selling "Duchess Trousers" and repairs for "10¢ a Button, $1.00 a Rip." The Bank of Shubuta, Drs. Hand and Hand, Hudson's Drug Store and two others, the Shubuta Drug Company and the City Drug Store in Quitman, the livery stables of E. C. Moody and of W. B. Falconer, grocer A. T. Rogers, jeweler J. R. Warrington, Frank Sullivan's garage, and the Poole Hotel all advertise in the fair bulletin. Both E. C. Moody and Frank Sullivan advertise "Automobiles for Hire."

The prizes in the Ladies' Department were only $1.00 each, prizes given for the best specimens of food products, handwork, and art. Foods include "Best display of preserves," "Best display of pickles," "Best loaf cake," "Best loaf home-made light bread," "Best loaf corn bread," "Best pound home-made butter," "Best quart of home-made lard," "Best lye hominy," "Best home-made sausage," and "Best home-made soap." There were ten categories of art entries, including oil and watercolor paintings and "Best specimen of hand-painted china." Needlework entries were patchwork quilts, silk quilts, sofa pillow tops, crochet pieces, handkerchiefs, and "handmade battenburg."[19]

The chief operations officer of this fair was Charles C. Hand, the secretary and treasurer, who oversaw the daily workings of the fair and compliance with its regulations. Dr. J. A. McDevitt was the fair's president and business owner W. H. Patton was vice-president, with board members including sawmill owner W. H. Fields from Hiwannee and W. L. Brunson from Enterprise, but clearly these officers were advisory to Secretary Hand, younger son of Annie Case Hand and the elder Dr. Hand. Hand would have been 24 years old and just returned home to live in Shubuta briefly after finishing law school at the University of Virginia. Later, after serving in World War I, he settled in Mobile and became a prominent attorney and father of federal judge Brevard Hand, who now owns the Shubuta Hand family home in Shubuta. Management of the fair was exactly the right assignment for a rising young professional star from among Shubuta's leadership families.

A 1928 Travel Diary

The 1928 travel diary of "A Trip to the Tropics" found in "Auntie's trunk" by her great-great-nephew when Miss Mary Weems moved to the Jackson nursing home from her Shubuta family home illustrates the opportunities Shubuta's upper class members had to learn from wide-ranging travel and cultural experience. Mary Weems and her sister, Sarah, as daughters of the banker, were central to that class. Their travel party was made up of the author of the diary, the young woman Annie Ruth Johnston and her parents, and none other than the same Charles C. Hand of the 1914 Shubuta fair, his wife, the former Irma Weems, who was born and brought up in Shubuta and was a distant cousin of Mary and Sarah Weems, and their son, Charlie.[20]

Starting in New Orleans after staying the night in its glamorous Monteleone Hotel, they traveled to Havana and spent several days sightseeing in Cuba. Then they went to Panama, through the Panama Canal, spent some time in Panama City, and docked in Honduras for loading bananas before returning to New Orleans and home by way of the train to Mobile.

The exuberant young writer misses nothing. She records that in New Orleans the group went to the "Saenger Theater to see Richard Dix in [the movie] 'Warming Up.'" The theater building is "the most beautiful show house I have ever seen." She likes the ceiling, which is painted to look like a star-filled sky. She tells that the next morning the group has breakfast at Gallatoire's, a fine New Orleans restaurant, before boarding their United Fruit Company steamship *Parisimina*.[21]

On board ship she writes again of every detail, describing the other passengers, their activity, and their food, including the menu for one of the daily seven-course dinners served to them. The sightseeing, taxi trips to the interior of Cuba and around Havana, travel through the locks of the Panama Canal, shopping in Panama City are reported as marvelous for all the party. However, on their way to Honduras a hurricane overtakes them and frightens them terribly with their ship pitching and rocking for several hours. Johnston's mother and Mary Weems have to take to their cabins, very ill with seasickness, and even the fathers look pale, though the young diarist reports happily that she was not affected. Mary Weems, though, invoking Shubuta, was sickest of all, and the writer recounts, "Miss Mary Weems about midday in a moment of despair gave expression to this lament, 'I would give a thousand dollars if I were in Shubuta now.'"[22]

A Civil Rights Movement Worker's Letters and Pictures

Coincidence happens, but hearing about Shubuta at Cambridge University strained even my strong belief in synchronicity. This was the most stunning coincidence of my experience.

Tony Badger, my host professor for the spring of 1993, had invited me to attend a session of his seminar where American history professor John T. Cumbler of the University of Louisville was speaking. Professor Badger introduced his visiting speaker as a former civil rights movement worker, and this particularly interested him because he was beginning a four-year project with his own American history students at Cambridge on the U.S. civil rights movement. A former civil rights movement worker in Nashville myself, I introduced myself to John Cumbler after the lecture and eagerly asked where and when he had been in the movement.[23]

Modestly, he said he was active toward the end, the summer of 1965, and had not accomplished much, he insisted, "in a little town in Clarke County, Mississippi, Shubuta."

Shubuta, Mississippi!

John Cumbler had given Tony Badger letters he had written to his future wife, Judith Kwait, as a 19-year-old University of Wisconsin student that summer of 1965, and eventually he had copies of them sent to me along with photographs he had taken that summer. Those pictures and letters from 1965, together with e-mail correspondence between Cumbler and me in the 1990s, provide remarkable documentation of the civil rights movement coming to Quitman and Shubuta and the opposition it experienced.

Cumbler was recruited in Madison, Wisconsin, along with a friend, Hartry Fields, by John Sumerall, the Mississippi Congress of Racial Equality (CORE) field secretary, who was originally from Quitman. Cumbler had been active in the Students for a Democratic Society (SDS) at the University of Wisconsin and had participated in protest marches of the SDS, but he had received no training as a civil rights movement worker.

The host black woman he best remembers is a Mrs. Johnston from Quitman. He met and talked with no local white people. He feared for his safety a lot of the time and felt he could not go out much into public spaces. For instance, he wrote Judith right away that he had to get someone to mail his letters so he could not write to her as often as he would have liked. He wrote her that this was active Ku Klux Klan country, a fact he was about to experience directly within a week of his arrival when his friend, Hartry Fields, was hit and got his glasses broken in the recruits' first confrontation with the KKK. Fields had to return home to the North.

The three summer recruits included a black graduate student from Berkeley and Cumbler working with Sumerall and the local Quitman people under the auspices of the Mississippi Freedom Democratic Party. At one point, two teachers came, one black and one white, to work in the Freedom School. Another white civil rights movement worker came for a week for supplies, and the group worked with movement people in other towns working on Head Start, and hosted briefly a lawyer and a reporter who were with the movement. Otherwise, they were on their own under Sumerall's leadership.

The projects John Cumbler worked on were a Head Start preschool program, Freedom School for older children and adults, voter registration, and a co-op grocery store for Shubuta's black community. Among these, only Head Start made any real progress and moved toward establishment that summer, but it already had local black support and leadership in Shubuta. Because he had organizational skills and experience with cooperative stores, John worked on the grocery store project, once being sent to Jackson to gather information about establishing a co-op.

In his letters, he writes that the group was "boycotting" in both Quitman and Shubuta, but he also writes of the few people who were willing to come to meetings. Two hundred people promised to come to the first one, but about fifty showed up. His group's voter registration effort made some progress in getting people to be willing to register, but when they took them to the registration office, the office would always be closed. He spoke in the letters several times of his discouragement over what he perceived to be the apathy of the black people. However, looking back thirty years later he said, "I didn't appreciate that these people all worked, were tired and scared."[24]

Cumbler was appalled at the living conditions of the black people in Shubuta, Quitman, and the rural areas surrounding them. He noted that in Shubuta there were a night watchman and a road sweeper for the paved roads in the white area, but only dirt roads and no care for them in the black neighborhood in which he stayed. He comments that a person having an indoor toilet is called well off, but that most of the black people's houses have outhouses. He continues, "Most houses don't have running water, but only a pump outside or a faucet if they can afford it. A lot of the people who are well off only make $50 a week[,] if that, and they do this by both the man and wife working. No one down here has proper dental care." The photographs he took reinforce these images: a small black boy in the middle of a dirt road, a black baby standing beside a large zinc washtub, a wooden outhouse with the door sagging open, shabby houses with dirt yards swept clean, row after row of tar-papered shotgun houses, a man plowing a garden walking behind a mule, rows of vegetables in a garden growing right up to the side of a small unpainted house—and the Hanging Bridge.

People in his group experienced violence against them several times, and they were repeatedly confronted by the KKK. Once, the visiting white woman worker at their office was shot in the arm from a drive-by shooting and was refused admittance at the Quitman hospital. They had to take her to Meridian to the emergency room and they were quite worried about a black man being seen driving a white woman on the highway in their car. Two days later two black students were fired at inside the office.

When the lawyer was visiting and they stopped at a gas station, they were refused gas and someone heckled, "We were treating *our* niggers fine 'til you northerners came down here and started causing trouble."

Another day after they had entered and been served at a Quitman restaurant in an integrated group led by Sumerall, some white teenagers followed them and taunted from their cars, "You damned niggers stink the place up." When they stopped the cars, scuffling ensued between the MFDP workers and the taunters, and Sumerall was hit on the back of the head and Cumbler was kicked. When the patrol officers came, Sumerall was arrested and fined. This was reported in the county newspaper, and Cumbler sent a torn-out copy of the story to Judith.

In the middle of the summer it was decided that Cumbler would move to Shubuta for the rest of the summer, but before they could get him moved, they got a call from Shubuta in the night from the people with whom he would stay. He writes,

> they had been threatened by the Klan, and about 15 white folks drove by every 10 minutes threatening to blow up the house or shoot. About nine of us went there with guns and guarded the house for the night. We had about 15 people over night guarding that house.[25]

A flyer distributed from Quitman and included in John's letters to Judith begins, "nigger's beware!" It goes on to say, in the spelling, punctuation, and vocabulary from the original, "All nigger's will be shot and killed if any demonstrations accure in Mississippi, All kinky headed darkies better stay on your guard, and kut out all this smart allic demonstration . . . If you find your car windows dash in and it burn up, or your wife hanging on a light pole, or kids strung up in the outdoor toilet, it will be alright."

The group particularly worried about the safety of the director, John Sumerall, for, after they integrated a movie theater by going up into the balcony where previously only blacks were supposed to sit, and fighting broke out, John wrote to Judith that the Klan put out a statement saying they were going to kill Sumerall. He introduced this scary topic with the only levity in the letters: "Mississippi has more dangers than the KKK. Mosquitoes down here are unbelievable. I have bumps and bites all over me. Despite the heat, you have to sleep under blankets to get away from *some* of them."

The ending of this period was as abrupt as its beginning for John Cumbler when he went back to the University of Wisconsin in the fall and was united with Judith, feeling that he had done very little that he set out to do as a summer volunteer in the civil rights movement. He was wrong, though. What one person did might have been only a little; but the combined efforts of civil rights activists everywhere, black and white, local and outside volunteers, including local Shubutans like Pearlie Mae Hozie, Bertha and O'Dell Cameron, and Cleo Powe Cooper, and the legal changes that the federal, state, and local governments enacted brought about desegregation.

Restitution of Dignity in Death at the Hanging Bridge

By the 1980s the end had come to legal segregation of facilities, schooling, and occupations, but some customary racism and symbolic race-injustice lived on. Nowhere was the memory of the racist past more sore than at the beautiful woodsy riverside site in Shubuta, the Hanging Bridge. Now at the well-kept wood-and-metal bridge on a gravel road one sees only trees and sandbars and a lovely curve in the river where the road leads into the deep forest to the hunting and fishing club lodge of a group of Shubuta men known for many years as the Hanging Bridge Hunting and Fishing Club. In 1993, former Shubuta mayor Florence Busby showed me the sign that now hangs in the middle of the bridge with one word painted out to read now "Bridge Hunting and Fishing Club." By court order from a case brought by the NAACP in the 1980s, Florence Busby told me, the club was required to change its name.[26]

TROPE 9: OL' MAN WEEMS'S NICKELS

Many stories of Shubuta memory group together around George S. Weems, the town patriarch and banker as Shubuta entered the twentieth century, and financial leader for decades during Shubuta's local economic boom time as a timber cutting, sawmilling, and trade center for the region's farming and logging activity. He had earned his own money in cotton milling, farming, and storekeeping before the coming of the sawmills.

The 1937 obituary of him in the *Mississippi Messenger,* headlined "George S. Weems Passes By Death," reads in part, "In the business circles of Shubuta, Clarke, and Wayne counties the deceased was an outstanding character. In 1902 he founded the Bank of Shubuta and for 33 years served as its president and for thirty years was a successful merchant."[1]

The 1902 newspaper account of the founding of the Bank of Shubuta and the cottonseed mill, the Shubuta Oil and Manufacturing Company, reports that the establishing meeting was in George S. Weems's home and took only one hour to set up the bank and the mill. Mr. Weems was one of the major shareholders in the bank and the oil company along with two other men, W. L. Weems, a cousin, and S. H. Floyd.[2]

George S. Weems's wife, Mary Virginia, known as "Mollie," was born a Hand, a member of another leading family of the town. A family portrait from about 1904, taken on the large porch of their tasteful home, shows the two of them with their seven children and her father, who had been a Confederate Army colonel. George Weems's Bank of Shubuta has been very secure down to the present time, when it is a branch of a regional banking company. It is still often repeated in Shubuta with great pride, and has been for decades, that the Shubuta bank did not close during the Depression; and the Weemses are known to have been wealthy throughout the twentieth century.

There is consistency in his personal life with his business life of saving and retaining money. Weems stories are stories of frugality, even stinginess. As a woman in her nineties, Elsie Jones Cross remembered watching as a young woman employed in the Hudson Drug Store as George S. Weems's grandchildren would dance around him on the street begging for nickels. "He wouldn't give them anything but nickels," she said, laughing. One of these grandchildren, Mary Virginia Weems French, remembers a little differently, but still recalls the emphasis on frugality. As a child, she says, she was allowed to sweep the sidewalk in front of the bank for a dime, but she was expected to save a nickel of the money and spend only the other nickel.

Elsie Cross also tells about going to the Weems house as a girlfriend of Mary and Sarah Weems and being required to appear at the breakfast table on time and fully dressed. The household manners required that everyone be up and dressed and in the dining room for breakfast at the set time. George S. Weems's eldest great-granddaughter, Mary Sue Mitchell, recalls that such manners prevailed through her parents' generation of Weemses. Her husband was astonished, she says, to be reminded by her grandfather, Robert C. Weems, that he was to wear a jacket and tie in the dining room.

The hall from which one entered that dining room in the Weems house was graced with the grandfather clock, the clock that chimes the different sounds of Westminster, Canterbury, Winchester, and York Cathedrals. Elsie Cross tells of watching from the drugstore as six men carried a big crate that looked like a coffin from the train station, up Eucutta Street, to the Weemses' house. Rumor spread that someone had died or was dying at the Weemses. It turned out to be the arrival of the clock.

Yet this capitalist of the bank, this purveyor of aristocratic manners, and this begetter of a large and publicly successful family, is again and again remembered for his thrift. A family neighbor remembers with sympathy for one couple of Weems's aged children that George S. Weems was almost miserly with his money. She recalls that he did not give this couple money in his lifetime, and this son was left as a bequest only a little stock in a Mobile bank, so that his wife had to sew for other people to help make their living.

Another interviewee says, "Ol' Man Weems would never spend more than a nickel. He would take the train up to Enterprise to do business, and he would buy his lunch—cheese and crackers, or something like that—and he would just spend a nickel. If it cost more than a nickel, he wouldn't have it."

The stories of George S. Weems are almost a classic case of a late-nineteenth-century and early-twentieth-century American capitalist—successful in business by skillful investment and profit-making strategies, extravagant in domestic lifestyle, but tight with other people and close with everyday expenses. These stories may or may not have been true of George S. Weems himself, but as legend, they give Shubuta its version of the contradictory character of that American elite, the successful white male capitalist. He made a lot of money and with it was able both to hold economic and political authority in the town and to set the social standards for behavior, but he was impatient with other people who did not follow the standard and practices he set for himself as their own.

Chapter 5

Interviews: Shubuta Memory in People's Own Words

> *What we owe the future*
> *is not a new start,*
> *for we can only begin*
> *with what has happened. . . .*
>
> —Wendell Berry, "At a Country Funeral"

To learn about Shubuta afresh, interviews with lifelong Shubutans were by far the most informative for me. Starting with the first interview with Janette Hudson and the subsequent early ones with Cassandra Cameron and her parents, with Cleo Powe Cooper, and Otis Bumpars, I learned about Shubuta in the present time as well as its history. The individual versions of Shubuta life in the words of old timers are among the best material I found. In this chapter, I will often quote extensively from my interviewees and thereby give accounts of their lives around Shubuta as told to me by Aubrey and Ollie Jones, Charlie D. Meeks, and Elsie Jones Cross. All of them are dead now, so I was quite fortunate to be able to talk with them when I did.

Aubrey and Ollie Jones

Aubrey Jones liked to say that he was the first middle-class mayor of Shubuta. It is true that he was not college educated and a professional person like most of his predecessors were, nor was he a holder of large amounts of land or wealth. Still, he owned a farm near the Red Hill community, a mile or so out of town where his parents had moved in 1905 when Shubuta was a booming sawmill town and where he had been born and had grown up; and he was a very successful Shubuta businessman by his midlife, owning the Shubuta farm supply and feed store. Also, his people were among the first white people to settle in the vicinity, his great-grandfather Samuel Jones having come in a wagon train in 1836 to the Frost Bridge community. Eventually, after the

1862 U.S. Homestead Act, his family homesteaded the land on which Aubrey Jones lived.[1]

The earliest settlers on the land around Shubuta, as on much of the land gained by United States purchases or treaties with the Native Americans, was bought from the U.S. government with sale receipts going for public revenue. The lands around Shubuta were sold in Georgia and South Carolina and the price seems to have been 25¢ an acre. There was controversy over the land in the West not being free to U.S. citizens, though most southern states opposed free land. However, in 1862 the U.S. Congress passed the Homestead Act granting a 160-acre tract to a citizen or the head of a household who claimed unoccupied land and lived on and cultivated it for five years. A person also could claim and cultivate land for six months and pay $1.25 per acre for the parcel under the act. After the Civil War, unoccupied or government land around Shubuta was homesteaded in one of these two ways.

Samuel Jones was a Methodist minister who is credited with having established several churches and religious institutions in the area, among them the Frost Bridge Camp Meeting, a summer camp revival center still in operation, one of the few in the country; the Hebron Methodist Church, which has one of the oldest continuous congregations and cemeteries in Wayne County; and the Shubuta Methodist Church, which Aubrey Jones contended his great-grandfather founded in a brush arbor in 1840, but about which there was dispute in the congregation for most of his life.

Aubrey Jones's wife, Ollie, was also a lifelong Shubutan, having been born on Eucutta Street in the house where she and Aubrey spent eight months out of each year for several years during their retirement when they were beyond 80 years old. Some of her Cooper family members were on the first wagon train that came from South Carolina and settled near Shubuta out beside where the Hanging Bridge is. Her father was a well digger, and he dug most of the wells that supplied the Shubuta homes and many others in the region with their water in addition to the celebrated town well that was first located in the middle of Eucutta Street. The town well was known as Cooper's Well.

Ollie Jones's parents and their first daughter, Bea, had lived in a substantial house near the river when the 1900 flood came and washed the rising waters under the house so deeply that it toppled and fell in. After that they moved to another house nearer the town center where Ollie's second sister,

Pug, long the town clerk for Shubuta as an adult, was born and lived briefly. Then they built the house on Eucutta Street where Ollie was born, grew up, and also lived some of her late life years.

Her mother and Aubrey Jones's mother were friends in Shubuta when their children were infants, and Aubrey often joked that he and his wife had been sleeping together a long time, for their mothers put them in the same bed as babies. They were married when both were 23, in a simple ceremony at the Methodist parsonage.

Ollie Jones had gone to the "normal college" in Hattiesburg for a teacher-training course of a few months, and then she taught in a one-room school for a while before she and Aubrey were married.

Aubrey Jones worked in stores, as an auto mechanic and on the farm as a young man. He was an effective businessman and before long bought his own store. In the 1940s he bought a prime building in Shubuta, the big warehouse that had belonged to Will Patton, and established a store selling "fertilizer and feed and stuff" to farmers. The building had been constructed around 1902 from timbers salvaged from the 1900 flood destruction of the upper river bridge.

In the prime years of their lives, Aubrey and Ollie Jones brought up their two daughters, Edith and Claire, and Aubrey took the civic responsibility of serving as mayor and later as town clerk. In 1947, they built their big modern house up on Highway 45 where very popular New Year's Eve parties were held every year by their daughters.

Edith Jones went to college at Mississippi State College for Women (MSCW, "the W") in Columbus, and Claire went to a business college in Meridian. After college, Edith was a stewardess on the passenger train that ran through Shubuta. She made a round trip from St. Louis to Mobile every ten days, she remembers. Her parents and the whole town would be at the station sometimes when she would come through. There would be weeks she would save up her dirty clothes between trips, drop them off with her parents in the morning on her way to Mobile, and pick them up "washed, starched, and ironed" in the afternoon on her way back to St. Louis.

In his late fifties, Aubrey decided to move to Florida, and he bought a grocery store and a small orange grove in Plant City, Florida, keeping his and Ollie's primary home there for the rest of his life. Aubrey and Ollie kept the old Cooper home in Shubuta, though, and returned in retirement to spend eight months of each year in the town of their birth. Aubrey Jones also kept the best town keepsakes and pictures of Shubuta of anybody in town, and the tape recording he made about the Shubuta of his youth provided an invaluable oral history of Shubuta as it began to change with the times he saw.

There is a story that Aubrey, Ollie, and Edith Jones told me, and also Edith's childhood best friend, Syble Meeks, told me in another interview, that encapsulates the Jones family's closeness as well and Syble and Edith's friendship. I give it the title "Boogie Woogie on the Church Chimes."

When Edith Jones and Syble Meeks were growing up as best friends in Shubuta in the 1940s, the center of the teenagers' social life, as well as their spiritual life, was the Shubuta Methodist Church. Both of their fathers were lay officers in the church, stalwarts of their congregation, both middle class economically—Aubrey Jones, Edith's father, mayor of Shubuta some of those years, Charlie D. Meeks, Syble's father, shoe shop owner, merchant, and shoe repairman. But the Shubuta Methodist Church was at least as dominant in their lives as the town government or business was. Mr. Meeks was the leader for the young people's group, the Methodist Youth Fellowship.

The Shubuta Methodist Church along with its school and the Jones home was an active sponsor of pleasurable activities for white teenagers. Syble Meeks remembers:

> We did all kinds of things with the MYF [Methodist Youth Fellowship] ... parties ... picnics ... went to Lake Waulkaway to swim. We rode in the back of Mr. Ben Evans's pickup and dragged our feet in the dust all the way. The roads weren't paved. You *had* to go swimming then. It didn't cost but 25 cents. We would go over there and stay all day. Now that's one of the things you remember.[2]

Besides the Sunday School lessons and the music and the worship services, Syble Meeks remembers the parties her church's young people had. "There were Claire and Edith Jones, Ben and Peggy Evans, Barbara Reynolds, Mamie Elise and Wallace and Tom Calhoun in the early days. Tom Hudson was a little younger. People came from all around. Some would come over from the Baptist Church."[3]

She remembers with great pleasure the New Year's Eve parties at the Joneses's house: "We would square dance. There were games people could play. Or just talk."[4]

Many social activities, games and parties and dances, took place in the Jones family's spacious home just on the outskirts of town. New Year's Eve parties were teenager specials under the talented supervision of Ollie Jones. Chaperoning their teenagers was certainly a heavy obligation of the teenagers' parents of the 1940s, but Aubrey and Ollie Jones were popular parental chaperones of the teenagers of their daughters' set, some of them Baptists as well as Methodists.

Aubrey Jones tells in an interview how much he enjoyed providing pleasure for his daughters and their friends and how he trusted his daughters:

> I was always glad we had the house. I was making a little money then. We had the picture show. The house was in an H—had a 20-by-40-foot living room in the center. We named the farm Happy Valley Farm. All her friends [his daughter Edith's]—the rich folks here in town— were all there [for the New Year's Eve parties]. The rich folks didn't want to have it at their house because they didn't want to mess their houses up. I always figured with the young folks, if it was too good for them to use, they didn't need it. These girls—they enjoyed their teenage years because they had it. And Ollie and myself would be back in our bedroom and go to sleep—and just let them go because we knew they knew how to behave themselves. Edith has always been strong as an ox—little boy playmates on her end of town: she could whip every one of them. She'd tear them up. They would build frog houses, and she would have to catch the frogs. So, I knew she could manage the parties.[5]

Interviewed with her father, Edith Jones Adams remembers,

> It was '47 when we built the house up on the farm. That was my senior year. I lived in that house until I went off to the "W" in September.... Claire's birthday—my sister's birthday is January first. It was a combination birthday party and New Year's Eve party. The college kids would come home for Christmas holidays. You know, we knew a bunch in Quitman, some in Laurel and Waynesboro—all around the area. We

just got to where we would have New Year's Eve—it was really a dance. It was formal. I mean: we would have a *formal dance.* Of course, all we had was a record player and records. And we would have just fruit punch and cookies. That's all we had. It was a social event. Up there on the farm. We had a big patio, so we could dance outside. We had the groups we would invite.... You could see the house sitting up off Highway 45, see the flood lamps out on the patio. So from Highway 45, this house with all the lights on was really bright. And Daddy said he was going to put him a sign out on 45 that said, 'This ain't no juke joint!' Everybody would think it was a roadhouse sitting back there! With the car lights in the first dark, there was a steady stream of lights of cars driving, of people coming, and the car lights with the people coming, car lights with people winding their way from 45 up to that house. Then, right after midnight, right after the new year, the party would break up and everybody would go home.[6]

Syble Meeks remembers one New Year's Eve when the Jones girls' party and the Methodist Church of which the Meekses and the Joneses were a part both provided fun for the teenagers. This was a night they did not all go home from the party just after midnight.

One year on New Year's when Robert Langford was the preacher, we had a party and we thought it would be fun to put a record on the chimes up at the church, so we went down there and put boogie-woogie on the chimes. It was Barbara, Donna Stallings, Ben Jr., and me—that was the group that was in on it. I went to ring the bell, and they left me! They went off without me, so when the preacher and the others came running out, they saw it was me. I was the one left there. With boogie-woogie playing on the church chimes! I was the one who got caught![7]

The stories of the Jones girls' parties and even the New Year's Eve prank are stories of family affection and trust and fun, of development of social ease and gracefulness among young people, of community building and playful amusement. Even so, they are stories of protection of young white people in a way young black people did not experience it in a southern town at the same time. It is a bit of an irony that the offending music that aroused the town after midnight on the staid and formal Methodist Church's bell tower loudspeaker meant for its worshipful music was boogie-woogie, the piano jazz that was black people's music.

Aubrey Jones was mayor of Shubuta in 1942 at the time the Lang and Green black teenagers were lynched.

Charlie D. Meeks

Charlie D. Meeks had the shoe repair shop on Eucutta Street in Shubuta from 1941 almost to his death in 1993. Well into the 1990s "harness repairing" was painted on the glass storefront along with the painted announcement about shoe repairs and sales. Mr. Meeks's shoe shop was the last of the local service businesses to close in Shubuta, he the last of the tradespeople to serve Shubutans with the work of his hands for most of his adult life. For a while after he left the shop, his daughter and only child, Syble, who had helped him sell shoes part-time for many years, kept the shop open for the sale of shoes; but when he was gone, not only shoe repair but a local, small-town way of life where a full array of shopping and services in locally owned and operated shops and offices were available on Main Street was gone, too.[8]

Charlie D. Meeks was born and died, having lived most of his life there, on his "old home place" a few miles north of Shubuta on Highway 45 in the DeSoto community. In the house where he had lived all of his married life and much of his childhood, I visited him and Syble on a 1990 evening.

I began the interview by asking him how he came to be a shoemaker, how he came to cobble shoes.

"My granddaddy was a shoe fixer," he said, "and Mama said I just inherited it from him. From that I just went ahead and worked on them. I would just try to do it."

In 1941, after having done farm work as a boy, and some farming and some logging and crosstie cutting, as well as selling cars, as a man, he bought the shoe repair equipment owned by the Nettles family and located in the back of the hardware store at that store's present location, moved the equipment across Eucutta Street, and opened for the business of shoe repairs.

"I would just take the shoes and fix them. Half-soling was very easy [on] that old stitcher. That old-model pedal stitcher that is still there."

Syble injected, "During World War II, he made Edith Jones and me a pair of sandals. He just traced the outline of our foot, cut it out and put a little heel on it and made a sandal. He put some straps on it and a little buckle." Leather was hard to get, and goods were rationed during the war. The two girls were among the few who had sandals. Asked if they saved them, the reply was no. Syble's father did not normally make shoes, he only repaired them. In the 1950s, he started to buy and sell manufactured shoes.

Mr. Meeks repaired saddles and harnesses for people's riding- and work-animals, as well as shoes. He mused, "[I] worked many a night making wagon lines for people. That was a big item back then. The loggers logged with teams, mule teams. Many a night a man would come in and want some wagon lines. I stayed down there and made wagon lines for him to have to work with the next day."

What were wagon lines?

They were the lines to guide the horses or mules or oxen. On the work animal's collar, there would be "a place to run the lines through. The men would load the logs on the wagon and pull it out with oxen or mules, or one mule or ox." The driver would guide the animal by means of the leather strap lines in his hands, pulling them taut when he wanted the animal to stop, tugging to the left or right when he wanted the animal to move left or right. "They could just talk to that old ox and tell him what to do, and he would go out there and turn around and come back and pull it off." "Gee" meant pull or go to the right, "haw" pull to the left. "Ho-o-o-o!" meant stop, a version of "Whoa."

I asked Mr. Meeks about his schooling. He said he went to school in DeSoto, went to the two-teacher Oak Grove School when he was a "little fellow." He said that on the way to school he "waded knee deep in branches when they were up. Getting back home, too. We wore pants just under the knees, knickerbockers, buckled just under the knees."

"You just took off your shoes and waded through the flooded branches?"

"Sometimes didn't even take off the shoes."

At school, with all the grades together, there were not many good readers, and children who could read better would be asked to read before the whole school. Children who could work out arithmetic problems would "go up to the blackboard and work out a certain problem." He said, "I remember one day a boy said, 'Oh, Charlie Meeks is good. Get him up there to do it.'" He got it right, and "they all just clapped."

What mattered most to Mr. Meeks like many Shubuta people were work, family, and church. I asked him about his meeting his wife, Gladys Cooper Meeks, and, not surprisingly, church and family merged in his answer.

"It was at district [Methodist youth] conference up on the hill over there at Cooper's Chapel Church. I saw her come in the door. She was always prissy, anyhow. She came a-prissing in the door and sat down.... She just never could get fixed just right, didn't look like. Just kept twisting around like she wanted someone to look at her, I reckon.... I said, 'There's my gal.' So I asked for a date and she gave me a date. From then on, we just kept a-going."

They were married eight months later. "Do you remember your honeymoon?" I asked.

"Not much about it," he said. He was 26, she 24. It was 1926. They were married at her home at three o'clock in the afternoon and "had a little Ford roadster. We got in that little Ford roadster and left and went to Laurel, spent the night, and it started to rain. Rained the whole time we were on the honeymoon. Couldn't go anywhere because of the flooding. No paved roads, roads flooded everywhere. We went on down to the coast and stayed a day or two with my sister and her husband. My sister was a teacher on the coast."

For decades, Charlie Meeks was the Sunday School teacher and youth group leader for the Shubuta Methodist Church. That church and his work for it were as much his life as the shoe repair he did for his livelihood. Syble tells about his teaching the teenaged boys in Sunday School, "He taught Jim Pace, R. L. Toney, Dave Owen, that group, in Sunday School." They went places every Sunday morning. Instead of staying in the church building, he would "carry them out somewhere in the car," he said. "They would be on the fenders and everywhere else. Couldn't get in the car there were so many of them. They would be all over the car. We would go way out in the woods somewhere. Everybody would carry a lunch. Or we would go down to the underpass at the railroad on the grass or to the lake.

"Jim Pace is dead now, died real young. R. L. Toney is here in town. Dave Owen, Miss May Owen's son, is dead, too. Hyman McCarty was in that group, too. He has done real well with his chicken farms."

I met Hyman McCarty at Miss Mary Weems's funeral. "Miss Mary's" friend from the 1920s, Elsie Jones Cross, was at the funeral, too. Mrs. Cross gave me one of my best interviews for my work.

Elsie Jones Cross

My aunt Erma, who so often went with me on my Shubuta interviews, was my father's younger sister and closest sibling. She was gregarious, generous, warm, and loving, quite unlike my stern and unforgiving father in temperament and personality. One of the joys of my midlife reconciliation with my homeplace and family of origin was recovering the mother-figure support and companionship of this special aunt. The day after my mother died, a member of my brother's family took some framed embroidery works and needlepoint pieces out of my mother's home; and I, the only daughter, feeling entitled to my mother's things, had a hissy fit. My aunt Erma and I found a half-finished needlepoint piece of birds and other wildlife and a dog and a gun, obviously started for my hunter-brother; and to share in my indignation and to right the wrong we perceived had been done to me, Aunt Erma took the half-finished needlepoint work to the expert needlework artist and her close friend, 90-plus-year-old Elsie Jones Cross—"Miss Elsie"—and she finished it so expertly that one seeing it now, nicely framed on my bedroom wall, could not tell where my mother's work ends and Mrs. Cross's begins.

My aunt Erma was a great supporter of my Shubuta project. She introduced me to people and found materials for me, and she went along with me sometimes when I interviewed people. I delighted in her being my most enthusiastic supporter, and so it was quite special for her to share with me her friendship with Elsie Jones Cross and to accompany me to interview her.

On the day of the interview, I gathered up my copies of the Sanborn Fire Insurance Company maps of Shubuta from 1885, 1890, 1900, 1906, 1912, and 1926; my photocopies of numerous 1918 and 1922 issues of the Shubuta newspaper, the *Mississippi Messenger*, that had been given to me by Syble Meeks; and I headed out. I drove out to Matherville and fetched Aunt Erma in my car, and we went to Quitman, where Elsie Jones Cross lived at the time, for the interview.[9]

Elsie Jones Cross and Erma Gay Graham Mathers, both widows in their late life, had been friends for a very long time. The two women were called by almost everybody, including sometimes one another, "Miss Elsie" and "Miss Erma Gay," with that traditional respectful title in the rural South. They were 94 and 83 years old at the time of this interview; and while they lived fifteen miles apart and now seldom saw one another, they talked to each other nightly on the telephone. Elsie Cross had lived in Shubuta from 1915 to 1923 as a single young adult, some of Erma Gay Mathers's high school years, 1921 to 1925, when she lived in town with her aunt, Mollie MacPhearson. Both of them lived for most of the rest of their lives in nearby villages oriented to Shubuta as "town."

Elsie Cross lived at Langsdale for thirty-one years after her marriage to Robert Cross at 33 years old in 1928, and Shubuta was still her town for those years, since she lived only four miles east of town in the Lang House on the old Lang Plantation.

The community of Langsdale still centered around the house in which the Crosses lived, the antebellum plantation house that had been built by Clem Lang. Elsie Cross moved into the Lang House as a bride, and she and Robert Cross lived there until they retired in 1959, when they moved to the county-seat town of Quitman. In one of the rooms of the beautiful and well-kept white galleried and pillared Lang House, Elsie Cross kept the post office for Langsdale for twenty-six years.

Erma Gay Mathers lived five miles farther east beyond Langsdale from Shubuta and was the postmistress for Matherville for some of the same years Elsie Cross served in Langsdale. Her post office was in the Mathers general store next to her house, a location that had once been the commissary for the Horne Plantation begun by John H. Horne early in the nineteenth century, contemporary with the development of the Lang Plantation.[10] The villages of Langsdale and Matherville no longer have post offices. A mail carrier now comes to Langsdale on a rural route from Shubuta, and the same carrier delivers to Matherville a bag of mail made up by computerized scanning 120 miles away in Jackson, addressed to post office mail boxes in the "Matherville Branch" of the Shubuta post office.

In Matherville, the plantation house, no longer standing, was similarly grand to the Lang House and had been across the road in Matherville from

Aunt Erma's store–post office and home. Her own house was not a grand one, though one steeped in history, beginning as a one-room log building that had first been a schoolhouse and added onto several times; but the house next door to it was the fine old dwelling that had belonged to her father-in-law, Thad L. Mathers, the doctor and community leader who had given Matherville its name.[11]

His third wife, "Miss Anna," the stately and aristocratic great-granddaughter of an Alabama governor, had lived alone in that house for many years after her husband died and her sons and stepchildren had grown up. The parlor of the old Mathers house held a splendid grand piano beside which "Miss Anna" stood, elegantly white-haired and dignified in her grief, for the memorial service for her son, Leon, killed in World War II. Not long after, she welcomed to her home to live with her for a while her German-born daughter-in-law with a child from a previous marriage in pre-war Germany, the two of them by then the "war bride" and adopted daughter of another of "Miss Anna's" soldier sons, Chester. Such was the World War II domestic irony of mothers and sons: for one mother's heart, both loss of a son by wartime death and new family members from the enemy side.

Erma Gay Mathers had come to Matherville as a teacher, had married one of "Miss Anna's" stepsons, Walton Mathers, and lived there the rest of her life. Born and brought up in the Hiwannee community five miles south of Shubuta, Erma first met Elsie when Erma was a high school student and Elsie was a woman in her twenties working in the stores on the main street of Shubuta and living first with her parents and then boarding with a Shubuta family.

Later, Elsie Cross and Erma Gay Mathers were parishioners together as married women in the Geneva Presbyterian Church in Matherville. Cross, a Baptist as a child and as a young woman, joined the Presbyterian Church with her husband. Erma Gay Mathers, too, became a Presbyterian with her husband, Walton, after growing up a Methodist in Hiwannee. The two couples attended services together nearly every Sunday for at least three decades at the beautiful pine-shaded church, which was in view from the Mathers houses across a green pasture. In retirement, Elsie Cross went to a Baptist church in Quitman. Erma Mathers was in her later life, as she was for many years, a central figure of the congregation and the natural local leader of the Geneva Presbyterian Church in whose cemetery lay buried her husband, a child lost at birth, her parents-in-law, and other Mathers family members and community friends.

Elsie Jones Cross was born in Michigan in McComb County north of Detroit on 3 September 1895. Her parents, Laura Belle Broughton Jones and James Putnam Jones; her two-years-younger brother, Robert James; and she came to Mississippi with the sawmill business when Elsie was 7, first living in Meridian, then DeSoto, and then Shubuta. Elsie's father was the first cousin of John Brownlee, the Shubuta sawmill owner; and James Jones joined him in the business in 1915.

Elsie Jones, after graduating from high school in Meridian, took a six-week "normal" course, teacher-education of the time, qualified to teach, but only substitute taught one year after moving to Shubuta at age 20. After the first year, she quit her job and helped her family clear the land and build the house and barn on a 120-acre place in the country that her father had bought, the family living in the barn after it was finished. Then, she went to work in the stores, one period of time in the Hudson Drug Store in town.

When I interviewed her in Quitman more than seventy years later, she was mother of a daughter, grandmother of three people, and great-grandmother of six. When I asked her to talk with me and with her friend, my aunt Erma, about Shubuta and the years of her young adulthood she spent there in the 1910s and 1920s, she answered my questions in her rich, husky voice, typical of the sound of speech we called in my childhood "a cultured voice," a voice trained to sing or to speak with the correctness, gracefulness, and inflections of the southern upper classes. A woman of great intelligence and personal warmth, and with a remarkable memory, Elsie Cross's faculties were quite sharp after her more than 90 years. Occasionally, she had to ask me to repeat because of some hearing loss. Otherwise, she spoke right up.

"It was a happy town," Elsie Jones Cross said of Shubuta in the 1920s.

What did young adults do for fun in Shubuta in the 1920s? I wanted to know.

She talked about roller-skating. She loved to roller-skate. She said the movie theater in Shubuta had a skating floor on the second story, and the young people went there and had skating parties. There were movies shown only once a week.

Much of their recreational activity took place in families, even with young adults. They played croquet on their lawns. Sometimes the young people in groups of their peers or with their families would take walks along the railroad tracks or down to the Shubuta Cemetery, in a magnificently beautiful spot on the Chickasawhay River, as Florence Busby as well as Elsie Cross remembered. Walks were frequent year-round in the temperate Shubuta climate; and on Sunday afternoons, dressed-up families often promenaded through the tree-lined and -arched streets down to the river. Another form of recreation, especially on Sundays and in the late afternoons, was to walk down to the railway station to meet the trains when they made their stops at Shubuta or to wave to the passengers or the engineers as they went by. Near the cemetery in Elsie Cross's youth there was a sandbar large enough and suitable enough for a swimming hole launch—they weren't called beaches there in those days—and the drop into the water was not from a diving board but from a natural-growing thick and sturdy grapevine wound high in an overhanging tree.

Young people in Elsie's social class had parties where they played board games and cards. They played musical chairs. One night when her family lived out in the country, a young man, Frank Brown, got so scared playing with the Ouija board, a game that alleges to predict fate, that he was too frightened to go home. The women had card parties for a game called "42," and she was sometimes invited to go and play. Her boss at the Hudson Drug Store, Mr. Floyd Hudson, told her that she must tell him when she was asked and take the time off to go and play "42" with the ladies.

The Hudson Drug Store had a soda fountain and sold ice cream over its marble counter, and young people and families alike, especially women in groups or teenagers, would come for the soda fountain service when Elsie worked there.

Young women went to each other's homes and spent the night. Mary and Sarah Weems were good friends of Elsie's, and she spent many nights in their home. One weekend when Elsie and her family were still living in the barn on the farm, she invited her friends Sarah Weems and Mable Ulmer for the weekend. "We had the best time," she said. "We had the best time staying in the barn and . . . just wandering around in the woods."

About the elder Weemses, she remembered, "The Weemses were gracious host and hostess. We had lots of parties there, and I spent many nights there. Mary and I were real close friends. Sarah and I were together really more than Mary. Of course, the first year I was in Shubuta I had more spare time [1915, when she was 20], and Mary worked in the bank, you know. Sarah and I ran around a lot together."

I asked her what her Weems friends' mother was like.

Elsie Cross replied, "She was just real sweet. But, I would say, rather retiring. She didn't get out much, she mostly stayed in. . . . Oh, yes, Sarah brought her out to see my Elizabeth when she was a few days old. [This would be about fifteen years later.] And I never knew Mrs. Weems to visit any and I was just thrilled to death to see her."

George S. Weems, the father and bank founder, she described as "kind of gruff." She said of him, "Well, if you spent the night at his house, you had to be at the breakfast table in the morning. He'd expect to see you at the breakfast table. Then you could go back to bed or do anything you wanted to. But, he expected you at the breakfast table. So, we all had to be there."

She dated one of the Weems brothers. They and her own family had traveled by horse and buggy during her growing-up time, but she remembers that some of the Weemses were among the first people in Shubuta to have cars, her own family having gotten a Ford somewhat later, in 1920: "George and Lutie Weems [George S. Weems Jr. and his wife] had a car and his younger brother, Fred Weems, who was working away in Atlanta for the telephone company, would come home, and we would often go to Stafford Springs. There was a big hotel over there in Stafford Springs, and they served delicious meals. Sometimes a group of us from Shubuta would drive over to Stafford Springs to have a meal."

My memory is jarred pleasantly. For the first time in many years, I remember being taken to a hotel restaurant in Stafford Springs, Mississippi, as a very young girl, perhaps 10 years old, when "Miss Susie" Weems and Robert C. Weems invited me to their house to "play with" three of their visiting granddaughters and go to Stafford Springs for dinner—the noon meal universally in the South at that time—with them and the Weems's daughter, Alice.

Returning to the present and the interview from my reverie, I asked Elsie Jones Cross about the family of her birth and her father's sawmilling.

She said that even after the family had gotten their car in 1920, her father would go out into the country to his sawmill using the horse and buggy. Though the Brownlee mill in Shubuta was a stationary sawmill, her father's mill in DeSoto in the early years and later in the Shubuta area was a portable one, "one you moved to one section of land and then another, instead of it being in one place and loggers bringing all the logs there to the mill. They moved the sawmill to the timber."

I asked her if they logged with horses or mules.

She replied, "They logged with oxen when they first started. The sawmill was pulled on a wagon with oxen or an ox pulling it.... The man who did the logging for him lived in DeSoto at the time we did and he followed us. His father was a sawyer and sawed for my daddy, and they followed us to DeSoto from Vimville, way south of Meridian, and he had worked for my dad up there and then came to DeSoto and then he followed us down here."

On another day on another visit with my aunt Erma with one of her contemporaries from childhood, Norma Kettler Chapman, I was given a photograph of some sawyers in the woods with their team of oxen, the oxen's long horns prominent over their docile faces looking into the camera. In the picture "Miss Norma" gave me, the team of oxen numbers eight. They are hitched to a wagon bearing three thick logs, pictured in a woods bare of timber standing more than a few inches in diameter. With the oxen, three sawyers pose, sitting on logs at the front of the picture, their heavy jagged-toothed crosscut saw with its opposing strong handles displayed prominently between two of them. Men and oxen seem to have done their work of clearing the woods of its large trees.

I turned back to Mrs. Cross and asked her about her mother's work in the home.

"She looked after the house. We usually had someone do the washing. Once in a while we would have someone in for the day to do the cleaning. She made the bedclothes and did embroidery and crocheting, but she didn't do quilting. She made the sheets, made her clothes and my clothes until I could sew. They bought the men's clothes, but she made everything for her and for me."

I did not learn whether the Jones family had a cook, but Elsie did talk about her mother's breadmaking. Unlike most Shubutans, "we didn't have much cornbread because we were Michigan people! My mother made light-bread [what southerners call white loaf bread], you know. And biscuits. You didn't go to the store and buy bread back in those days."

Speaking of food and sleeping arrangements in discussing her boarding in the home of a Mrs. Everett when she worked in Shubuta in the 1920s, Cross said, "They served three meals a day. And when I boarded there, I slept in the room with Mrs. Everett and her daughter, Alles [this "Alles" later became the mother of my interviewee James Brewer].... Alles and her mother slept together. I had my own bed. When I moved to the Poole house, I had a room with Eleanor Fairchild, whose mother was a Poole."

Mrs. Everett and Mrs. Poole were sisters, the latter the keeper of the Poole Hotel after Elsie boarded in her home. Elsie remembered, "Mrs. Poole especially made the best angel food cake. She made apple pie. I know we had fried chicken and rice! She catered for parties, too."

I asked if they had special recipes of their own for southern foods like cornbread.

"I imagine they did," she said. "We had turnip greens and cornbread. I have a recipe that Mrs. Robert Hand gave to my mother—nut bread, I believe it was. Annie Hand."

The cookbook published by the Shubuta Parent Teacher Association in 1925 has a nut bread recipe from Mrs. A. P. Hand, "Miss Rhoda," Annie Hand's daughter-in-law. Annie Hand is represented in the book with a recipe for "Green Corn with Chicken," a kind of casserole made with chicken and fresh picked and scraped-off corn. The nut bread recipe reads, "One egg, 1 cup sugar, 1 cup milk, 1 cup raisins, 1 cup nuts, 1 teaspoon salt, 3 cups flour, 3 teaspoons baking powder. After mixing, set to rise 20 minutes; bake in slow oven from 30 to 45 minutes."[12]

Her daughter, Caroline Hand, the one who lived to be past 100 and taught schoolchildren for many years, contributed one of the fancier recipes in the book, one for "Daisy Appetizers," in which white bread is cut into the shape of daisies and hard-boiled egg-salad mixture is put on top to make open-faced sandwiches with the egg yellows for the center and the egg whites for the daisy petals. Lots of Weemses and Pooles and Heidelbergs and Pattons are included in the book, and "Mrs. Elsie Jones Cross" has a recipe for "Polish Eggs," a deep-fried eggs, cheese, and bread mixture. The recipe says, "One-half cup of grated cheese, 6 eggs beat slightly, 1 3/4 cups diced bread, 1 teaspoon minced onions, 1 teaspoon parsley, 1 tablespoon cream, 2 tablespoons shortening, 1/2 teaspoon of salt, one-eighth teaspoon pepper. Mix all together and drop by spoonful in deep hot fat. Fry until light brown."[13]

These foods represent party foods and special meals of the leading social class in the town. Elsie Cross told me about a women's club party at a much later time, sometime in the 1950s, when the building that had been the depot was moved to the town park, across the street from the ice house. Mr. Spinks at the ice house would make ice cream for the "ladies," so once when she and Nerva McCaskey were hostesses, they worked out a deal for him to come over with the ice cream when they signaled by putting a big card in the window.

Interested in other everyday-life and domestic matters of Mrs. Cross's young adulthood, I opened copies of the *Mississippi Messenger* from 1918 and asked my two wonderful old women to look at pictures of advertising and clothing. We looked at pictures of women workers in trousers. Elsie Cross thought that was for women in war work: "I guess the ladies had to do factory work while the men were in the service. Wore regular work clothes." She remembered that during World War I, "ladies would knit sweaters or scarves, afghans and things to send to the soldiers, and do things through the Red Cross. I remember I started two sweaters and somebody else had to finish them because I was knitting too tight, so couldn't get the thread off my knitting needles, so somebody finished both of them."

A funny story occurred to her from World War I Shubuta: "Let me just tell you something funny about Dr. McDevitt [who was a medical officer in the armed forces in the war]. He was always joking! He wrote his wife when he was about ready to come home from France, and he said, 'I'm bringing two kids with me.' And Mrs. McDevitt came over to our house and she was bemoaning the fact that she didn't know any French and she didn't know what she'd do with these children. And when he came home, why, it was a pair of kid gloves!"

A relative of Shubutans, Edward Phillips, wrote from "Somewhere in France, July 16, '18" during the war, on the subject of receipt of the women's

Red Cross knitting: "Mama, there is nothing you can send me the 30th of August—my 21st birthday— ... I have plenty of good, warm clothing, a Red Cross sweater, etc. While I would like a box of good eats from home, I can't get them. The French sell us a good many things, mostly, cookies and sweets, but they are high and we get plenty without having to buy from them. So don't think we are not well cared for."[14]

I turned the subject to Elsie Cross's wedding. She said, "We were married at home, at my parents' house, and had about fifty guests. [They had finished building the house while living in the barn.] I had it nicely decorated because it was Christmas time, and my neighbors had helped me decorate, and we had a little refreshment after the wedding. Annie Laura Phillips, the music teacher in Shubuta, played the piano, and Mary Weems sang solos. Sarah Weems played for her to sing. And Brother Phillips was our preacher [the Reverend J. M. Phillips, minister of the Shubuta Baptist Church, and father of Annie Laura Phillips and Oscar Phillips]. My parents and my brother were there, and my brother stood up with Robert and Virgie Smith with me. Virgie Smith was a friend of mine who came to work for Long Bell [the big lumber company in Quitman], where I was working then, in 1928 [and for five years before]. After the wedding reception was over, we went over to Laurel and spent the first night at the Pinehurst Hotel over there, and the next two nights we spent in New Orleans, and the next two in Mobile with the Brownlees. From there we went on out to Langsdale where we went to live."

"And tell me about the Lang House," I asked.

"We lived there in that house for thirty-one years, and I had the post office then. I was the postmaster there in the house. I had it in one room of the house. So I could go right out of my kitchen into the post office! The post office served around thirty families, or something like that, in the Langsdale community. And the mail carrier business was bidding and whoever bid the lowest got to carry the mail from Shubuta. The mail went from Shubuta to Langsdale, Matherville, Carmichael, and then on to Melvin, Alabama. ...

"Well, of course the house ceilings were high, twelve feet downstairs and eleven feet upstairs. On the main floor there was the living room and the dining room and the kitchen with one bedroom and a hallway all the way through. Robert's father had changed it all considerably before I went there. He had added a room that they could use for the post office, and he also had a store. And then he enclosed a south verandah that he could use as a kind of sun room. After his wife died, he moved his bed into that little sun parlor. And then there were four—three bedrooms upstairs. With the one bedroom downstairs.

"And we didn't have running water [indoor plumbing in the kitchen or bathroom]. No one had running water until way late!"

How was it decorated? Was there wallpaper?

"Plastered and painted, no wallpaper. Well, they did have a border around the top, but that was extra. Then the window facings and everything were unusual. The window facings were unusual because they were wider at the bottom than they were at the top. The front windows were from the ceiling to the floor."

I asked if her daughter was born in the Lang House.

She was and lived there all through her childhood and youth. Elsie remembered the financial details about the birth. "When my child was born, she was born at home, and I had Doctor Mathers and a midwife. Dr. Mathers charged $13 and the midwife charged a dollar a day. I guess they did the same thing in Shubuta, Dr. Hand and his father. I was amused at Dr. Albert Hand—one man and his family had a child, and they had had several children. Dr. Hand remonstrated them about having so many children, you know. Just a short time after that he [the doctor himself and his wife] had twins, and they had four children really close together!"

Asking the women to take one last look at the street map of Shubuta from 1926, I asked about the shops on the commercial block of Eucutta Street. There were the bank and the store they knew as the Rogers' store, "General Merchandise" on the map, the doctors' offices, and a cotton warehouse. South of the depot by the railroad tracks were the Shubuta Oil and Gas Company and a cotton gin. At the other end of the street was a little shop labeled "Printing," the town newspaper publisher's shop, and a blacksmith's shop, Mr. Knapp's blacksmith shop, they said. They remembered another bank, the People's Bank, and two or three dry goods stores, one owned by some people called Braswell. The hardware store was Weems and Shriver's. Then we saw the millinery shop on the map.

"Mrs. Fairchild had a millinery store," Mrs. Cross remembered.

"What kind of hats did she make?" I asked.

"Oh, I had such pretty hats," she replied, "I remember when I had one made of rose chiffon, about this big," gesturing with broadly cupped fingers, "and it had flowers on it, a pretty hat. I suppose she had some shipped in—made of straw, but she made some of them, made mine."

Did she sell lots of hats?

"Yes, most women wore hats for dress-up occasions or all of the time. We would not think of going to church or anywhere without a hat. For going to church you had to have a hat."

It was a thoroughly informative and delightful interview.

Not wearing a hat that day, or any day for a long time except for protection against the cruel Minnesota winter, I smiled happily with Elsie Jones Cross in her good memory of Mrs. Fairchild's hats, gathered up my archival newspapers and maps, and thanked her for her good conversation. Before she let me go home, though, she poured tea and served the cake that she had waiting for my aunt Erma and me.

TROPE 10: OVER THE PRAIRIE TO
MATHERVILLE WITH MY CHILDREN

Sometime late in the 1990s, I decided to sell my inherited house in the country near Shubuta. My husband was not going to retire there with me; and our children, Natasha and Stiles, both entering their thirties, soon to be married, and having moved back to Minneapolis, were not going to want to use their grandparents' Mississippi house as a vacation home or retreat place as I had for the several years since my parents' deaths. So, I sold it, and all three of my immediate family members went with me to Shubuta for the weekend just before the closing . . . to help me prepare to let it go. The Place. My place. My homeplace and my father's homeplace before me and his father's place before him and before him the place of the old Irishman who rode a white mule and had homesteaded it. That was my great-grandfather and his spunky bride, Margaret, married to him with one day's notice for leaving her Ireland home; and before the U.S. government and the Treat of Dancing Rabbit Creek, the place belonged to the Hiwannee Choctaws who followed the brave chief Yowannee.

It was May and lilies-of-the-valley and purple iris were blooming in our Minneapolis home garden, and I took lily-of-the-valley and iris cut-flowers in bags of ice on the airplane with my family along with gourmet shop delicacies and good white wine for our weekend. I had had lilies-of-the-valley in my bridal bouquet and Wilson in his lapel boutonniere for our July wedding at the Shubuta Methodist Church, flowers ordered by the florist from Quitman, but I had never seen lilies-of-the-valley growing until we moved far north to Minneapolis. Now the bulbs and their fragrant white blooms take over some of our flower beds every May. This May I made a large bouquet of them for our trip and mixed them with purple iris that some previous owner of our Minneapolis house had planted and that grow nearly wild along our north fence. We had sweet-smelling Minneapolis lilies-of-the-valley and iris all over the Mississippi house for that last weekend of mine there; and when we went to the Hebron Cemetery, where my parents and other Graham relatives are buried, and to the Matherville Cemetery, where Aunt Erma and Uncle Walton and other Matherses are buried, I took small vases of fresh flowers from my northern garden and put one on my mother's grave and one on Aunt Erma's grave.

Natasha made a tasty shrimp dish for our dinner on our first night and then late that night—or maybe it was the next night—my two adult children invited me to come outdoors in the moonlit darkness and sit cross-legged on the grass to watch fireflies with them like they had done there as children and like they knew my brother and I had done when we were children. "We used to take glass jars and punch holes in the lids," I told them for the hundredth time, "and then we would catch the 'lightning bugs' and put them in our jars and watch them light up right there in our hands. Sometimes we would take the jars of bugs indoors and to bed with us.

"The barn was over there, and the pasture for the cows was beyond it, and Daddy and Aunt Bessie would go out early in the morning and call up the cows and milk them before the rest of us got up. And some springs Carson Creek would rise so high that Daddy would have to go out in his boat on the floodwater to the pasture and get the cattle safely in with the boat.

"And I would sit outside under these trees or on this grass almost year round reading books: book after book after book after book."

Natasha and Stiles had brought out a bottle of wine and glasses for each of them and me. We sat silently drinking our wine for a while in the dark on the soft green grass out near the machine shed and the pecan tree my father had planted. My adult children were indulging me in the finest of communion. Silent tears ran down my cheeks in the darkness, tears of pure joy.

"I want to go out to Matherville tomorrow," Stiles said, "and see Aunt Erma's house." When Stiles was a small boy, Aunt Erma had allowed him to make pecan candy with her.

The car trip around Wayne and Clarke Counties the next day was not planned precisely, but it hit all the high spots, anyway: Waynesboro and the elementary school where my mother had taught the last years of her career, the consolidated high school where Mary McCarty teaches now, the successor school to the all-white one where I was not allowed to play basketball by my father because of his strict morality about girls' legs showing in front of men, but where I had been introduced to good theater and good literature by my role-model teacher Christine Hicks and had loved learning everything there was to learn, and from which I had graduated as valedictorian.

"And you were homecoming queen," my son reminded me. When they were still children, they had found my high school annuals and that was what impressed them. Truth be told: me, too.

We stopped at the Hebron Cemetery on our drive and walked around the Graham graves, James with his Confederate States of America tombstone, Margaret with no birth date, only "came from Ireland in 1850." We drove through Chapparel where some oil wells had been pumping a little wealth into the community and where the first Shubuta mayor from out in the country, Randy Waller, had been born. We looped back to the town of Shubuta and went first to the Shubuta Methodist Church.

Though we all four were dressed in most unchurch-like shorts and shirts, we went in, went into the pulpit and all around the front rows. "I sang solos from here a few times," I told them, "but I wasn't such a good musician. Public speaking and theater were more my interests. It did make a major difference in my life, though, that the minister, 'Brother Speed,' invited me to direct the girls' choir and Gary Boutwell to direct the boys' choir when he was moved to another church just before our senior year in high school.

"For our wedding, I stood there, and your dad stood there, and we had memorized our vows, which startled many people in the congregation, though they said things like, 'Wasn't that just like Gayle?'"

Wilson was wandering around at the back of the church. "This is a Rembrandt print," he commented. The plaque beside it said it was a gift of Robert C. and Suzie Nunnery Weems.

We took photographs in and around the church with our cameras and then rode on through town. I showed them the other churches in town, the business district, both the black people's and the white people's cemeteries, and some memorable houses. Then we drove on out of town. I took them down to the Hanging Bridge and told them all that I had learned about it. We drove to the bridge that was last called the Shubuta Bridge, also closed to traffic now, and then turned around and drove out the Matherville road out of town. We drove to the Lang House and I told them about the building of the house by slaves, the skill of the slaves all over the region in carpentry, and the carpentry legacy that Falconer, Lang, and McCarty black men of recent times had from the plantation slave builders. I told them about

Elsie Cross, who had lived there and kept the post office, and about my interview with her.

In some ways the most exhilarating part of the ride was the drive out to Matherville. The land between Shubuta and Matherville is a stretch of prairie with open spaces and grasses unlike the darker earth along the waterways. I told the children that we used to say we were going over the prairie to go to Aunt Erma's house. When I was a child, I thought that what "prairie" meant was "going to Aunt Erma's." I remembered that once as a very young child I was riding in the back seat of a car with Aunt Erma's mother-in-law, "Miss Anna," a University of Mississippi graduate and a very proper lady. She was very, very wrinkled and white-haired and always very correctly wore a hat, attaching it to her white hair bun with a hatpin. I must have said something wrong, though I remember the experience wholly pleasantly, for she said to me, paying close attention to me, making me think I was valued, "Gayle, you must always be respectful to an old woman with white hair and wrinkles like mine!"

As we drove on the road to Matherville, I told them about the local Choctaws, the treaties that took their land, the settlers from the seacoast white families with their black slaves, the diary of the young Evans boy who had been the first white child in the mission school for the local Indians.

I told my children about the physical geography, the history, and the people on this prairie between Shubuta and Matherville. "Do you remember laughing with Aunt Erma one time until tears ran down our faces when she told us about her friend, Mary Claire, the one who was afraid of being alone after her husband died? She pushed a big piece of furniture against her bedroom door, a chifforobe, and then it fell over one night and she could not get out of her room. She phoned Aunt Erma, who also lived alone but was known to be resourceful, to come over and try to help her get out. Mary Claire Helton was a descendant of Colonel John Horne, the owner of the large plantation that was the original founding place of Matherville.

"Colonel Horne had helped support the railroad being built through Shubuta, supplying both money and slave labor for it."

"Mom," Natasha said, "You need to get this book written really soon. It should be required reading for every school child and everybody else in the area!"

With that confirmation of the first order, I drove on to Matherville, happy in my work. The story I was telling my children is a story I have learned well enough to tell others, I was being assured. We went to the cemetery. We put the little vase of lilies-of-the-valley and iris on Aunt Erma's grave, just as we had done on my mother's at Hebron.

Hornes are buried in that cemetery at the Geneva Presbyterian Church, I continued to reminisce, as are "Miss Anna," her doctor husband after whom the village was named, their soldier son, Leon, brought home dead from World War II, and her stepson, my uncle Walton. Florence Busby remembers Leon as her brother's best friend when they were growing up and as a wonderful music-maker on the guitar.

Under the pine trees in the churchyard, their shades come and go and their living memories give us back both knowledge and love.

I can tell the story, the story of my town, and let it go. My children will remember, as will perhaps others to come. The story told will hold in memory. The Place is a place of memory, too.

Chapter 6
The New Shubuta

> *If you put* the *question to me, I hear it as, "What about* us"—...
> *living in a country we are in the difficult, thrilling process of creating. That we must create; for despite its natural resources, its sophisticated infrastructure, its advanced technology, what we want never existed for us before: a truly human society.*
>   —Nadine Gordimer, from "My New South African Identity"

Shubuta stories serve as shorthand narratives that define the town. On the face of them, the stories are accounts of a town's tri-racial past, stories of organization and explanation, stories of conflict, hatred, and lawlessness, stories of creativity and building, stories of interpretation and regret, amusement and development, stories that provide particulars of the narration of cultures, peoples, and institutions in the United States, stories that make a town. They are also stories of the damage of violence and mortal crime, as the Hanging Bridge stories show; they are stories of the power to establish and run the government and economy of a place, as the mill and bank establishment stories and "Ol' Man Weems's Nickels" show; but they are also the narration of power to name and categorize, even to decree who people have been, against all odds of probability or truthfulness, as in the sour meal stories about the Shubuta Choctaws and in the stories of slavery and racial segregation in the region.

There are the black community insider stories that Otis Bumpars told me of the 1942 lynchings of the Green and Lang boys and of the Lang boy's grieving father, Bumpars saying of the man, "He wasn't saying nothing to nobody." And white Janette Hudson's telling and judgment of that same event with her report that one boy's mother was seen around town just wringing her hands for years afterward.

While it is far too facile to say that Shubuta stories are simply racist, sexist, and elitist—some of them are that, but they are more—they are also parables of contemporary American life, each a story with a moral to it of where we have come from, where we have been. The stories of social disorder, hatred, and shame are mediated with stories of forgiveness, love, and social reformation.

Authentic Choctaw memory also lives in Shubuta alongside stories buffooning the Choctaw people. The town's name is still Choctaw, as is the name of the dark stream where even today mists rise smokelike from it early on a hot summer's morning. And the blood of Shubuta's Choctaws runs no doubt in Oklahoma families, runs mixed with the white Shubuta ancestor of James Johnston who drove Indians to Oklahoma, but stayed there, married to one.

It may be a new day for southern small towns simply because of a mass-market economy in the United States, or because of global communications and transportation systems that have moved them nearly off the map, but I believe it is truly a new day morally in Shubuta as well as in other southern towns because we know now that the stories that we tell are blended stories, shared stories of European Americans, Native Americans, and African Americans, all our past and our destinies, intricately interwoven with one another. Thus even the stories of shame, in the telling, can be transformed into shared stories of shared sorrow and thus of victory and of promise.

My interviewees were among the people who showed me the possibilities of promise as well as the records of the past. When I asked for their whereabouts in a phone call to Town Hall as I prepared the manuscript for completion I learned that Harry Laffitte was still postmaster, Clyde Brown was serving his third term as mayor, and all of the same aldermen had been re-elected at the last election. The police chief had retired and Shubuta no longer had a police chief. Cassandra Cameron had been "let go" and there was no librarian in the building across from Town Hall, though "two or three" had succeeded her, and a search was being conducted for a new one. Meals were being served at the Nutrition Center by a new person, Almeda Clark.

The current population of Shubuta was 675.

Mary McCarty, Cleo Powe Cooper, Janette Hudson, Phyllis and James Johnston, and Patsy and R. L. Toney among my interviewees still lived in Shubuta and were active in town life. Linda McInnis and her husband had moved to an assisted-living residence in Waynesboro, and Florence Busby was reported to spend most of her time in Atlanta with her children.[1]

Nothing has changed and everything has changed. McCartys and Coopers and Toneys and Johnstons still get their mail at the Shubuta post office.

New Shubuta stories from the recent past still tell of pride in place but they also tell of hope for a wider vision and a better world. They can be like the fiction that Eudora Welty writes about in *The Eye of the Story,* where "something happened" in "the heart's field."[2]

The Firehouse Christmas Program

My story of the Firehouse Christmas Sing-Along is one indicator of the new Shubuta. As Otis Bumpars said, "After the desegregation and everything, things got a lot better." It is in some ways a typical story and a reminder of the ambiguity of the end of legal separation of white and black people in a small U.S. southern town. Nothing is ever quite settled. The lines between right and wrong, good and bad, black and white are far more often blurred and windingey rather than straight. This is one of the many things I learned in my 1990s Shubuta journey seeking knowledge.

When I first went back to Shubuta as a researcher, I carried with me the memories of thoroughgoing racial segregation, which had been absolute well through my college years up to 1961. Now the reality of desegregation is a whole generation past. However, before the legal and social changes of the 1970s that followed the 1960s civil rights movement when I was already an adult, public schools in the U.S. South were funded separately for white and black children. Shubuta had two public schools, just as it had two cemeteries in the town, and in those public schools teachers and principals, all black at the black school and all white at the white school, both prayed at the beginning of the school day, just as they led their pupils in the Pledge of Allegiance to the U.S. flag. School prayer, the pledge to the flag, and racial segregation were all both legal and customary in the United States. A generation ago in Shubuta when the adult black people were not full-fledged citizens, and were not allowed to register to vote or to serve on juries, it was unthinkable that one might hold office. A generation ago black people were required to enter through back doors of public buildings.

Today, though some of them are sent to private white academies, the children of Shubuta, black and white together, are bused to the public school in the county seat town, Quitman; and black Cassandra Cameron held the keys to the public building that houses the library and seniors center through several years of the 1990s. Today Mayor Clyde Brown is black, the recently retired chief of police and the postmaster are black; but all of the town's churches are made up of congregations that are either all black or all white. Public life is desegregated. Some private life, however, especially collective religious worship, is largely segregated still.

When I returned to Shubuta to work on my research, I attended worship services in the sanctuary of my beloved Shubuta United Methodist Church. In my lifetime, the national denomination had merged with the Evangelical United Brethren Church and changed its name from the Methodist Church to the United Methodist Church, but the Shubuta congregation had shrunk considerably from my teenaged years of intense involvement there. I remembered the time my husband and I were home from Boston for a summer vacation visit to my parents after we had served as directors of a civil rights movement voter registration project in Nashville and how apprehensive we felt when my mother told me warily, as if not even connecting our efforts and commitments with what she was telling, that "some of those outsiders stirring up trouble" might bring "some Nigrahs" to our church that Sunday morning. My husband and I worried with one another. Should we just stay home from church? Or should we go and be prepared, as our conscience would require, to walk out of church to demonstrate with the civil rights leaders against the church holding my parents and all those Johnstons and Toneys, Weemses and Hands, Stanleys and Meekses and Hudsons who had known me all my life and had celebrated our wedding with us in that church and given us wedding presents and parties in a very recent summer? No outsiders came, so we were not put to the test.

On Sunday morning, 17 December 1989, the third Sunday in Advent, when I was sitting in church about twenty-five years after that time of worry, Dr. Shaw Gaddy announced from the pulpit of that same Shubuta church that there would be a community sing-along that afternoon at the town firehouse, that choirs from all the churches in and around Shubuta would be singing, and that we were all invited to come. This public program was being announced in all the churches in and around town.

I attended the program that afternoon and saw strikingly demonstrated the new ambiguity of public and private racial connection after the end of segregation in this annual Shubuta public town event. It was also a fascinating lesson in the melding of the public and the religious values and expectations of one community.

Now, Shubuta had no fire truck for a long time, and the corrugated metal building, built in the hopes of acquiring one, has big sliding garage doors and resembles a truck stop more than a public building. It contrasts considerably in style and taste with the two nineteenth-century church buildings at the center of town. The Christmas program, too, had little resemblance to what is usually an American public event.

And what was the town Christmas program? In a United States agonizing over prayer in the public schools, skeptical of public displays of religion, and in a mood to interpret the constitutional separation of church and state to mean the absence of religious expression in public places, in Shubuta, Mississippi, the town Christmas program in the town firehouse was church choirs singing hymns and music of the Christian Nativity. Gathered in the firehouse, sitting and standing, black and white people were together, mingled, but the performers were racially separate. The program was introduced by Randy Waller, the mayor, sitting in his wheelchair, and was in every way a civic event—held in a town building, scheduled by the town offices, introduced by the mayor. The program was also one wholly of Christmas music, hymns, carols, and choral specials. The church choirs of the Tribulation Baptist Church, black, the Shubuta Baptist Church, white, the New Mount Zion United Methodist Church, black, the Saint Matthew Baptist Church, black, and the Assembly of God Church, white, each sang for the town program.

The people were all in one room, familiar with one another, friendly, conversing, sitting down together, and having a good time, but they sang separately, church choir by church choir.

The Last of the Shubuta Weemses: Miss Mary Weems's Funeral

On a chilly February day in 1992, Hyman McCarty was at Miss Mary Weems's funeral at the Shubuta United Methodist Church and at the graveside service in the Shubuta Cemetery that followed it. The tribute he paid her in life of the half-million dollar scholarship fund for Millsaps College in her honor, which he had come to Shubuta to her eightieth birthday party and announced, he continued by his respectful presence at her funeral, which was held in the 150-year-old church in which both of them had grown up and been shaped in their values of religion, education, and ethics.

Mary Sue Mitchell, Mary Weems's great-niece, Chip's mother, had come from Jackson and helped arrange "Auntie's" funeral. Mary Weems's niece, Sue, was there, as well as other representatives of three generations of the Weems family, none of them from Shubuta. Mary's friend of her youth, Elsie Jones Cross, came with a companion from Quitman. Women of the church had prepared a lunch in the fellowship hall of the church building with the tables decorated with winter red-blossoming branches of flowering quince shrub.

The formal Methodist funeral service was conducted by the Reverend Dr. Gaddy in full clerical garb and was in the same sanctuary where infant "Mary Virginia Weems Jr." had been christened by Bishop Charles Betts Galloway. There were about twenty people in attendance.

The small number attending the service signifies quite powerfully the closing of an era that was marked by Mary Weems's death. Laws have changed, customs and practices have changed, business and communications and education have changed, even culture and people have changed.

Even more significant a meaning was conveyed by the visitation the previous day at the Freeman Funeral Home on Skyline Drive in Waynesboro. Mary Weems had been brought up in a time when bodies were prepared for burial in the family home by women of the community. As an adult living in Shubuta, she had been very familiar with the substantial historical home on North Street, "Silk Stocking Row," that served as Will Patton's funeral parlor and where family and community members sat attending the body around the clock before a burial service. At the end of her own life, Mary Weems's body's preparation for burial having been out of a commercial mortuary in the next larger town is an indicator of how greatly the times have changed and the people with them.

Janette Hudson had phoned me to tell me the visitation would be from three o'clock until nine o'clock p.m. I drove to Waynesboro about six o'clock, thinking I would see many people as they came and went paying their respects. When I went into the funeral home, I learned that there were two parlors where bodies lay for reviewal, Mary Weems's being in the back parlor.

There were busy comings and goings and a buzz of conversations in the front of the building, the hallways and beside the front parlor. The deceased there was a grandmother from a large family out in the country. When I went down the hall and approached the back parlor, I realized it was much quieter, and then when I entered the room, I was shocked. Save for the body of Mary V. Weems and me, there was nobody there.

Great-Niece Sally

The Weems money and Weems descendants, as well as the effects of Weems generosity like the scholarship fund set up by Hyman McCarty, are literally spread all over the United States. The last Robert C. Weems, the one born in 1910 to "Mr. Bob" and "Miss Suzie," who wrote of putting up signs saying "Your Money is Safe in this Bank" for the family Bank of Shubuta with his father only to have hunters use them for target practice, lives in Reno, Nevada. His sister, Gin, lives in Gig Harbor, Washington. One great-great-great-granddaughter of the bank founder, Gin's granddaughter, lives on Lake Minnetonka in Minnesota. The one of her female cousins who went to the Kennedy School of Government at Harvard, Sally Kay Mitchell, now lives in Los Angeles. None of them lives in Shubuta, though some live in Jackson. One of them is Sally McDonnell Barksdale, chip off the old philanthropic block.

Sally and her husband, Jim Barksdale, former CEO of the computer Web-browser company Netscape who sold it to America Online, are pictured and featured in an issue of *Newsweek* on "The New Philanthropists." The picture is a gorgeous half-page image with Sally at the center, Jim beside her, half a dozen young black children gathered around in a Jackson schoolroom of Lee Elementary School, everyone laughing, with a red-covered book of *The Town Mouse and the Country Mouse* in Sally and Jim's hands. The text tells that the children have been reading aloud, everyone in turn, with the Barksdales coaching on enunciation and inflection and the occasional missed word. The article describes how the Barksdales chose thoughtfully, after Jim sold his company, to establish a foundation where they could provide hands-on service to fill a significant need in the state of Mississippi. They decided that literacy and a comprehensive reading program could serve people better than anything they could think of, so they established a $100 million endowment to advance literacy in Mississippi. Their effort with the problem is not just giving money, however. They regularly go into elementary schools and read with children, as they were pictured doing in *Newsweek*.[3]

While the press's emphasis is on entrepreneurial Jim Barksdale's money and initiative, I am quite certain that Sally's Weems relatives and ancestors prepared the way for Sally Barksdale to be a full partner in the literacy initiative. And I am told by his mother that Sally's nephew, Chip Mitchell, archivist of "Auntie's trunk," now a University of Virginia history graduate, works for the Barksdale foundation in Oxford, Mississippi.

Toney Hunting Camps

While there are no Weems descendants living in Shubuta after "Miss Mary's" departure and subsequent death, another of Shubuta's affluent families, the Toneys, do have members who live in Shubuta still, and they enjoy both their family business and the recreation that the Shubuta area affords in hunting and fishing.

Patsy Toney drove me through all of Shubuta and out and about in the vicinity of town more than once. One time she and Florence Busby drove me around to see all the businesses that operate in Shubuta and also to see housing developments on the roads running out into the country. Another time she responded to my request to see the country churches located in the rural area near town. Once she took me to meet some members of the medical board she chaired, the Outreach Medical Services, a U.S. government program that supports the clinic in Shubuta. One of them was Mary McCarty, another was Suzie Shirley.

At Suzie Shirley's house, Leon Shirley, Suzie's husband, and two other men came in from having hunted all day. They had been hunting deer but hadn't killed anything.

This led Patsy Toney to think about hunting, so when we got back into her car, she took me to see hunting camps in the woods around Shubuta.

These would be the Toney Woods, akin to Morgan's Woods in Eudora Welty's fictional Morgana. Landowners' woods good for hunting around Shubuta would include the Jones Woods, the Atkinson Woods, or the Stanley Woods—though in Shubuta the woods would more likely be called "the place"—the Toney Place, Aubrey Jones's Place, and the like.

Patsy told me that their hunting was very important recreation for the Toney men and their friends who were invited weekends to come from all over and also to the black people "who lived around the place." Saying we were riding in her car instead of mine because it "knows the way," she commented on how much hunting was enjoyed by a great many people in the community. We drove by a grouping of homes belonging to a black family named McDonald, and she said that when the father in the family became ill he said, "Oh, now I can't go hunting with the Toneys!"

Patsy Toney was a Baker from Brandon, Mississippi, before she married R. L. "Tuddy" Toney and came to live with him in Shubuta. R. L., whose initials stand for Robert Lee after the Confederate general, is the younger son of J. E. "Jake" Toney Sr., whose family came to Shubuta from Franklinton, Virginia, in 1910 and who founded the Shubuta Tie and Timber Company in 1919, the business still in operation. The family business supplied an extensive market for railroad track crossties and other wood products for many years and continues to thrive as a woodyard, shipping pulpwood and other logs and lumber from its location beside the Shubuta railroad tracks. J. E. Toney Sr. ran the business until his death in 1945. R. L.'s older brother, J. E. Toney Jr., was also in the business and lived in Shubuta with his family until his death in 1958. There is a fresh 1998 grave in the Shubuta Cemetery for "Little Jake," son of J. E. Toney Jr. Patsy and R. L.'s three sons are named Buddy (R. L. Jr.), Brad (Tracy Bradford), and Barry (Barry Stuart).

The Toney men loved to hunt, and as their numbers grew and new generations came, they established campsites and deer stands, along with club organizations for hunting, as other men in the area do. In fact, some property is now bought and hunting lodges built for using the land for recreational hunting only. The clubs are both sites on woodland properties and membership groups. The Toney club members are from a circle of friends and relatives of both R. L. Toney and his older brother, Jake.

Once Patsy Toney took me to a trailer house cabin on one property that was not a clubhouse but a young man's home at the time. He had a feeding station with ears of dried corn out for deer very near the home. Two other cabins in the woods Patsy and I drove to are clubhouses for the deer hunters, one a "boys' camp," and another where the women go, too, and stay with the men sometimes. At different times she took me to each of them, first to the "boys' camp" with its lined-up cots and bunk beds dormitory style and with its pin-ups of buxom female persons on the wall and the refrigerator door. In the hunting camps, the men typically do their own cooking. Over at the camp where the women are invited, more comfort and domesticity is evident—couches and curtains and dishes and glasses, as well as a lovely water view of the pond on which it sits.

The day of our stop by the Shirley house was a cold winter day and the last day of hunting season. Patsy and I drove out to still another campsite where the men had a big campfire going in an old oil drum. No hunting paraphernalia was in sight. Rather, they were busy warming their hands and generally trying to keep warm. But, no hurry. Warmth was more important than hunting deer that particular day. Camaraderie in the woods was the real point.

Shubuta News from the Senior Nutrition Center, Cleo Powe Cooper and Cassandra Cameron

On two different Shubuta visits in 1997, 16 January and 8, 9, and 10 December, as I had several times over the decade, I sat through their lunch time and talked with the Shubutans who come to the Senior Nutrition Center in the small room attached to the library at the back of the building. I saw Cassandra Cameron who oversaw the food program along with the library at that time and I rode along with Cleo Cooper as she drove her route delivering the meals, as she did each day.

The black man who brought in the containers of food was named Green, and I wondered if the boy killed at the Hanging Bridge was one of his relatives, but I did not ask.

At the food service, available to Shubuta's older people, poor and well-off alike, there are culturally automatic gender, racial, and religious behaviors.

There were regulars present, about fourteen to sixteen people each time, all of them white, who sat at a women's table and a men's table in the room at the nutrition center, among them Kathleen Stallings, Linda McInnis, Alton B. Miller, Jeff Kettler, and Mark Mason. When Cassandra finished putting the food on the hot trays, the women all got up and put on plastic gloves and served the plates with Cassandra, assembly-line style. Everyone waited until all the plates were served and a prayer had been said before beginning to eat.

Mark Mason was the one asked to "say the blessing." Mason, a retired military officer, is among the town's most financially secure; and he and his wife live in the "old Ben Evans house," one of the best houses in town. He said his wife was not there because she was preparing to entertain her Sunday School class for the Shubuta Baptist Church.

At the tables the people laughed and joked with each other companionably, some teasing about the fact that one of the women helping to serve had almost put gravy on the rice pudding dessert. "Well, it is just plain white like plain rice," she laughed in her defense.

One of the days that I rode with Cleo Cooper to deliver meals, she pointed out other people's houses on our way. By then some of them were already familiar to me. Taking pride in the reelection of Clyde Brown, the first black mayor, she showed me his house as we drove by, a modest brick home in the north section of town. Another similar house she pointed out as "our police chief's house." She reminded me that both these officers, as well as the postmaster, are African Americans. She shared town news with me as we drove along, an item of which was that Mary McCarty was up in Tupelo that day, accompanying Oseola McCarty on a book signing for *Simple Wisdom for Rich Living*.

Linda McInnis was not well that day, so Cleo Cooper drove up to her back door on Eucutta Street to deliver her food, "dinner," the noon meal. Mrs. McInnis was glad to see me along with Mrs. Cooper, and she told me that she was rooting some cuttings from the gardenia plant I gave her on a previous visit.

Another stop on the route was Pearlie Hosie's house, and Mrs. Hosie came out to the car and handed Mrs. Cooper some money for the food. Some other recipients did not seem to be paying, suggesting that the food program is free to those who cannot pay and the food is paid for by those who can.

One black woman named Howze gets dressed up every day to greet Mrs. Cooper when she brings the dinner, Mrs. Cooper told me. That day was a relatively warm December day, about 60 degrees Fahrenheit, and Mrs. Howze came out to the car in a knit blouse and neat and attractive cotton culottes. Both Mrs. Cooper and Mrs. Howze had on knit caps on this warm December day, Mrs. Howze's a bright, almost luminous, chartreuse, probably hand knitted.

Mrs. Cooper told me about the conditions of some of the other people as we drove to deliver the food—this one confined to bed, this one on some kind of machine, this one not able to see in one eye, one woman's son "seventy-years-old and only able to lie on his stomach his whole life." We passed many trailer houses and modest homes, some near dilapidation, but all of them—and this was winter—had lovely plantings in front, flowers still blooming; shrubs with deep greens, red berries, and colorful seed pods; and ornamental grasses, reminding me collectively of Alice Walker's tribute to her own black mother and grandmothers, "In Search of Our Mothers' Gardens," where she said they were women who made beauty with flower-growing and courageous lives at homes where there were many limits. The same could be said as well of these Shubuta women's gardens.

Behind one trailer home a row of collards grew with a row of white plastic bottles like Clorox bottles put up behind them. Cleo said that kept the deer away—the collards taste good to deer like they do to people, she surmised.

Cleo, the generation of grandmothers to Cassandra Cameron, asked me if I knew that Cassandra had had a baby that October. I did not, but I did know of her wedding from a previous visit with her back in January.

At the January visit, Cassandra had asked me if I wanted to see the pictures from her wedding. Yes, I said, I love wedding pictures! She said she had married Dewey Shope in November of 1996, and there they all were in the wedding pictures: Cassandra in a tea-length lace gown with a full train and a matching headpiece, bridesmaids in turquoise dresses, the groom in formal whites, the best man and other men in the wedding party in black, Cassandra's 3-year-old serving as flower girl, her daughter at 13 a member of the wedding party, the Tribulation Baptist Church decorated with flowers and blue and white candles, the groom keeling before the bride, taking off her garter.

The groom in the pictures is a fair-complexioned redhead. Cassandra Cameron had married a white man.

A New Federal Post Office Building Rises

In April of 1999, a new United States Post Office building was opened in Shubuta. I visited it on 19 April that year. Harry A. Laffitte, an African American man who has been Shubuta postmaster since 1996, was the person behind acquiring the new building. He said that working conditions in the old space had become impossible, that many springs when there was flooding there would be standing water a foot high in the back of the building. The street-level old space was in a privately owned connected store building on Eucutta Street for which the U.S. Postal Service had paid the Waynesboro owner $600.00 per month rental since 1968.[4]

The new building on Highway 45, just around the corner and across the street from the old one, is free-standing and has its own parking lot. Like many U.S. Postal facilities, Harry Laffitte explained, this building was built by a private contractor and leased by the federal government. The lot was bought from the Methodist Church next door, a lot where a house known as the Spinks house had stood.

Laffitte was justifiably proud of his new building, and on the day I visited with him the week after the building opened, several people came in to do postal business—to buy stamps, mail packages, or collect their mail with their new keys to their new mailboxes. I met the assistant post officer, Rhonda Davis, and Florence Busby drove up and came in to mail some letters. We greeted one another and commented on how pleasant the new building is.

At a lull in his business at the counter, Laffitte explained to me that the Shubuta operation is a regional one and that this post office is a consolidation of those from Carmichael, Matherville, and Langsdale with the Shubuta one. Regional mail carriers go out on routes from this facility each day, one more than one hundred miles, one sixty-nine miles and expanding, one south into Wayne County, and one east all the way to Melvin, Alabama.

The new post office building is perhaps a good image for the new Shubuta at the turn of the twenty-first century, indicating that the culture of the town is now national rather than local. It sits on Highway 45, the new "Main Street" and also the only road through town that is a federal highway. Customers can readily come there in their cars and park, as Americans do all over the country at shopping malls and post offices. It sits across the street from the Shubuta Kwik Stop, a convenience store with gasoline pumps, and the Southeast Mississippi Bank, which is the long-ago merged branch of the successor bank to the Bank of Shubuta founded by George S. Weems.

In many a small town in the United States, the only agency of the federal government is the United States Post Office, the only federal officer, the postmaster. Thus, by office, Harry Laffitte is the nation's chief representative in Shubuta. Yet, this officer and the institution he presides over are the same in communities all over the country, major and medium-sized cities, neighborhoods, villages, and towns. The services are the same, the creatively designed postage stamps sold are identical, the organization the same.

With a new post office building as its emblem, Shubuta heads into the twenty-first century alive and well. With the 1849 establishment of the United States Post Office being the first signal of official government recognition of Shubuta—the town was not chartered until 1867 by the State of Mississippi—how fitting it is that the U.S. Post Office is the signifier of Shubuta once again serving as a regional center in the new century!

Shubuta has changed, diminished in some ways, certainly lost much of its local focus. It has lost some fine old buildings and all its schools. Most local businesses have been replaced by chain or regional ones. It has changed demographically, town and country, black and white, in some ways. Shubuta has scattered sons and daughters all over the United States and to some extent the world and it has kept fewer at home. It has embraced all its citizens with the rights to vote, to hold office, and to function freely socially and economically under the law. It has seen new buildings go up and has sent its children on buses to larger, consolidated schools. It has participated in government programs, local, state, and federal, for medical services, library services, and programs for its poor and elderly. Its population, though changing in some make-up, has remained in the range of 500 to 650 for several decades; and numerous people have not ever moved out of Shubuta for their entire lives.

Yet, the Chickasawhay River still runs the same on the east side of town and forks away into Shubuta Creek, where the dark mist still curls up as it did when only the Choctaws knew this land. The river and the town and the stars in the sky are still there, but a new post office building has risen on Highway 45. Shubuta has changed and changed and changed, but Shubuta has been the same, too, for well over a hundred and fifty years. Shubuta is a beautiful town, beautiful town, beautiful town. Ugly town, too. Shubuta is a beautiful town. Home. Homeplace. Home.

Notes

Introduction: Beautiful Town . . . Ugly Town

1. *Shubuta, Mississippi: Area Profile, 1991*, pamphlet compiled by the Mississippi Department of Economic and Community Development, 1. Also, *Shubuta, Mississippi, Clarke County, Mississippi*, Community Profile pamphlet (Quitman, Miss.: Chamber of Commerce, n.d. [about 1990]); Diane Brown, telephone conversation with author, 7 Dec. 2001, Shubuta Town Hall; *Clarke County Mississippi, 1926*, pamphlet (n.d., n.p.), from the personal archives of Aubrey Jones. Also, Aubrey Jones tape and "Shubuta, 120 Years Old," *Clarion Ledger–Jackson Daily News*, cited in the Notes on Sources.

2. Helen Phillips, letter to the author, 21 April 1990, 3; "The Victory, Thanksgiving and Business" advertisement, *(Shubuta) Mississippi Messenger*, 22 Nov. 1918, n.p.; "Mr. Ed Graves Celebrates 108th Birthday, Laurel, Miss.," *Impact*, 31 July 1996, 1, clipping provided by James Johnston. Trading in Shubuta is also discussed on the audiotape on Shubuta made by Aubrey Jones and in a letter to the author by Helen Phillips, Meridian, Miss., 21 April 1990.

3. "The Victory, Thanksgiving and Business" advertisement.

4. William Thomas Sellers, conversation with the author, 10 Dec. 1997, Shubuta Senior Nutrition Center.

5. "Diary of Annie Ruth Johnston on a Trip to the Tropics during the Summer of 1928," 23, carbon-copied typescript of a thirty-seven-page manuscript from the Weems family archives saved from "Auntie's trunk" in Shubuta, the possessions of Mary V. Weems, by Don Allan "Chip" Mitchell and used by permission of Mary Sue Mitchell (archives hereinafter cited as "Auntie's trunk").

6. Janette J. Hudson, "Shubuta United Methodist Church, Homecoming, 1987," mimeographed seventeen-page booklet produced by the church.

7. "My Graduation Journal," Shubuta, Miss., 1925.

8. Frank L[edyard] Walton, *Shubuta: On the Banks of the Chickasawhay* (Shubuta, Miss.: Shubuta Memorial Association, 1947); "Festivities Begin Shubuta Bicentennial," *Wayne County News*, 1 May 1975, sec. A, pp. 1, 9; *Mississippi Messenger*, 2 Aug. 1918, ad, p. 5 ("Local News"). While I have no memory of a newspaper in Shubuta, the *Mississippi Messenger* was a daily paper, begun in 1879, edited by C. A. Stovall, and was a thriving enterprise for several decades. Syble Meeks gave me a large number of copies from 1918, 1920, and 1922.

9. Helen Phillips letter, 2.

10. Obituary, "Mrs. Elsie Jones Cross," *Tuscaloosa News*, 18 Feb. 1999, n.p., clipping from her daughter, Elizabeth Cross McLeod.

11. "Financial Statement, Town of Shubuta," *Mississippi Messenger*, 18 Oct. 1918, p. 4.
12. Bob Weems, e-mail message to author, 26 May 1999.

Trope 2: Auntie's Trunk

1. His official name is Don Allan Mitchell. His Shubuta genealogy is son of Mary Sue McDonnell Mitchell, eldest daughter of Alice Weems McDonnell, daughter of Shubutans Suzie Nunnery Vaughan Weems and Robert C. Weems, oldest son of Shubuta bank founder George S. Weems and Mary Virginia Hand Weems; "Fire Levels Shubuta Landmark Friday," *Clarke County Tribune*, 24 May 1989, n.p., clipping from "Shubuta" file, Mississippi State Department of Archives and History, Jackson, Miss.; information from Mary Sue Mitchell and Don Allan Mitchell interview, 7 Sept. 1990, from informal discussion with Mary Virginia "Gin" Weems French, 16 Nov. 1998, Fox Island, Wash., from e-mail to author from Robert [C.] Weems, 26 May 1999, and from Robert C. Weems, "The Weems Families of Shubuta," four-page typescript memoir, Reno, Nev., 4 Aug. 1996.
2. Twelfth Census of the United States, Schedule No. 1: Population, Clarke County, Mississippi, Beat 2, Shubuta town, Arthur R. Shumaker, Enumerator, 26 June 1900, Sheet No. 20.

Chapter 1: Shubuta's People

1. "By W. H. Patton" [Early Shubuta], one-page typescript from "Auntie's trunk."
2. Lisa Spencer, "A Sociological Oral History of Clarke County, Mississippi," including cassette-tape interviews (M.A. thesis, Mississippi Oral History Project of the University of Southern Mississippi, 1987), 42.
3. Ibid., 65–66.
4. Ninth Census of the United States. Inhabitants of 2 District of Clarke Co., Mississippi, 22 Day of June 1870, 27–37.
5. Ibid., 101.
6. Ibid., 102.
7. Program for Closing Exercises, Shubuta Male and Female Academy, Wednesday Evening, 30 June 1880, single sheet from Phillips Family Archive, Shubuta Public Library.
8. Twelfth Census of the United States, Schedule No. 1: Population, Clarke County, Mississippi, Beat 2, Shubuta town, Arthur R. Shumaker, Enumerator, 26 June 1900, Sheet No. 17.
9. 1900 Census, Sheet No. 18; "Shubuta" subject file, Mississippi State Department of Archives and History Library, Jackson, Miss., archived typescript for entry in *WPA County History for Clarke County, Mississippi*.
10. 1900 Census, Sheet No. 20; Shubuta Institute and Military Academy Catalogue, 1899–1900, and Prospectus, 1900–1901 (Brandon, Miss.: E. B. Tabor, Book and Job Printer, 1900), 20, photocopy from the personal archives of Aubrey Jones.

11. 1900 Census, Sheet No. 20.
12. "Dr. Robert McLain Hand," in Robert Stephens Hand and Thomas Edwards Hand, *Handbook-2: Descendants of Obadiah Hand (1760–1837), Sixth Generation in America* (Decorah, Iowa: Anundsen Publishing Co., 1987), n.p., Biography ID # 127.
13. 1900 Census, Sheet No. 20.
14. "Bank and Oil Mill for Shubuta. Shubuta Oil and Manufacturing Co. Shubuta Bank," clipping dated in ink, 1902, in the Phillips scrapbook, n.p., Phillips Family Archive, Shubuta Public Library.
15. "George Stephenson Weems Sr.," in Hand and Hand, *Handbook,* Biography ID #137, p. 1.
16. "Bank and Oil Mill" clipping, Phillips scrapbook.
17. Ibid.
18. Ibid.
19. Ibid.
20. Gradie Pearl Dansby, "From the Rocking Chair: Another Safe Story," *Clarke County Tribune,* 9 Dec. 1987, n.p., Society section, clipping from archives of Nerva McCaskey.
21. Ibid.
22. "George Stephenson Weems Sr.," in Hand and Hand, *Handbook,* Biography ID #137.
23. Otis Bumpars, interview with author, 30 April 1996, Shubuta.
24. Aubrey Jones on tape about "Shubuta."
25. Information in this section comes from Rosalie Primm, "Antebellum Homes: Hand House Recovering From Neglect," *Clarke County Tribune,* 23 April 1981, n.p., and "Hand House," Historic Sites Survey, No. 29, State of Mississippi Department of Archives and History, Shubuta files; "William Brevard Hand," Martindale Hubble Legal Directory, www.martindale.com; site visit and photographs in Shubuta with Patsy Toney; and Hand and Hand, *Handbook.* In occasional variations of dates, numbers, and names in my sources, I took the *Handbook* genealogy as authoritative. For example, the county newspaper article said Annie and Robert Hand had eight children, their grandsons' book that they had seven.
26. All information and quotations in this section from Cleo D. Powe Cooper interviews with the author, 30 April and 28 May 1996, and subsequent informal visits including 5 Nov. 1998.
27. Rick Bragg, "All She Has, $150,000, Is Going to a University," *New York Times,* 13 Aug. 1995, pp. 1, 11.
28. Ibid.
29. Atlanta: Longstreet Press, 1996.
30. Quotation and subsequent ones from Mary McCarty interviews with the author, 16 Jan. and 10 Dec. 1997.
31. New York: Basic Books, 1996. Other studies document the reverse black migration from the North back to the South. One is Nicholas Lemann, *The Promised Land: The Great Black Migration and How It Changed America* (New York: Vintage Books, 1992).

Newspaper reports of them include Haya El Nasser, "Southern roots pulling many blacks home," *USA Today,* 24 Feb. 1997, sec. A., p. 4, and Associated Press, "Black migration has reversed—toward South," *Minneapolis Star Tribune,* 29 Jan. 1998, sec. A, p. 4.

32. Mary McCarty, interviews with the author, 16 Jan., 10 Dec. 1997, and a subsequent informal visit 16 April 1999.

33. "H. F. McCarty: Caring Leader, Generous Benefactor," *Millsaps Magazine* (summer 1998): 28.

34. R. C. Weems to Mary Sue McDonnell, 8 May 1963.

35. R. C. Weems to Mary Sue McDonnell, 9 Dec. 1963.

36. R. C. Weems to Mary Sue McDonnell, 18 July 1964.

37. R. C. Weems to Mary Sue McDonnell Mitchell, 6 Sept. 1963, 22 Feb. 1965, 16 May 1968.

38. Shubuta Institute and Military Academy Catalogue, 1899–1900, and Prospectus, 1900–1901; James and Phyllis Johnston, interview with author, 30 April 1996; A. Johnston, "History of the Johnston Family" (seven-page typescript); "Percy Walker Johnston," in *Mississippi—A History,* ed. George H. Ethridge, historical, and Walter N. Taylor, biographical, pp. 1869–70, n.d., photocopy in family archives of James Johnston.

Chapter 2: Shubuta's History

1. "Experts say canoe may be 300 years old," *Wayne County News,* 29 Aug. 1985, n.p.; "Mysterious River Craft Exhibited in Shubuta," *Clarke County Tribune,* 22 Aug. 1985, n.p., clippings in "Shubuta" file, Mississippi State Department of Archives and History Library.

2. John H. Evans, "Reminiscences of Olden Times, 1809–1850" (photocopy of twenty-four-page typescript copy of a memoir from the East Mississippi Regional Library, Quitman, Miss.), 2–4; James Brewer, interview with author; Janette Hudson, interview with author; "The Pettis House," *Clarke County Tribune,* 30 Oct. 1980, n.p., clipping in "Shubuta" file, Mississippi Department of Archives and History; Aubrey Jones tape; Evans memoir.

3. James Brewer interview; Evans memoir, 7.

4. James Johnston interview.

5. Peter J. Hamilton, "The Yowanne, or Hiowanni, Indians," *Publications of the Mississippi Historical Society* 6 (1902): 408–9. Also, James F. Brieger, "Hometown Mississippi" (typescript compilation of place-names found in the East Mississippi Regional Library, Quitman, Miss., n.d.), 527.

6. "Experts say canoe," *Wayne County News,* "Mysterious River Craft Exhibited in Shubuta," *Clarke County Tribune.*

7. Charles H. Cole IV, "The Chickasawhay Country—The Story of Wayne County in Facts and Legends" (photocopy of thirty-eight-page typescript, in Waynesboro Public Library, Waynesboro, Miss.), 3.

8. Map Book 1, Chancery Clerk's Office, Wayne County Courthouse, Waynesboro, Miss.; Hamilton, "Yowanne," 408–9.

9. Walton, *Shubuta*, 10.

10. Ibid.

11. Mary Frances Bass, "A Study of Place-Names of Clarke County, Mississippi" (M.A. thesis, University of Alabama, 1941), 84–85. Her source is cited as: "Rowland, op. cit., Vol. II, 664"; Files, *C.[larke] Co. Tribune*, 29 Sept. 1933.

12. From James Johnston interview.

13. Bass, "A Study of Place-Names," 85. Her source is cited as: "Rowland, op. cit., Vol. II, 664"; Files, *C.[larke] Co. Tribune*, 29 Sept. 1933.

14. Clarke County Tax Assessor's Office, Tax Records of Deeds, Registration of Deeds, Clarke County Court House, Quitman, Miss.

15. Survey map from Wayne County Chancery Clerk's Office, Land Deeds, Book 1; Norma Kettler Chapman, interview with author, 31 Aug. 1990, Hiwannee, Miss.

16. Bass, "A Study of Place-Names," 84.

17. George Dougharty, Field Notes, Government Survey, #1905 [first entry dated 29 May 1820], Wayne County Chancery Clerk's Office, Wayne County Court House, Waynesboro, Miss.

18. Dougharty Field Notes, 29 May 1820.

19. Ibid., 15 July 1820.

20. Evans memoir.

21. Cole, "The Chickasawhay Country," 4.

22. Ibid.; H. H. Daniel, "St. Bernadette's Catholic Church," in "History of Wayne County, Miss. Churches and Cemetery Records 1800's–1915" (photocopy of eleven-page typescript, East Mississippi Regional Library, Quitman, Miss.).

23. Brewer interview; Evans memoir, 7.

24. "Historical [Clarke County]," 29 Sept. 1933, n.p., clipping in Phillips scrapbook.

25. Ibid.

26. Aubrey Jones interview, 14 March 1990; Evans memoir; 1870 and 1890 U.S. Census records; Hand and Hand, *Handbook*.

27. "William Powe," in Hand and Hand, *Handbook*, Biography ID #39, p. 1. Also, James F. Brieger, comp., "Bucatunna," in *Hometown Mississippi*, 2nd ed. (n.p., n.d.), 523, duplicated copy from Mississippi Department of Archives and History.

28. "John Britton Hand," in Hand and Hand, *Handbook*, Biography ID #19, p. 1.

29. "The Pettis House," *Clarke County Tribune*, 30 Oct. 1980.

30. Ibid.

31. A. Johnston, "History of the Johnston Family" (mimeographed eleven-page paper, in James B. Johnston family archives), 26 Sept. 1907, 1.

32. "Obadiah Hand," in Hand and Hand, *Handbook*, Biography ID #1, p. 1; Brieger, *Hometown*, "Matherville," 528.

33. H. H. Daniel, "History of Clarke County, Miss., Wills 1834–1900, Land Grants & Cemetery Records, 1834–1915" (photocopy in East Mississippi Regional Library, Quitman, Miss.), 26–46. Comprises lists of names with dates of persons buried in each cemetery.

34. Clarke County 1840 Census of Slave Inhabitants, Beat 2, signed John M. White, Asst. Marshal, microfilm in East Mississippi Regional Library, Quitman, Miss.

35. Brieger, "Langsdale," in *Hometown,* 92.

36. James Brewer, interview.

37. Clarke County 1840 Census of Slave Inhabitants, Beat No. 1, 5th day of August, 1850, signed by John M. White, Asst. Marshal, microfilm in East Mississippi Regional Library, Quitman, Miss.

38. Mary McCarty interview.

39. "Antebellum Homes: Hand House Recovering from Neglect," *Clarke County Tribune,* 23 April 1981, n.p., clipping from Mississippi State Department of Archives and History, Historic Sites Survey file; Florence Busby interview; Postal Records of the General Services Administration, Judicial, Fiscal, and Social Branch (NNFJ)-83-F-7895, National Archives and Records of the United States, Washington, D.C., photocopy of inquiry report provided by James B. Johnston, former postmaster, Shubuta.

40. Clarke County Census of Slave Inhabitants, 5 Aug. 1850, signed John M. White, Asst. Marshal, microfilm in East Mississippi Regional Library, Quitman, Miss.

41. "Captain Thomas Jefferson Woolverton," in Hand and Hand, *Handbook,* Biography ID #48.

42. W[illiam] H[inkle] Patton, no title, half-page photocopy of typescript on 1850s and 1860s Shubuta, in "Auntie's trunk."

43. "William Hinkle Patton," in *Goodspeed's Biographical and Historical Memoirs,* vol. 2, *Mississippi* (n.p., n.d.), 560–61; "Shubuta" clippings file, Mississippi State Department of Archives and History.

44. *Weekly Southern Republic* 4, no. 18, Shubuta, Miss., Saturday, 4 June, 1864.

45. Georgia D[ees] Phillips, Recollections from the Civil War of Captain W. C. Phillips by the Rev[erend] J[oshua] M. Phillips, Shubuta, Miss., 11 May 1932, manuscript in Phillips Archive, Shubuta Public Library. Since Georgia Dees Phillips wrote regularly for the *Mississippi Messenger,* this may have been a manuscript prepared for publication.

46. James B. and Phyllis Johnston interview; "The Civil War: 14th Regiment Infantry—Shubuta Rifles, Enterprise Guards, Quitman Invincibles," *Clarke County Tribune,* 12 April 1984, sec. B, p. 1.

47. Shelby Foote, *The Civil War: A Narrative,* vol. 2, *Fredericksburg to Meridian* (New York: Vintage Books, 1963), 819–20.

48. Ibid., 916.

49. "Wanted," *Weekly Southern Republic,* 4 June 1864, 4, microfilm copy in Meridian Public Library.

50. Ibid., 3.

51. Ibid.
52. Phillips ms., 4.
53. *Goodspeed*, 560–63.
54. "W. H. Patton's Anniversary," n.p., n.d. [Sept. 1930?, probably from the *Mississippi Messenger*], clipping in Phillips scrapbook, Shubuta Public Library.
55. "Shubuta, Miss., May 1900," Sanborn-Perris Map Co., Ltd., microfilm copy in Mississippi Department of Archives and History.
56. "Shubuta, Miss., June 1906," Sanborn Map Co., ibid.
57. "Shubuta, Miss., March 1912," Sanborn Map Co., ibid.
58. "Shubuta, Miss., Jan. 1926," Sanborn Map Co., ibid.
59. Walton, *Shubuta*, 7.
60. Rosellen Brown, "Paranoia on Main Street," *New York Times*, 2 Aug. 1995, sec. A, p. 12.
61. Ibid.
62. Robert Earl Shirley, letter to author, n.d. [postmarked 1 April 1994]; Janette Hudson interview.
63. Photocopy of town map showing lot deed-holders, Shubuta, Clarke County, Miss., n.d. Dates of deed transactions as early as 1866 and as late as 1896 appear on this map. This copy came from Linda McInnis, whose own copy is a photocopy. An original is said to be owned by R. L. Toney. Its likely date is around 1900.
64. "Captain Thomas Jefferson Woolverton," in Hand and Hand, *Handbook*, Biography ID #48, p. 1.
65. Elsie Jones Cross interview, 2 Feb. 1990.
66. *Mississippi Messenger*, 2 Aug. 1918, ad on "Local News" page (p. 5).
67. Microfilm copies of Sanborn Fire Insurance Company maps of Shubuta for 1885, 1890, 1900, 1906, 1912, and 1926, Mississippi State Department of Archives and History Library.
68. Dr. A. P. Hand, "The History of Shubuta as written by Dr. A. P. Hand for the Clarke County Centennial Edition of the Clarke County News" (photocopy of two-page typescript, in archives of Nerva McCaskey; second two-page typescript of Shubuta history from 1973, no author listed, also from McCaskey archives).

Chapter 3: Church and School, Depot and Town Hall

1. Site visit, 28 May 1996.
2. Site visit, 10 Dec. 1997.
3. Otis Bumpars, interview with author, 30 April 1996, Shubuta; Cassandra Cameron, interview with author, 16 Jan. 1997; Linda W. McInnis, "Shubuta Baptist Church History" (1981), 4.
4. Cassandra Cameron interview, 16 Jan. 1997.
5. James Brewer, interview with author, 10 Nov. 1990.

6. "Assemblies of God," *Columbia Encyclopedia*, 5th ed. (New York: Columbia University Press, 1993), 166.

7. Carl Fox, General Solicitor, Gulf, Mobile, and Ohio Railroad Company, to Miss Ruth White Williams, Regent, Horseshoe Robertson Chapter, DAR, West Point, Miss., 5 July 1955; Carl Fox to Robert C. Weems, Shubuta, 15 Nov. 1957. Used by permission of Mary Sue Mitchell.

8. Carl Fox to R. C. Weems, 15 Nov. 1957; Florence Busby interview, documents shown to the author and read during the tape-recorded interview; photocopy of map of Shubuta town lots with transference of deed dates indicated, n.d., in family archives of Linda McInnis.

9. *Gulf Mobile and Ohio Railroad: The Rebel Route* (2 Jan. 1941), pamphlet, in "Railroad—Gulf, Mobile, and Ohio" clippings file, Mississippi State Department of Archives and History ; "What Became of the Rebel," *Jackson Daily News,* 11 Aug. 1970, n.p., clipping, ibid.

10. Information in this section from site visit by the author to the Shubuta Town Hall with town clerk Libby Owen, 17 Jan. 1997. Lists of Shubuta mayors and postmasters and their terms provided by Harry Laffitte.

11. Diane Brown, telephone conversation with author, 7 Dec. 2001, Shubuta Town Hall.

Trope 7: The Hanging Bridge

1. Rosalie Primm, "Antebellum Homes: The Pettis Home," *Clarke County Tribune,* 30 Oct. 1980, n.p., clipping from personal archives of Aubrey Jones.

Trope 8: The Phillips Archive

1. Clipping, n.p., n.d., in Phillips scrapbook, Phillips Archive, Shubuta Public Library [most likely from the *Mississippi Messenger*].

2. Ibid.

3. Ross A. Collins, M.C., to the Reverend J. M. Phillips, 8 Dec. 1937, in Phillips Archive, Shubuta Public Library.

4. Helen M. Phillips to the author, 21 April 1990; "Shubuta" clippings file, Mississippi State Department of Archives and History; clipping , n.p., n.d., in Phillips scrapbook.

5. "Pageant Depicts Clarke County in Its Early Days," clipping, n.p., n.d., in Phillips scrapbook.

Chapter 4: Documents: Shubuta Memory in Maps, Pictures, Letters, and Buildings

1. John T. Cumbler, e-mail letter to author, 21 Aug. 1995, 1.

2. John T. Cumbler, e-mail letter to author, 14 April 1995.

3. Designated historic sites are the Sumrall-Albritton House on Highway 45 South, the Hand House at North Street and the railroad tracks, and the Price-Patton-Pettis House at the corner of North and 2nd Streets. Nos. 28, 29, and 30, Historic Sites Survey, State of Mississippi Department of Archives and History.

4. John H. Evans, "Reminiscences of Olden Times."

5. Ibid., 1, 9–10.

6. Ibid.

7. David G. Sansing, *Mississippi: Its People and Culture* (Minneapolis: T. S. Denison and Co., 1981), 155–57.

8. Manuscript letter, headed "Mrs. Georgia D. Phillips, Shubuta, Miss., May 11, 1932," composed as the "son's reminiscences [sic]" of the Reverend J. M. Phillips, 3, in Phillips Archive, Shubuta Public Library.

9. Ibid.

10. Ibid.

11. Sansing, *Mississippi*, 156–57.

12. Phillips ms., 1–2.

13. Ibid.

14. Ordinance No. 89, 15 Sept. 1920, Ordinance Book, Town of Shubuta, Office of the Town Clerk.

15. Ibid.

16. Program bulletin for First Annual Fair, Clarke-Wayne Fair Association, Shubuta, Miss., 3, 4, 5, 6 Nov. 1914, p. 23.

17. Ibid., 5.

18. Ibid., 7, 23.

19. Ibid., 34–35.

20. "Diary of Annie Ruth Johnston."

21. Ibid., 1.

22. Ibid., 23.

23. Information in this section from John T. Cumbler letters (thirty-six pages of handwritten letters, two to three pages each), n.p., n.d. [June–August 1965]; twenty-six black-and-white photographs of African American residential areas in Quitman and Shubuta [June–August 1965]; e-mail letters from John T. Cumbler to author, 14 April, 21 Aug. 1995.

24. Cumbler e-mail letter, 21 Aug. 1995, 1.

25. Cumbler letters, n.d. [about mid-July 1965].

26. Florence Busby, interview and site visit with author, 3 Sept. 1993.

Trope 9: Ol' Man Weems's Nickels

1. "George S. Weems Passes By Death," n.p., n.d. [most likely from the *Mississippi Messenger*], clipping in Phillips scrapbook, Shubuta Public Library.

2. "Bank and Oil Mill for Shubuta. Shubuta Oil and Manufacturing Co. Shubuta Bank. Both the Creatures of One Hour's Conference Among Local Capitalists," n.p., dated in ink 1902 [most likely from the *Mississippi Messenger*], clipping, ibid.

Chapter 5: Interviews: Shubuta Memory in People's Own Words

1. Aubrey and Ollie Jones, interview with author, 14 March 1990, Jones home, Shubuta; Aubrey Jones audiotape about Shubuta; interview segment with Edith Jones Adams with her parents, 14 March 1990.
2. Charlie D. Meeks and Syble Meeks, interview with author, 13 March 1990, Meeks home, Shubuta.
3. Ibid.
4. Ibid.
5. Aubrey Jones interview.
6. Edith Jones Adams interview.
7. Syble Meeks interview.
8. Charlie D. Meeks and Syble Meeks interview.
9. Interviews with Elsie Jones Cross, 2 Feb. 1990, and with Elsie Jones Cross and Erma Gay Graham Mathers, 14 March 1990.
10. June Stagg, "Matherville Community Has a Proud History," *Wayne County News*, 29 March 1973, sec. F., p. 1.
11. "School History," in Matherville Elementary School Annual, n.p., n.d. [1952?]. The school was a "one-room school" in the 1950s.
12. *The P.T.A. Cook Book*, rev. ed. (1925; reprint Shubuta, Miss.: Parent-Teachers Association, 1949), 4, 5, 7, 21.
13. Ibid., 8.
14. "Edward Phillips Says People of France Bear Burden without Murmur," n.p., n.d. [dated internal to the text 16 July 1918], clipping in Phillips scrapbook, Shubuta Public Library.

Chapter 6: The New Shubuta

1. Diane Brown, telephone conversation with author, 7 Dec. 2001, Shubuta Town Hall.
2. Eudora Welty, *The Eye of the Story* (New York: Vintage, 1979), 118.
3. Anamaria Wilson, "Sally and Jim Barksdale: The Gift of Literacy," *Newsweek*, 24 July 2000, 58–59.
4. Clarke County Tax Assessors Registration of Deeds, Map of Sec. 4C, Bk. 12, Par. 13, corner at the highway, Edna McCoy Fike, owner.

Notes on Sources

The gradual building of my understanding for the study of the town of Shubuta, Mississippi, came first through interviews and site visits with Shubuta people who live there now, who lived in Shubuta in the past, or who have close relatives and ancestors who were Shubutans. Next came archival sources, personal ones given to me by individuals and families and public material found in state, county, and local libraries and county courthouses. Third, I used books, newspapers, and scholarly articles both for background information and for specific knowledge about Shubuta itself.

From 1989 through 1999, I had formal tape-recorded or note-taking interviews with James Brewer (10 March 1990); Otis Bumpars (30 April 1996); Florence Busby (4 Sept. 1993); Cassandra Cameron with Bertha Cameron and O'Dell Cameron (6 Feb. 1990); Cleo Powe Cooper (30 April, 28 May 1996); Elsie Jones Cross (2 Feb., 14 March 1990, 10 Sept. 1993); Jane Hudson with Janette Hudson, Linda McInnis, and James B. Johnston (5 Sept. 1993); Janette Hudson alone (4 Feb. 1990); James and Phyllis Johnston (30 April 1996); Aubrey and Ollie Jones (14 March 1990); Edith Jones Adams with her parents, Aubrey and Ollie Jones (14 March 1990); Erma G. Mathers with Elsie Jones Cross (14 March 1990); Mary McCarty (16 Jan., 10 Dec. 1997); Linda McInnis (5 Sept. 1993); Don Allan Mitchell and Mary Sue Mitchell (10 March 1990); Charlie D. Meeks and Syble Meeks (13 March 1990); Helen Phillips (5 Sept. 1990); and Patsy Toney (10 Sept. 1993, 17 Jan. 1997), as well as numerous informal visits with these people and other Shubutans, both African Americans and European Americans.

Overview information about the town throughout the book comes from: the Phillips Family Archive in the Shubuta Public Library; the files of the East Mississippi Regional Library in Quitman, Miss.; the 1870, 1890, and 1910 U.S. Censuses and the 1840 and 1850 Clarke County, Mississippi, slave censuses; church archives and site visits to the Tribulation Baptist Church, the Shubuta Baptist Church, and the Shubuta United Methodist

Church; clippings files of the Mississippi Department of Archives and History, Jackson; personal archives lent to me by Linda McInnis, Cassandra Cameron, Erma G. Mathers, Nerva McCaskey, Janette Hudson, Aubrey and Ollie Jones, James B. Johnston, Don Allan Mitchell and Mary Sue Mitchell, and Norma Kettler Chapman.

Sometime in the late 1980s former mayor Aubrey Jones tape recorded his recollections of Shubuta in the first decades of the twentieth century, when he was a boy; and a copy of this recording was made available to me. I used Frank L[edyard] Walton, *Shubuta* (Shubuta, Miss.: Shubuta Memorial Association, 1947), a forty-eight-page local history, essentially a kind of boyhood memoir, commissioned by the white residents' cemetery association and written by a Shubuta-born New Yorker, who had been a major in the U.S. Army in World War I, and thus a patriotic promoter of his hometown at the post–World War II time of his writing the book.

Among primary written sources, a long letter to me from Helen Phillips (21 April 1990), donor of the family archive to the Shubuta Public Library, who grew up in Shubuta, was very useful. E-mail correspondence (26 May 1999) with Bob Weems, a man at the time in his eighties who had grown up in Shubuta, was very helpful, as were his e-mail messages (14 April, 21 Aug. 1995) and his 1965 photographs (twenty-six, black-and-white) and handwritten letters (thirty-six pages of two- or three-page letters) to his future wife from Shubuta by John T. Cumbler, who served as a civil rights movement worker in Shubuta the summer of 1965. In the East Mississippi Regional Library at Quitman, I found "Reminiscences of Olden Times, 1809–1850," by John H. Evans, a photocopy of a twenty-four-page typescript copy of a memoir, which proved quite valuable. "Diary of Annie Ruth Johnston on a Trip to the Tropics during the Summer of 1928," a carbon copy of a thirty-seven-page typescript from the Weems family archives, found in a trunk in the Shubuta home of Mary V. Weems and in the possession of Don Allan ("Chip") Mitchell, was made available to me by Chip Mitchell, and I found it to be marvelously informative. Mary Sue Mitchell gave me copies of personal letters to her from Shubutan Robert C. Weems, her grandfather (and father of Bob Weems, brother of Mary V. Weems, and great-grandfather of Chip Mitchell), dated from 2 Jan. 1963 through 7 June 1975, a wonderful cache of correspondence that provided many insights.

I studied county courthouse records of property deeds, wills, and court records, land surveyors' records, and historical and current maps in the chancery clerk's office in the Wayne County Court House in Waynesboro, Mississippi, and the chancery clerk's office in the Clarke County Court House in Quitman, Mississippi.

Other sources of local data for my work were Robert Stephens Hand and Thomas Edwards Hand, *Handbook-2: Descendants of Obadiah Hand (1760–1837), Sixth Generation in America* (Decorah, Iowa: Anundsen Publishing Co., 1987); "Shubuta, 120 Years Old, Boomed, Faded, Rebooms," *Clarion Ledger–Jackson Daily News*, 31 March 1974, sec. B, pp. 6–7; Charles H. Cole IV, "The Chickasawhay Country—The Story of Wayne County in Facts and Legends," photocopy of a thirty-eight-page typescript of unpublished county history, from Waynesboro Public Library, a copy given to me by Lester Milton Holcolm. A master's thesis by Lisa Spencer, "A Sociological Oral History of Clarke County, Mississippi," including cassette-tape interviews (Mississippi Oral History Project of the University of Southern Mississippi, 1987), was particularly valuable to me.

I used a published study about the Choctaw people who were the first inhabitants of Shubuta: Peter J. Hamilton, "The Yowanne, or Hiowanni, Indians," *Publications of the Mississippi Historical Society* (1902). Other general information about the Choctaws comes from: Carolyn Keller Reeves, ed., *The Choctaw before Removal* (Jackson: University Press of Mississippi, 1985); "Choctaw Indians—General," file, Mississippi Department of Archives and History; Paul Vance, "Mississippi Choctaw Indians," in *Mississippi Magic* (Nov. 1951), 9–11; "Mississippi Indians," typescript from WPA, *Mississippi: A Guide to the Magnolia State*; and John H. Peterson Jr., "Assimilation, Separation, and Out-Migration in an American Indian Group," *American Anthropologist* 74 (1972): 1286–92.

Pertinent maps of Shubuta are the most current town map, "Shubuta," MA Cu Shu, and the 1914 "Clarke County Soil Survey," MA CLA #1, Mississippi Department of Archives and History, Special Collections, Cartographic Records; and "Shubuta Quadrangle," U.S. Department of the Interior, Geological Survey. Also, I used the maps of the town of Shubuta made by the Sanborn Fire Insurance Company in 1885, 1890, 1895, 1900, 1906, 1912, and 1926, available on microfilm in the Mississippi Department of Archives and History.

I saw one copy of a newspaper published in Shubuta during the Civil War, the *Weekly Southern Republic,* 4 June 1864, on microfilm in the Meridian Public Library. I saw many clippings and a number of issues, from 1918 to 1922, of the *Mississippi Messenger,* given to me by Syble Meeks. This daily newspaper was published in Shubuta from 1879 for several decades, at least into the 1930s.

General information about Mississippi, its regions, and Shubuta is drawn from Ralph D. Cross and Robert W. Wales, eds., Charles T. Traylor, chief cartographer, *Atlas of Mississippi* (Jackson: University Press of Mississippi, 1974); James W. Loewen and Charles Sallis, *Mississippi: Conflict and Change* (New York: Pantheon Books, 1974); David G. Sansing, *Mississippi: Its People and Culture* (Minneapolis: T. S. Denison & Co., 1981); and *Mississippi: The WPA Guide to the Magnolia State,* Golden Anniversary edition, with a new introduction by Robert S. McElvaine (Jackson: University Press of Mississippi, 1988).

Several studies of towns and cities, as well as some town fiction and creative essays, have provided models and theories for scholarship about a place and people in which the author has personal investment, as I have in this work. Foremost is the village study by South African–born black fiction writer Bessie Head, *Serowe, Village of the Rain Wind* (London: Heinemann, 1981), in which she presents the cultural and national history of her adopted Botswana by means of interviews and biographies of Serowe villagers. Her model, in turn, is sociologist Ronald Blythe's English village study, *Akenfield.* The Dutch Americanist Rob Kroes writes of cultural adaptations from Europe to America in his work on Amsterdam, Montana ("Windmills in Montana: Dutch Settlement in the Gallatin Valley," *Montana: The Magazine of Western History* 39, no. 4 [autumn 1989]: 40–51), from his unique perspective from the original Amsterdam. Henry Glassie's *Passing the Time in Ballymenone* (Philadelphia: University of Pennsylvania Press, 1982), especially his preface on how he did his work in the Irish village he studied, has influenced my work, as has the ethical insight on the social values of community in Kai T. Erikson's *Everything in Its Path: Destruction of Community in the Buffalo Creek Flood* (New York: Simon and Schuster, 1976). My Mississippi compatriot Eudora Welty created a fictional town, Morgana, in her story cycle, *The Golden Apples,* from which I have learned much about

U.S. southern towns; and poet Kathleen Norris in her memoir biography of a place, *Dakota: A Spiritual Geography* (New York: Ticknor & Fields, 1993), has helped me think of place and spirit in new ways. New histories by Englishmen, Roy Porter's *London: A Social History* (London: Hamish Hamilton, 1994) and Simon Schama's *Landscape and Memory* (New York: Alfred A. Knopf, 1995), have inspired my confidence that historians writing about their places of origin and ancestry can do so with delight and depth, as well as with judgment. Even Manhattanite Ann Douglas's *Terrible Honesty: Mongrel Manhattan in the 1920s* (New York: Farrar, Straus, and Giroux, 1995) suggests that commitment to understanding one's own place adds the richness of feeling to fact. Here, too, as in other places, I have found useful David A. Hollinger's theory in "Postethnic America" (*Contention* 2, no. 1 [fall 1992]) and *Postethnic America* (New York: Basic Books, 1995), in which he argues that the cultural history of the United States is ethnic, while the political history of the United States is national. This is useful for me in arguing that the regional and racial histories of the U.S. South are peculiarly ethnic while also participatory in a common U.S. national political history.

Epigraphs heading each chapter come from Wallace Stephens, "Anecdote of the Jar," *The Palm at the End of the Mind: Selected Poems and a Play*, ed. Holly Stevens (1967; reprint New York: Vintage Books, 1972), 46; Josephine Humphries, "Southern Discomfort," *New York Times Book Review*, 17 March 1996, 13; Garrison Keillor, *Lake Wobegon Days* (New York: Viking, 1985), 4–5; Kathleen Norris, *Dakota: A Spiritual Geography*, 20; "'Tis a Gift to Be Simple," nineteenth-century Shaker song; Wendell Berry, "At a Country Funeral," *Collected Poems, 1957–1982* (San Francisco: North Point Press, 1985), 159; and Nadine Gordimer, "My New South African Identity," *New York Times Magazine*, 30 May 1999, p. 40.